ooo

W H E N the circus came to town, Mr. Jones took his whole family.

There, to their surprise, following the elephant parade with a shovel

and pail, was long-lost cousin Irving. After the show, the family hurried

back to the animal stalls where Irving was cleaning out the cages.

"Come home, come home," cried Mrs. Jones.

"We'll find you a job," said Mr. Jones. "Anything is better than

this!"

The children held their noses.

"What?" shouted Irving, drawing himself up proudly despite the

straw in his hair and the dirt on his hands. "And quit show biz?!"

ALSO BY MICHAEL LYDON

*Rock Folk*

*Boogie Lightning*

# How to succeed in
# SHOW BUSINESS
## by really trying

### A HANDBOOK FOR
### THE ASPIRING PERFORMER

## BY MICHAEL LYDON

### PHOTOGRAPHS BY ELLEN MANDEL

DODD, MEAD & COMPANY
New York

*With thanks to Donna Brooks, and to the Ottendorfer, Tompkins Square, and Lincoln Center branches of the New York Public Library.*

*In memory of Seymour Peck and Saul Rosen*

*for*

*WILLIAM HICKEY*

*and*

*JULIA WORTMAN*

*two of many teachers*

# CONTENTS

# iNTROdUCTION

Y O U 'V E been playing guitar with a friend and thinking, "Let's start a band!"

You've been taking ballet classes since you were six; now you're beginning to wonder, "What will I ever do with it?"

Drama club was the most fun you had in high school, but you're asking yourself, "How could *I* make a living as an actor?

If any of these apply to you, you are, whether you know it or not, considering a career in the performing arts. In other words: show business!

*Show business*—the words sparkle with bright lights and tinsel. Fame, wealth, glamour, hope, heartbreak, and unique excitement— show business has it all. If the bug bites you, you may never be the same. Like countless generations of actors, singers, dancers, jugglers, and clowns, you may become a lifelong trouper, following your artistic star through whatever triumphs and disappointments await you.

Right now, you're not sure the bug has bitten you. Maybe it has, but what can you do about it? The world of TV, movies, theatres, and record companies seems so big and faraway, even if you live near entertainment centers like New York, Los Angeles, and Nashville. You've heard enough stories about how hard it is to "break in"; how will you ever get your chance? Of course, a few stars become rich and

New York City: in the theatre district

famous, but the unknowns are "starving artists." Show business is a risky business—your parents or friends may have pointed that out to you already—not safe and down-to-earth like teaching, accounting, or computer programming.

And what would you do in show business anyway? Hundreds of people can already sing better than you, play faster, leap higher, and they already have years of experience. What is your unique gift, that indefinable something you have that nobody else has? And if you have that something, will anybody like it—like it well enough to pay you for doing it?

If any or all of these questions, worries, and indecisions are bugging you, relax. They face and have faced every show biz hopeful there ever was or will be. You are not alone.

Show business does look dauntingly complex to a beginner. The performing arts consist of three major arts: acting, the art of make-believe; dance, the art of movement; and music, the art of sound. Each of these consists of innumerable disciplines and traditions. Classical music encompasses great diversity: chamber music and symphonies, art songs and grand opera. Ballet, modern, tap, jazz, ballroom and the new "break" dancing are a few of dance's idioms; folk dancing is as varied as the peoples of the world. In this century, film acting has been born as a new acting discipline.

There are also the variety and circus arts: juggling, acrobatics, clowning, animal training, magic, ventriloquism, ice-skating, as well as burlesque and the fire-eating, sword-swallowing oddities of the sideshow.

Show business is organized around all these specialized arts and the artists who work in them. There is a union for stage actors, the Actors' Equity Association, and one for film actors, the Screen Actors Guild. There are managers and agents who handle the careers of jazz musicians exclusively, others who work only with child actors or concert pianists or ballet dancers.

One nightclub has belly dancers and oud players from the Mideast; another is a forum for new stand-up comics. Radio stations often pick all their music by "format": the records they play are within defined limits of disco, album-oriented rock, adult-contemporary, easy listening. A movie theatre that has built a reputation for showing the latest foreign films is unlikely to present a festival of Burt Reynolds car-crash comedies.

The public, from its side, is many audiences. There are the "under-thirty-fives" and the "over-thirty-fives," and closer limit groups like the "thirteen-to-twenty-five record-buying audience." There are big-city and small-town audiences, white audiences and black audiences, East Coast, West Coast, and mid-America audiences. Ballet has an audience that may know little of what's going on in modern dance. A fan of country fiddler Roy Clark may never have heard violinist Yehudi Menuhin. There are TV watchers who seldom go to the movies, just as there are moviegoers who have never seen a professionally performed play.

You are a beginner. The vision of all these separate avenues is overwhelming. You may have some idea of what you want to do, but you know little of what you can do, less of what you may have to do to survive, and nothing of what will actually happen. Which path will you take? Where will it lead you?

The premise of this book is that show business is complex but fundamentally unified. Show business is one world of the performing arts: a world of many nations, all closely linked.

Shows begin with the impulse to perform, to put on a show. The impulse is the same for all performers: to strut their stuff before the public. The show that results depends on the individual who feels the impulse.

The arts of performance have become, over centuries of evolution, crafts that require years of training and study to master. Each has its own methods and goals, but all are alike in the degree of discipline they require for precise control of the mind and body.

These links of desire and craft create a kinship that performers feel for each other. Actors, musicians, and dancers, jugglers, clowns, and magicians know that they share a life based on the love of performing. They often work together, and many, many times their disciplines overlap. They learn from and inspire each other.

Show business reflects this artistic unity as well as diversity. Few of its organizational divisions are rigid. Many actors, for instance, belong to Equity and the Screen Actors Guild as well as AFTRA, the American Federation of Television and Radio Artists. A manager helping a dancer plan a long-term career may develop singing and acting opportunities for him or her as well. If one format is not earning a radio station top ratings, it can switch to another overnight.

The public keeps more of show business' colorful spectrum in mind than it is consciously aware of. People absorb information about the performing arts as if by osmosis, from images on the airwaves and in magazines, newspapers, billboards, and store displays. They know best what they like best, but have some familiarity with nearly everything.

And for the performer, there is ultimately only one audience: whoever will look and listen. Once a performer leaves his own living room, he never knows who may experience what he creates. Anyone might be there in the dark—a child, a stranger come by accident, an old friend. Since it could be anyone, it might as well be everyone. Every performer addresses the universe.

Seeing all the performing arts as a unity is a realistic and helpful perspective for a young performer. It can keep you close to your fundamental motivations and goals at the same time that it widens your outlook, your sympathies, and your sense of your own possibilities. Some elements are common to all the arts. You will be able to learn about your own art by analogy with the others. To make one such analogy here: like an orchestral musician, you will be able to play your part better if you are aware of the harmony of the whole symphony.

A unified view also makes it plain that show business is not a never-never land far away in "Hollywood" or on "Broadway." It begins in you, and it can grow in any community as large as a small village. Amateur night at the church or community center, the school play, the boy's club marching band, Madame Yvonne's School of Ballet, Tap, and Modern—these are show business' outposts and recruiting centers. This is where you begin.

But to make what you do there a real beginning and not just "fun while it lasted," you need to think and plan.

You need to plan because there are few "slots" in show business— jobs where a boss tells you what to do and how to do it. Performing artists make their own jobs and create their own careers. You will need to plan your own learning, training, sales, and career strategies. Without planning, you'll waste time and money, miss some opportunities under your nose and be unable to take advantage of others when they appear.

You need to think because learning the skills of performance requires the consistent application of focused mental energy. Like scientists, performing artists are continual experimenters, stretching and studying their bodies and their imaginations, putting what they've learned to the test of performance, evaluating the results, and trying again. The audience gets out of a performance what the performers put into it. Whether you act, sing, or juggle Indian clubs, only focused thought—what am I doing, why am I doing it—will make it come alive across the footlights and through the camera.

This book is designed to help you think and plan. It is written by someone who has gone through and is going through the same trials and tribulations you are. It will not solve every problem nor keep you from making every mistake, but I hope it keeps you from charging up every dead end blindfolded.

Good luck!

. . . . . . .

INTRODUCTION

. . . . . . .

HOW TO SUCCEED IN

SHOW BUSINESS

BY REALLY TRYING

# chapter 1

○ ○ ○ ○ ○ ○ ○ ○ ○ ○ ○ ○ ○ ○ ○ ○ ○ ○ ○ ○ ○ ○ ○ ○ ○ ○ ○ ○ ○ ○ ○ ○ ○ ○ ○ ○ ○ ○

# THE
# basics

THE first show, according to one hoary theatrical legend, occurred on a rainy night back in the Stone Age. After a dinner of mammoth haunches roasted over an open fire, the cavemen and their mates squatted dully in the feeble light, picking their teeth. All but Og, who, figuring there must be more to life than hunting, eating, sleeping, and scratching, decided to liven up the party.

Ducking into a darkened corner of the cave, he dropped his furs and, using mud as glue, covered himself with feathers left over from dinner the night before. Then he took a deep breath, leapt out into the light, and danced around the fire, flapping his arms and clucking like a madman.

His friends and neighbors looked on stupefied until one grunted with dawning comprehension, "Hey, Og's a chicken!" Then everybody got it, and the cave rang with raucous laughter and the sound of greasy hands clapping in appreciation.

In fact, Og the Human Chicken was such a success, he was back the next night—with his agent!

Like most legends, this one is both fanciful and true. Og's chicken act, though mythical, does contain the essential elements of all shows—as well as their essential paradox.

Leilani Jones making up for *Little Shop of Horrors*, Orpheum Theatre, New York City

· · · · · · ·

The elements: a performer at work and an audience entertained; action and reaction; light and dark; surprise and discovery; imitation and recognition. Og had a vision and he made others see it. His show was his insight made real.

What did Og's cavemates see? They saw an imitation of life: Og pretending to be a chicken. They saw Og *and* his assemblage of life elements—sound, feathers, mud, a man in motion—selected and used to make a living picture. They saw more than plain life: they saw life organized, animated, and intensified by Og's imagination. Og did not become a chicken, but his audience saw a chicken in Og. They saw pretend life that was true to life.

This is the paradox: a show is an illusion that conveys truth. The illusion is the magic of a show's appeal, the truth its ultimate value.

The word *show*, from the Old English *shewen*, is both a verb and a noun, and is closely related to the word *see*. It's primary meaning is visual: "to cause or permit to be seen . . . to put on view," says *Webster's*. Stores catch the eyes of passers-by with attractive *show windows*. School kids let their classmates see their pet frogs and then talk about them in *show and tell*.

Since we rely so much on our eyes to tell us the truth ("seeing is believing"), show has come to mean to *demonstrate*—"I'll show you how"; *to prove*—"The facts will show"; or *to guide*—"Show me the way."

From these definitions it's a short step for show to mean an arrangement of things to be seen that will tell something or make a point. For instance, if I draw a skull and crossbones and put it on the page, I am showing you a skull and crossbones. But if I put that skull and crossbones on a bottle, I am showing you that the bottle contains poison. In effect, I am showing you what cannot be seen, or as Webster puts it, "revealing or displaying an inward disposition, feeling, or trait by appearance or behavior."

Even unconscious acts—a yawn, tensed eyebrows, scratching the head—and semiconscious details of dress and personal style show much about us. My brother John and I used to play a game we called "Sherlock Holmes." Sitting on the subway, we'd pick people out and construct their biographies and occupations from everything we could notice about them. We never knew how right we were, but we trained our eyes and imaginations and had fun besides.

People make a show, however, when they purposely act in a way to show those around them what they think and feel. This is what Og was doing, and we all do it. A little boy thinks the girl next door is getting stuck-up because she has a new bike, so he puts his thumb on his nose, waggles his fingers, and shouts, "Nyah, nyah, nyah, nyah!" The little girl tosses her head and pretends not to notice, showing how grown-up she is. The boy's mother comes out onto the step with her hands set on her hips, arms akimbo, to show she's not one bit amused. The father shows his anger by lowering his voice to its gravest pitch. The boy may show his defiance by stomping noisily off to his room and slamming the door, in which case the mother may throw up her hands as if to say, "What ever will I do with him?"

We all also *show off* from time to time, making a marked display of ourselves so that others will admire us. We use big words, recount heroic exploits, tell jokes, predict confidently who's going to win the World Series, and hint that *we* know what's going on between Vera and Jack—all to be, for a moment at least, the center of attention. Outward show sometimes conceals inner feeling: we put on phony smiles and say thank-yous we don't mean to keep our true emotions from showing. Sarcasm is a kind of double show: we make an obviously false show of what we don't feel to display our true feelings all the more clearly. "Oh, gee, you're *so* generous," we say, our tone and expression caricatures of sincerity, to show how little we appreciate the last morsel of an ice cream cone that was supposed to be shared equally.

Shows of everyday feeling are the raw materials for the art of making shows. As a cabinetmaker transforms planks of maple into intricately inlaid boxes, or a sculptor transforms rough stone into vibrant figures, show artists take the postures, gestures, and sounds with which we all communicate and transform them into art: acting, dance, and music. The actions of the show artist communicate because we recognize in them the daily language of showing common to us all. As the great jazz trumpeter Louis Armstrong put it: "What we play is life."

An artistic show, however, is not an ordinary show. It differs in its quality of observation and distillation, and in its purpose. An actor shows us a defiant little boy, not because he wants to defy the audience as the boy defied his parents, but because he wants to show what a defiant boy is like. Perhaps he had once been such a boy or is the father of one. His artistic show is based not on the need to defy but on the desire to show the audience something he has observed to be true and has found the means to recreate in art.

This is how shows, through illusions, convey truth. The truths shows convey are not only emotional ones. Jugglers and acrobats, dancers too, show us truths about the physical world: gravity, weight, momentum, and the limits and possibilities of our bodies. Music shows us the many faces of time, and the mathematics of vibrations and their complex relationships. Magicians show us that seeing isn't always believing; quick hands can truly fool the eye.

The truth any show conveys is difficult to put into words, perhaps impossible. Many artists feel it can be fully expressed by nothing except the show itself. "Trouble begins," said George Balanchine, the Russian-born dancer who became America's greatest choreographer, "when we try to explain things that are unexplainable. You cannot describe with words something for which there are no words. Poetry, art, religion—you cannot explain these things. You say, 'That girl is beautiful.' You say, 'She is like a rose.' But what *is* a rose?"

To that question Gertrude Stein once replied, "Rose is a rose is a rose is a rose." So it is with shows. Independent movie producer Samuel Goldwyn is said to have told screenwriters who wanted to load their scripts with meaning, "If you want to send a message, use Western Union." A show doesn't carry truth like a train carries coal; its truth is the show, the assemblage of action, color, and sound. A jazz quartet working in close harmony, each player making his own statement while listening sympathetically to the others, embodies freedom and equality without a word being spoken.

A show's truth begins in the minds of the artists who create it— playwright, composer, choreographer, director, costumer, set designer, and lighting designer as well as performers having their own idea of what that truth is. The audience receiving the show's truth are individuals who take it in according to their own knowledge and need. Any show's truth is open to countless reactions and interpretations.

Artists often disagree with each other, and audiences with them all, about what a show says; truth to one is arrant nonsense to another. Librettist William Gilbert and composer Arthur Sullivan matched witty words to witty music in a series of brilliant comic operas, but their collaboration was marked by bitter quarrels over their work. A baffled and angry Parisian audience rioted the first time they heard Igor Stravinsky's eerie *Sacre du Printemps;* fifty years later Beatle fans started happy riots in total appreciation while their parents covered their ears and wondered what "Yeah yeah yeah" meant. For many showgoers, following and joining critical controversies is sport equal to the shows themselves.

Beyond these differences of opinion, can shows convey actual falsehood? Yes and no. False show is possible. Hitler supported his totalitarian regime with propaganda films and broadcasts that preached the lie of racial superiority. More innocently, commercials manipulate show elements of comedy, music, and dance as easily as they manipulate statistics to prove their product better than their competitor's nearly identical Brand X.

False shows mislead us, like a bottle of poison labelled not with a skull and crossbones but with a cow grazing contentedly in a pasture. If we believe them, we're in trouble. False shows, however, cannot stand the test of time. As Abraham Lincoln said, "You can fool all of the people some of the time, and some of the people all of the time, but you can't fool all of the people all of the time."

True shows, on the other hand, are based on the truth of life itself, ongoing, eternal, and far more powerful than any human attempt to distort it. "Movement," said the great modern dancer Martha Graham, "cannot lie." True shows are helpful guides. By renewing our aspirations, opening our eyes and ears to new beauty, and simply by making us laugh and cry, they help us live and love life more fully.

All show truths are not grand; banal shows that repeat tired formulas and stale situations tell us plainly that we humans do not live constantly at the highest peaks of inspiration. Even the most commonplace truth, however, can be fresh when made real by a performer honest to his own vision. After all, Og's companions had seen hundreds of chickens before Og leapt feathered and squawking out of the dark.

The performing arts have a long and proud history. Og or no Og, shows did begin in the Stone Age, the era of the earliest cave paintings, and they have continued to evolve ever since. The many phases of this evolution, wrote Richard Southern in his excellent book, *The Seven Ages of the Theatre,* are like the many layers of an onion. One does not replace another; each makes the whole more pungent.

The great forces of life seemed to contain messages for early man, but the messages were hard to understand. The phases of the moon, thunder and lightning, the migration of the animals—what did they mean? But if men could give form to these elemental forces, shape them in human terms, perhaps then, as *images,* they could be understood.

The earth, men sensed, gave them birth and sustained them with its fertility. The earth was their mother. A full-breasted, full-hipped figurine like the four-and-a-half-inch-tall "Venus of Willendorf," found in an Austrian cave and believed to be over twenty-five thousand years old, was an image of the Earth Mother. For the pygmies of the African rain forest, whose culture anthropologists believe has changed little since prehistoric times, an elephant hunt may be a two-week trek that ends in failure. But their Dance of the Hunt, in which a tribe member masked as an elephant is symbolically caught and killed, concentrates in a day-long image all the underlying excitement, danger, and triumph of a great group effort to kill a powerful beast and feed the tribe.

Over centuries, pageants of the seasons and crucial moments in life—birth, initiation, marriage, coronation, and death—became intricate rituals whose details of song and dance, costume and mask, were administered and preserved, generation to generation, by priests and shamen. These rituals had a "dominating religious element," according to Southern, and they often took place in great open-air temples like Stonehenge in England and the pyramids of Mayan Mexico.

A new phase began when the dancers, musicians, and actors of ritual became aware of the art of their techniques independent of their religious meaning—"professionalism," Southern calls it. This phase was reached in Egypt by 2300 B.C. when Pharaoh Pepi II imported a famous dancing dwarf from Nubia. In Mesopotamia about the same time, musicians led a privileged life at the court of Hammurabi.

Professionalism became fully established in ancient Greece and particularly in the sophisticated city of Athens. There, between 500 and 400 B.C., a ritual festival for Dionysius, the god of wine and fertility, became a theatre festival. Poets competed for the prize of a laurel wreath with tragedies and comedies. The actors were professionals paid by well-to-do citizens. Among the prizewinners for tragedy were Aeschylus, Sophocles, and Euripides; for comedy, Aristophanes and Menander. Of their prodigious output (Sophocles alone wrote one hundred and twenty dramas) only a few dozen plays survive, but on their work much of Western theatrical tradition is based.

The very words theatre, drama, music, chorus, scene, orchestra, choreography, antagonist, and protagonist are of Greek origin. So are the words comedy and tragedy and their laughing and weeping masks, still universal symbols of the theatre's power to evoke and express emotion. In the Greek tragedies, hero and heroine (also Greek words) were often drawn from legend, but the playwrights and actors made the sufferings of Prometheus and Ajax, Antigone and Electra, deeply human. In the comedies not even the gods were safe from satire, and Aristophanes in *The Clouds* shows the great philosopher Socrates as a nit-picking buffoon.

At first Greek theatres were wooden structures with no clearly defined stages. Later they became elegant stone amphitheatres with tiered seats, defined stages and backstage areas, painted scenery and machinery for moving it. By the time of Christ, Greek civilization had declined, but the Romans, basing their own plays on Greek tradition, built Grecian-style theatres throughout the Mediterranean world. Roman theatre went far beyond its Greek models in the lavish and bloody display of its spectacles. Chariot races, animal fights, and gladiatorial combats were staged in huge circular arenas. The emperor Vespasian built the Colosseum in 80 A.D. for these circuses whose magnificence, the emperor and his successors hoped, would blind the average Roman to the poverty of his lot. With the fall of Rome came the collapse of the Greco-Roman theatrical tradition. The theatres first became overgrown with weeds and then fell to partial ruins as warring European tribes used their stones for fortresses.

The first thousand years A.D. saw the founding of India's classical dance and drama, and the first puppet plays of Java, in which the moving shadows of the intricately carved figures are seen cast on a translucent screen. About 750 A.D., Emperor Ming Huang started China's first theatre for the training of professional actors. In Europe's early Middle Ages, however, theatre slipped back to more primitive levels. Show artists existed on the fringes of Christian society. Court jesters lived precariously dependent on the whims of kings and nobles, minstrels sang their lays in exchange for a meal and a place to sleep, and small troupes of players traveled from town to town, setting up rough booths in market squares.

Slowly a new tradition grew, again, as in Greece, nurtured by religion. The Catholic Church wedded its rituals to pagan seasonal festivals, making Christmas, Easter, and other holy days occasions for elaborate masses and costumed processions. In devising means to write down Gregorian chants, church musicians established the rudiments of modern music notation. Colorful passion plays, staged on the wide porches of the then new cathedrals, told gospel and Bible stories in the language of the people. The church also preserved the literature of Greece and Rome in its libraries.

With the Renaissance and its independent urban culture, Europe was once more ready for professional theatre on its own stages. Renaissance show makers first found inspiration in antiquity—in 1486, humanist philosophers in Italy revived the Roman plays of Seneca and Plautus—but they soon created fresh work, using folktales, historical events, and satirical views of everyday life as their starting points. Technological advances (Leonardo da Vinci designed a revolving stage), the invention of printing, the rise of literacy, and better roads and communication all helped spread the newly vigorous show arts. Chinese magicians, Hungarian gypsy dancers, *commedia dell'arte* companies from Italy, and Punch-and-Judy shows from rural England toured from city to city. Painted natives of the New World were displayed as sideshow oddities.

New theatres sprang up all over Europe. Shakespeare's Globe theatre, built about 1590 among the taverns of the common people on the south bank of the Thames in London, was one of the last open-air theatres. In the seventeenth century, theatres and concert halls built for aristocratic courts and for the guilds of city merchants and craftsmen were fully enclosed. These could be used year round and allowed the development of painted flats and elaborate scenery.

By the late eighteenth century, when the United States was young, the basic elements of the modern show arts were well established. The stylized dancing of the aristocratic courts had become ballet. Musicians, influenced by the great genius Johann Sebastian Bach, had adopted the tempered scale and its system of twelve interrelated keys built on the scale's twelve tones. With this system came the sharps and flats and five-line staves of modern music notation, new instruments like the pianoforte, and the wind and string instrument ensembles that led to symphony orchestras. Opera had grown from plays mixed with song into a new art that blended acting, music, and dance in a grand dramatic unity.

Puritan societies in Europe and America closed some theatres, frowning on the performing arts even as avocations in the home. Elsewhere the theatre was a lively forum for the revolutionary ideas of the day—freedom, equality, and the brotherhood of man. The French playwright Beaumarchais made a barber the hero of his *Barber of Seville* and *The Marriage of Figaro*. Figaro was a clever fellow quite able to dupe his masters. In one scene, Figaro tells the count he works for:

Because you are a great lord, you think you are a great genius . . . What have you done to earn so many advantages? You took the trouble to be born, nothing more. Apart from that, you're a common type. Whereas I, lost in the herd, had to exert more skill just to survive than has been spent for a hundred years in governing this country. And you want to tangle with *me*!

For such audacity King Louis XVIII banned *The Marriage of Figaro* for four years until popular demand forced him to allow a production in 1784. Many historians say its success hastened the French revolution, and the guillotining of Louis, five years later.

Artistically speaking, the nineteenth century is just yesterday. The symphonies of Beethoven and Brahms, the songs of Schubert and Schumann are still staples of the repertories of orchestras and concert recitalists. No opera season is complete without Verdi's *Aida*, Bizet's *Carmen*, or Leoncavallo's *Pagliacci*. Modern dramatic realism begins with the plays of Ibsen and Chekhov, and the modern dance with the experimental work of Ruth St. Denis and Isadora Duncan in the 1890s. The best-loved actress of the last century, Sarah Bernhardt, lived long enough to make a movie, *Queen Elizabeth*, in 1912.

Our own century has witnessed the birth of jazz, the theatre of the absurd, and the free-form, mixed-media events called "happenings," as well as two of the most important developments since shows began: broadcasting and recording. Now shows—the actual light and sound images—can be flashed around the world in an instant and captured forever in film and vinyl. Movies, television, radio, records, and electric instruments have created drastic changes in the show arts, for performers and audiences alike. Actors perform first for the camera, their audience miles away or months in the future. Dancers can break their movements into fragments, each photographed separately or from many angles. A single guitarist can create sound to shake a stadium, and in the recording studio musicians can overlap tracks of sound twenty-four layers deep.

At a play or a concert, the audience sit in their seats watching and listening to live action right in front of them. Watching television or a movie, or listening to a record, audiences may physically be in their seats, but they are responding to carefully prepared images of action. They see what the camera saw, hear what the microphone heard—in effect, they are in the camera, in the microphone.

The camera and microphone take us on magic carpet rides never before possible. We can travel to Tibet without leaving home, dance to popular music from Australia, laugh at Charlie Chaplin just as heartily as did the Little Tramp's first audiences sixty years ago. At the same time, the camera and microphone create a distance between audience and performer; even in close-up, a movie star is just a photograph. Only in live theatre is there, as Polish playwright Jerzy Grotowski put it, "the closeness of the living organism"—the age-old magic of audience and performer responding to each other at one place on earth, in one here-now, gone-forever moment of time.

And so the performing arts, live and recorded, exist side by side today. How far have we come from the ancient days of earliest ritual? Peel back a few layers of modern plot and circumstance in any play or film, and you'll find the same stories of initiation, love, and death. In all the centuries of music, time and tone have not changed; neither have space and the human body in all the centuries of dance. "In the end we can subtract so much of the technical refinements," Southern concludes, "but we cannot take away the centre of it all, the living player."

Generations of living players, however, have left us a legacy: their answers to unanswerable mysteries, the shapes they have given to sound and space, the evocative movements they created for their bodies. For every player living now, this past is an invaluable heritage, riches to be had for the asking, available now to make a future still unknown.

People are willing to pay to see a show, to trade something they have for the experience they are going to get. Therefore, making shows is more than a creative art, it is a business: show business.

"There's no business like show business," says Irving Berlin's wonderful song; it's true. All businesses have ups and downs and sudden changes of direction that economists cannot fully explain. Even the most nuts-and-bolt industry is subject to the whims of fashion— what plumbing supply wholesaler could have known ten years ago that hottubs would be a mid-1980s status item? Yet for mercurial instability and chronic uncertainty, show business is in a class by itself.

For one thing, it's impossible to quantify the human need for shows. Without food and water life stops; water utilities and grocery stores have at least that to go on. Without entertainment, life might be boring, but it would go on. Shows satisfy human needs that are basic but not absolutely essential. Shows are an "extra" for most people. They go to a play or buy a record as the mood strikes them. How often

Between takes: *Mr. Ricco* on location at University Art Museum, Berkeley, California

will the mood strike? Only one guess is certain: not with breakfast-lunch-and-dinner regularity.

Nor can show business predict what direction people will go when the mood does strike, what will be a hit, what will flop. In 1974, *The Great Waldo Pepper* was a colorful, action-packed movie based on the romantic days of the devil-may-care barnstorming pilots of the 1920s. Robert Redford starred and George Roy Hill directed, both fresh from the huge success of *The Sting*. Result: box office disaster. A few years later, *Chariots of Fire*, a low-key movie with unknown actors, an unknown director, and a story based on two obscure Olympic runners, was a worldwide smash. "Your odds in the movie business?" said the late Robert Lippert, a film producer and exhibitor. "You're better off at the crap tables in Reno or Las Vegas."

Not only in the movie business. In the 1920s, *Abie's Irish Rose* ran for years on Broadway after every critic had panned it as ludicrously sentimental. In the 1950s, the Russian Moisieyev Ballet danced before packed houses in America at the height of the Cold War. Decca Records turned down the Beatles in the early 1960s when Brian Epstein first brought their demo tapes to London. Decca executives felt, quite understandably, that four scruffy boys from Liverpool had little chance to break into the American-dominated world of pop music.

Even artists have little idea of what will work and what won't. Moss Hart, a playwright who wrote numerous Broadway hit shows (often collaborating with George Kaufman) and directed others (including *My Fair Lady*), discussed this problem eloquently in his brilliant autobiography, *Act One*. Performers and creators in all the show arts would gladly (or perhaps sorrowfully) second his sentiments:

> It is taken for granted that a cabinetmaker or a shoemaker, or a lawyer or doctor, for that matter, starting with a certain degree of talent for his profession, does, after the practice of that profession for ten or twenty years, learn how to make a good cabinet or a decent pair of shoes, or plead a case or diagnose an illness correctly. Not so the playwright. He is quite capable after twenty years of practice of having a left shoe for the second act when a right shoe is obviously called for, and is as unable to perceive the tumor in the third act that stares him in the face as the merest beginner. . . .
>
> If [this] maddens and seems inexplicable to the critics and the public . . . it frustrates and bewilders the playwright also.
>
> With each new play the playwright is a Columbus sailing uncharted seas.

Show artists hard at work do not always look businesslike. Movie director Billy Wilder once escorted a group of bankers who were financing his film on a tour of the set. When they got there, the cast and crew were playing cards, laughing and chatting between takes. The bankers were horrified to see the people whose salaries they were paying loafing on the job. Wilder, on the other hand, was delighted. "A very creative session," he said, knowing that a relaxed set would pay off in efficiency and in ad-lib touches that could make his movie come alive.

Yet show business is now a multibillion-dollar, worldwide industry. It manufactures a product—shows—and provides a service—entertainment. Show makers are the sellers; audiences, the buyers. Show makers try to stimulate demand for what they supply with advertising, promotion, brand names, and personality appeal. They follow up with attractive packaging and strategic marketing. Just like wholesale plumbers, they prefer profits to losses; some years they are happy to break even.

Show business is not a monolithic industry, but a grouping of many industries with major centers in the large cities of every country and many regional centers within each country. Some of its units are huge entertainment conglomerates with thousands of employees and thousands of shareholding owners. Others, like many neighborhood movie theatres and record stores, are "mom and pop" businesses that support a single family.

There are important segments of show business that are called "noncommercial": theatre arts schools, college concerts and productions, government and private foundations that make grants to artists, small experimental theatres, folk music coffeehouses, and endowed arts like opera and ballet that depend in part on public donation. Even public television, the country's fourth largest network, is considered noncommercial television. All, of course, are commercial in that they own or rent property, pay salaries, advertise, charge admission, or in

Clint Eastwood

some way exchange money for work. But they are not expected to earn profits. They are "nonprofit organizations," and their endowments and donations make up their losses.

There are possibilities for performing artists at every level of show business. One possibility underlies all the others: the possibility of making a living. A performer looks at show business as many possible sources of livelihood. A professional's career follows the path of paying work. This path can take sudden turns and shift levels.

After national success in the 1981 film *Atlantic City*, actress Susan Sarandon next appeared in *Extremities*, a small Off-Broadway production about a woman shattered by rape. The original cast of *Ain't Misbehavin!*, the Broadway show based on the music of Thomas "Fats" Waller, was first assembled for a workshop production of the musical at the nonprofit Manhattan Theatre Project. When John Houseman, in his seventies, made his acting debut in *The Paper Chase,* he had been a film, theatre, radio, and television producer; his job at the time was director of Juilliard's Theatre Center. After he won an Oscar as Best Supporting Actor for his role as a law school professor, he went on to use his imposing voice and presence in many television commercial celebrity endorsements.

Violinists in the Nashville Symphony often play country music sessions in the city's many recording studios. Jazzmen go direct from nightclub dates to months as composers-in-residence at colleges. Mezzo-soprano Marilyn Horne sang note-for-note copies of hit records for obscure record companies before she became an international opera star. She has declared succinctly, "You see, I'm not just an opera singer. I'm in the business of singing."

A performer can be employed by a company and paid a salary, or a performer can be an independent businessperson, a business unto him or herself, receiving fees for services rendered. Many performers, when they report their income for tax purposes, use Schedule C, the form for profits or losses from a business or self-employed profession. Successful performers often form personal corporations through which they do business. Actress Mary Tyler Moore's corporation, MTM Productions, has become a major producer of television shows, including "Love Boat" and "Hill Street Blues."

A performer's business is subject to the demands of any business, and to the peculiarly fluctuating uncertainties of show business. Besides learning all the skills necessary to create shows of value, performers must advertise and promote, package and market themselves and what they have to offer. For long periods they may find few buyers; show business' marketplace is crowded with performers offering excellent wares. Competition is severe.

There is statistically a miniscule chance that any performer at the start of a career will one day become wealthy, a star with the virtually limitless income of Paul McCartney or Clint Eastwood. There is an excellent chance that the beginner, despite determined effort, will not be able to make even a bare living and will eventually leave show business for another profession. In between there is the chance, which no one could accurately predict, that today's rookie will become tomorrow's seasoned pro, making a living that may be modest or well-to-do, but is secure enough for the performer to plan on show business as a lifetime occupation.

With that, I'll introduce myself briefly. I began show business as a profession in 1973 when I was twenty-eight. Being a singer, guitarist, harmonica player, and songwriter was a second career inspired by my first. A reporter and writer since college, I had become a free-lance writer specializing in pop music, interviewing performers like B. B. King and the Rolling Stones, whose music I loved, for the *New York Times*, *Rolling Stone*, and other magazines.

From the beginning, my performing partner has been singer, pianist, and songwriter Ellen Mandel. Now we're husband and wife. As the music and comedy duo Mandel & Lydon, we apprenticed in San Francisco area coffeehouses, then moved to New York where we've continued, working in clubs and colleges all over the Northeast and on television in New York and Boston.

Along the way we've studied acting, dance, voice, and music theory; accompanied choral groups and other singers; produced our own record; acted Off-Off Broadway; been extras in films; and demonstrated cookware in department stores to help pay the rent. Now, after eleven years and more ups and downs than we can count, we are in the last category: making a modest living and building with some confidence on our foundation of skills and experience. In the years to come, we hope, our talents and abilities—and our value and income—will continue to grow.

This is success in show business. If you decide on performing in show business as a career, and can develop as an artist while you make your living from your art, you will deserve hearty congratulations for a difficult achievement. All of this book is aimed at guiding and encouraging you to that success.

# VARIETY

PRICE $1.25

NEWSPAPER
Second Class P.O. Entry

Published Weekly at 154 West 46th Street, New York, N.Y. 10036, by Variety, Inc. Annual subscription, $65. Single copies $1.25.
Second Class Postage Paid at New York, N.Y. and at Additional Mailing Offices
©COPYRIGHT, 1984, BY VARIETY, INC., ALL RIGHTS RESERVED

34205

80 PAGES

New York, Wednesday, January 4, 1984

Vol. 313 No. 10          USPS 656-960

# WEBS' GROSS UP 12.3% TO $6.4-BIL

## 1ST QUARTER BULLISH AFTER RECORD '83

By JACK LOFTUS

While the three commercial television networks enter the New Year locked in a struggle for bigger slices of the advertising market, they can pause for a bit and look back on 1983 as a very good year — a $6.4-billion year to be exact.

That's according to figures from all three webs and represents a 12.3% increase in revenues in terms of total sales for all dayparts over 1982.

Just how all that translates to the bottom line won't be known until ABC, CBS and NBC put out their year-end results, but according to most estimates if the webs have been generally successful in keeping entertainment costs at a 10% growth rate, ABC Inc. should wind up the year with companywide profits up about 12% over 1982, CBS Inc. at roughly 14% and NBC probably much higher (but that's because the other companies have non-broadcast businesses).

Looking ahead to 1984, the first-quarter network sales market has finally taken off, and most experts expect the strong quarter to spill over into the rest of '84. If that prediction holds true, then the television networks may turn in sales revenues 18% higher than 1983.

As for national spot, 1983 estimates have it at 12% over the year previous (probably a bit lower than expected due to sharply reduced network prices in the fourth quarter which ran smack into national spot dollars). Local sales revenues look to be up 15.5%.

Again looking at '84, national spot is expected to bounce back and hit the 19% increase mark, while local will come in at 16%.

With all the moaning and groan-

(Continued on page 69)

## Murdoch Makes Bid For Warner; Curious Angles

Australian publisher Rupert Murdoch may have struck out once in his attempt to get a handle on the U.S. entertainment market, but he's apparently determined not to take a called second strike.

At least that is the way things looked this week, as the high-stakes battle for control of Warner Communications took one curious twist after another.

Strike one against Murdoch was the much ballyhooed Skyband, direct satellite to home service in the U.S. announced last May when the Aussie's News Satellite Television Ltd. signed a $75,000,000 six-year lease for five tv channels on a satellite owned by Satellite Business Systems. But that plan quickly

(Continued on page 76)

## Cannon Sets Sights On Amati Theaters, Rome's Major Chain

Rome, Jan. 3.

Cannon Group heads Menahem Golan and Yoram Globus are investigating the possibility of taking over the Amati exhibition circuit in Rome — the biggest single-city chain in Italy.

Cannon emissaries this week plan to meet with circuit reps to determine if the circuit can be acquired without corollary property. One of the two Cannon partners has been heard to say: "We know how to make and market movies, but we are still unfamiliar with property

(Continued on page 76)

## Argentine's New Gov't Giving Arts Positions To Recognized Figures

Buenos Aires, Jan. 3.

Buenos Aires cultural affairs have been entrusted by the new democratic government to well-known personalities from the arts, the letters and specialized fields. For instance, Pacho O'Donnell, formerly a blacklisted playwright, was appointed Culture Secretary by Mayor Juan Carlos Saguier. O'Donnell, in turn, chose a

(Continued on page 69)

## Kodak Intros 8m Vid System, Meets Standards

Eight millimeter video, the format that holds the potential to both unify and devastate the world's VCR marketplace, arrived in the U.S. Wednesday (4) via a new system introduced by Kodak.

Kodak's machines will hit the market in summer 1984 in the U.S. and worldwide in the fall.

Kodak is describing the system as "electronic home movies," but brochures for the unit also key in on its capabilities as a conventional VCR, where with add-ons, the unit "may be used to record your favorite broadcast programming."

Maximum running time for the Kodak sysem is currently 90 minutes, but the company says that will be increased as tape and

(Continued on page 69)

## Gold, Platinum LPs Down During '83; Total Awards Up

While a few albums sold far in excess of any 1982 titles, the total number of gold and platinum certifications by the Recording Industry Assn. of America barely increased from 1982 to 1983.

Total gold certifications rose from 154 in '82 to 158 last year, but the number of gold albums dropped significantly, from 130 to 111. Compensating for this decrease was the fact that certifications of gold singles, spurred by a

(Continued on page 78)

## Legal Confusion As 'Fraternal' Stunters Keep Women Out

By DAVID ROBB

Hollywood, Jan. 3.

The Stuntman's Assn. of Motion Pictures (SAMP), Hollywood's oldest, largest and most prestigeous stuntman's organization, does not allow women to join as members. It never has, and according to its president, it never will.

Stunts Unlimited, Hollywood's second oldest stuntman's organization, also has what amounts to a

(Continued on page 78)

HEATHCLIFF IS COMING TO TELEVISION!

Here comes HEATHCLIFF, next season's hottest syndicated strip for kids!

• 65 brand new daily half hours in production now for Fall '84.

• Top quality animation: $12 million production budget.

• Built-in audience appeal: This crafty comic-strip cat delights 80 million readers in hundreds of newspapers every day.

AMERICA'S LEADING TELEVISION SYNDICATION NETWORK

LEXINGTON BROADCAST SERVICES COMPANY, INC.
875 Third Ave., N.Y., N.Y. 10022
(212) 418-3000   Telex 640818

© 1983 McNaught Synd., Inc.

*chapter 2*

○ ○ ○ ○ ○ ○ ○ ○ ○ ○ ○ ○ ○ ○ ○ ○ ○ ○ ○ ○ ○ ○ ○ ○ ○ ○ ○ ○ ○ ○ ○ ○ ○ ○ ○ ○ ○

# THE *VARIETY* of show business

*VARIETY* is the national weekly newspaper of American show business. It covers the whole industry, reporting the latest developments in all the entertainment professions. Founded by Sime Silverman in 1905, *Variety* first focused on vaudeville and then expanded to include stories on Broadway theatre, Tin Pan Alley, and the growing movie industry. The paper was so successful among show business professionals that someone once suggested it could become one of the many fan magazines for the general public. No, said Silverman, *Variety* is for insiders. If everybody knew how the deals got made and how much people got paid, it would be like letting the public backstage before the show. Show magic depends on mystery for full effect; until the curtain goes up, the audience must sit suspensefully in the dark.

So *Variety* is still a tradepaper, telling the New York record producer, Burbank TV director, Nashville songwriter, Reno hotel owner, and neighborhood-movie-theatre manager in Bangor or Bakersfield what's cooking.

To talk to this far-flung tribe of troupers, *Variety* has developed its own language, English fractured along the same lines as Damon Runyan's wisecracking Broadway lingo. Even if you've never read *Variety*, you may have heard of its famous headline "HIX NIX STIX

*Variety* front page

. . . . . . .

19

PIX," the paper's way of saying country folk didn't like movies about country folk; they wanted big-city glamour, not their own reality. When a blizzard closed theatres in Buffalo, *Variety* headlined "BLIZ BOFFS BUFF BIZ." The stock market crash of 1929 got this page-one banner: "WALL ST. LAYS AN EGG."

*Variety*'s main office is a four-storey brownstone building just off Times Square in New York City. The paper has a total staff of close to one hundred reporters and editors, half of them in New York and the other half in nine bureaus: Hollywood, Washington, D.C., Chicago, London, Paris, Rome, Madrid, Sydney, and Toronto. Current circulation is about fifty thousand. *Variety* also owns *Daily Variety*, a separate newspaper published in Hollywood specifically for and about the movie industry.

You can get the latest issue of *Variety* by sending $1.25 plus $1.25 postage to

Subscription Department
*Variety*
154 West 46th Street
New York, New York 10036

In or near a big city, *Variety* is usually available at central libraries, large newsstands in the theatrical district, or at stands that carry out-of-town and special papers.

Get a recent issue of *Variety* and study it cover to cover, not to be able to answer a quiz on one particular story, but to catch the newspaper's flavor and down-to-earth point of view. Read the reports from Broadway and Hollywood, and the ones from Tokyo and Madrid. Look at the ads and see who is selling what to whom. Read the reviews, including the New Act reviews that cover artists on the rise. Look over the long columns of figures that detail how much movies are making at theatres all across the country. There will be items about opera stars and circus clowns, violinists and ventriloquists. Any issue of *Variety* is an excellent introduction to the whole spectrum of contemporary show business.

Take, for instance, the issue of Wednesday, January 4, 1984. A relatively thin, postholiday issue, it's still got eighty pages packed with news and ads. On page one, below the black sweep of the *Variety* logo, is a banner headline, "WEBS GROSS UP 12.3% TO $6.4 BIL." In other words, the three commercial television networks, "webs" in *Variety* lingo, have just released 1983 figures that show their total income for the year was $6.4 billion, 12.3 percent more than for 1982. *Variety* notes, "It was a very good year."

Page one's second big story ("Murdoch Makes Bid for Warner; Curious Angles") reports an attempt by the Australian newspaper magnate, Rupert Murdoch, to buy Warner Communications, the entertainment conglomerate that began sixty years ago as Warner Bros., a movie studio with stars like Al Jolson, Bette Davis, Lassie, and Bugs Bunny. Today, besides producing and distributing films, Warner owns cable TV networks, Atari video games, book publishers, and a dozen record labels. The "curious angles" include a maneuver by Warner to link itself to Chris Craft Industries as a way of avoiding a takeover by Murdoch, and speculation that Murdoch may really want to buy only Warner's film library. At press time, *Variety* reports, the outcome was still uncertain.

"Kodak Intros 8m Vid System, Meets Standards" is the third lead item. The Rochester-based film and camera company is bringing out its own home-video system. This new "Kodavision" will use eight-millimeter-wide tape designed to meet new international standards that may make the half-inch tape of Betamax and other systems obsolete.

Four stories on the lower half of page one report a drop in the total number of gold and platinum certifications for record albums selling over five hundred thousand and a million units: down from 189 in 1982 to 162 in 1983; a major movie theatre chain in Rome may change owners; Argentina's new government is giving jobs in cultural affairs to artists who were formerly blacklisted; and Hollywood's Stunt-man's Association still doesn't allow women members. As a fraternal organization, the association can keep its "men only" policy, but as an informal employment agency for TV and film producers looking for stunt personnel, the sex discrimination may be illegal. So far, however, stunt women have been reluctant to complain because, says *Variety*, "they still must rely on the men to hire them for the jobs they do get."

The rest of the front page is dominated by an ad, brightened by highlights in red ink, announcing that Heathcliff, the cartoon cat, is coming to TV in sixty-five brand-new half-hour episodes that will be ready for airing in the fall. The kids' show is being offered to broadcasters by Lexington Broadcast Services, "America's leading television syndication network."

Inside, on page two, wildly contrasting stories stand side by side in long narrow columns. The National Foundation for the Advancement of the Arts is holding its third national young talent search in

Miami, and a crime boss is headed to jail for thirty years after being convicted of skimming receipts at a Las Vegas hotel. A report from Paris says that Jean Paul Belmondo, who usually plays charmingly footloose adventurers in films, is in French court fighting to get his latest movie released as a video cassette. In London, the city council wants to ban entertainers who have performed in South Africa from playing in concert halls sponsored by the council. Under the headline "Hit The Jackpot And Sea Will Part" is a story about a new gambling boat, owned by a British-Israeli group, that will cruise the Red Sea.

On page three begins the "Pictures" section, the largest section in the paper—twenty-six pages on the movie industry. The section's first five pages are all news. "Calif. Anti-Piracy Law Cheers Show Biz" is the top story. A new law that went into effect January 1 imposes on convicted film (and record and video) counterfeiters fines of up to three times their profits and three times the damages they cause. California is the first state to pass such a law; Congress has twice failed to pass similar legislation.

Director-producer Francis Ford Coppola—*The Godfather I* and *II* are his best known films—will sell his Zoetrope Studios at auction February 10, hoping for a minimum price of $12.2 million. At a meeting of the National Association of Concessionaires, movie theatre snack-stand managers debated raising popcorn prices. Kirk Douglas has just finished a new Western, *Draw*, to be shown on Home Box Office; the International Animation Festival will be held in Toronto this year; and, sadly, William Demarest is dead at ninety-one. Demarest, "whose seventy year career spanned vaudeville, theatre, films, and television," was a character actor who played a lovable sourpuss in dozens of 1930s and 1940s comedies, including two classics directed by Preston Sturges, *Hail the Conquering Hero* and *Miracle at Morgan's Creek*. Later in his career he made a comeback as Uncle Charley on the popular TV situation comedy "My Three Sons."

After a huge two-page ad for the gangster film *Scarface*, announcing that it grossed $22 million in its first twenty-four days, come four pages of detailed reports of box office income from movie theatres all over the country. These give the theatre's name, size, ticket price, the movie being shown, and, often, a comparison to the week before, as well as the theatre's "nut"—its basic operating costs. New York's Astor Plaza, for example, which seats 1525 and charges $5, took in "a brilliant $85,000" on the comedy drama *Terms of Endearment*. The week before the same film earned $42,432 in that theatre. The theatre's

Movie Marquee, Salt Lake City, Utah

nut is $21,000, so for those two weeks there was a profit of $85,000 to be split between the Loews chain, which owns the theatre, and Paramount, the film's distributors. Burt Reynolds's *The Man Who Loved Women*, in contrast, broke even at the Art Theatre in Greenwich Village, earning $8500 against an $8500 nut.

*Variety* spices up these long columns of figures with humor. In the short paragraphs that introduce the numbers, the reporters call theatres showing *Educating Rita* "schools," those with *Return of the Jedi* "galaxies," and *Christine*, a movie about a killer car, is playing "garages." A week is a "frame" (sometimes a "spin" or "stanza"), and if a movie is held over for three or more frames, it's "showing legs."

Even without the jokes, these pages would have avid readers. Nowhere else can film makers and sellers get such instant reports on how their product, and the competition's, is doing in the marketplace. "My mother used to tell me I was wasting my time in show business," an actor once joked on the "Tonight Show," "but now she reads *Variety* and complains if the gross on my new movie is down in the third frame at some mall Cinema III in Pittsburgh."

The most closely read of all these pages is solid figures: the "50 Top Grossing Films." This is the movie industry's equivalent of *Billboard* magazine's "Hot 100" for the record industry. From the first week of release, executives, directors, actors, composers, and costume designers study the full-page chart to see how their film is faring. The better it does, the higher their own prestige and bargaining power for their next project.

Clint Eastwood's *Sudden Impact*, the third of his Dirty Harry series, is number one this week with a gross of $2.3 million (the grosses listed here are a sampling compiled by the Standard Data Corporation, approximately one third of the national total). *Sudden Impact* was also number one the week before with an even bigger gross—just over $3 million. *Terms of Endearment* is now number two and *Scarface* number three; the previous week their positions were reversed. The science fiction adventure *Return of the Jedi* is still holding strong in sixteenth place after thirty-one weeks on the chart; *48 Hours*, a comedy cops-and-robbers film, has also been listed for thirty-one weeks but it is last on the chart. Its total gross is $24 million compared to *Jedi*'s $68 million.

Dollars and deals, deals and dollars—*Variety* can seem hard-boiled on first reading. There are no photographs, no scandalous gossip, and no heart-to-heart interviews with flamboyant stars who reveal at great length that they long for privacy. *Variety* leaves celebrity psychologizing to the fan magazines. Its job is to see through the ballyhoo and press release puffery to the humming machinery that keeps the neon lights bright and shining. Like Detective Joe Friday, whom Jack Webb used to play on TV's "Dragnet," *Variety* wants "Just the facts, Ma'am."

Yet the very plainness of *Variety*'s perspective conveys a respect for show business and the skilled professionals at work in it. The review of a new Canadian movie, *Dead Wrong*, for example, begins by praising director Len Kowalewich for bringing in "a viable thriller for under $1,000,000 that looks as though it cost thrice as much." The camera work of Doug McKay is "crisp, imaginative lensing . . . every shot shows the eye of a craftsman." Editor Jana Fritsch had a tough job because the low budget meant there was little extra footage for her to choose from, but her cutting has "style." The actors are seen as craftspeople too. The central quartet in this film has "a tongue in cheek attitude . . . that is perfectly judged." Even in the reviews, however, economic considerations are not forgotten; for another film, *Rocking Silver* from Denmark, "foreign sales can hardly be expected."

After "Pictures" comes the paper's second biggest section: twenty-five pages of "Radio-Television." "CBS Skeds 18 Pilots" is the lead story. The network will fund the production of eighteen trial shows, a mix of half-hour comedies and hour-long dramas, to be considered as possible additions to the fall schedule. How many will be expanded to full series will depend on the success of current shows. Over in the coastal town of Monastir, Tunisia, rioting hasn't halted the shooting of "Anno Domini," a $30 million, twelve-hour NBC mini-series about the early days of Christianity.

NBC also lucked out on the New Year's Day football games. The Orange Bowl it was broadcasting turned out to be a 30–31 cliff-hanger, tense until the last second of play. ABC's Sugar Bowl was a low-scoring, ho-hum affair that many football fans deserted early to catch the action on NBC.

An article in the radio section reports that a New York City radio station changed from an easy listening format to Top-40 and emerged as the city's top station in the autumn Arbitron ratings. Another article says that New Hampshire used to have one TV station, but soon it will have four. Two pages are full of personnel changes at stations around the world. Polly Reynolds in Providence, Rhode Island, is switching from WEAN radio to WJAR-TV, replacing Gary Scurka, who "ankles" to KOUR-TV in Sacramento, California.

The big TV ads are for "Magnum PI," "Hart to Hart," and "Hill Street Blues." The advertisements are not meant to push the current series on the networks, but to offer the syndication to local stations. In other words, reruns. You can see "Happy Days," "Mary Tyler Moore," and "MASH" at two in the afternoon or two in the morning because, for a share of the retail profits, the original producers let syndication companies like Viacom or MCA-TV sell their shows over and over again. Successful syndication can double or even triple the earnings of a show's original run. "I Love Lucy" has been rerunning continuously for twenty-five years.

Syndicators also sell independent, low-budget shows like "Make Me Laugh," "Lie Detector," and "Heathcliff," the cartoon advertised on page one of this issue. A small ad in the Radio-TV section announces a new show, "Putting on the Hits," in which amateurs dress up like their favorite recording stars and sing along with their records. Twenty-six weeks of "Putting on the Hits" are available. A station can run it once a week for the twenty-six weeks, rerun it once, and have a year's worth of music and comedy that could be as popular as "The Gong Show."

Home video gets two pages. The big story is Michael Jackson's video "Thriller." It is so popular that record stores as well as video shops are selling it, a breakthrough that could push the rock-video boom to new heights. Other stories reflect home video's huge growth. Vestron, a two-year-old company that markets movies as video cassettes, is now grossing $40 million a year. Cassette rentals are increasing along with sales, and *Variety* estimates that the home video business is now grossing over $400 million a year. A full-page ad announces a new cassette for sale: *The Day After*, a movie made for television about the aftermath of atomic war in Kansas. The ad says the cassette will contain "scenes not previously viewed."

After two pages of International news from Tokyo, Rome, Glasgow, Rio de Janeiro, and other cities, there are four pages of "Music-Records." Michael Jackson is on top here too: his single with Paul McCartney, "Say," and the *Thriller* album are both number one. ASCAP—the American Society of Composers, Authors, and Publishers—is having a songwriting seminar in June that will be taped for the US Information Agency. Young songwriters will perform their original material and get evaluations from pros like singer Roberta Flack.

Ever since Glen Campbell had a hit with "Rhinestone Cowboy," a ballad about a country singer losing touch with his roots in the glittering world of Las Vegas and Los Angeles, Steve Weiss, who wrote the song, has been trying to get the song made into a movie. Now, *Variety* reports, his ten-year dream is coming true. The film is in production with Dolly Parton and Sylvester Stallone in starring roles, and 20th Century Fox will release it. One column over from this success story is a report that Beach Boy Dennis Wilson is dead at thirty-nine. One of the three Wilson brothers who founded the surf-rock group, drummer Dennis drowned in the Pacific Ocean near Malibu. His "simple pounding style fit the Beach Boys' fun music formula perfectly," *Variety* notes.

The Harmony Hut record stores, a popular chain in the mid-Atlantic states for thirty years, has been bought by the American Can Company another article notes. This is not ACC's first step into entertainment retailing; it already owns 363 Musicland, 37 Sam Goody, and 20 Discount Record stores. Buying the 24 Harmony Huts for $8 million gives the conglomerate a strong foothold in the important New Jersey-to-Washington, D.C. region.

*Variety*'s music reviews cover stars new, old, and in-between. A rave review about an upcoming rock-blues guitar player from Texas, Stevie Ray Vaughn, predicts that his "overwhelming virtuosity" may make him "a legend in his own time." Barry Manilow at Los Angeles's

Palace Theatre, Times Square,
New York City

Broadway's
Spectacular
Musical
Comedy!

GEORGE HEARN KEITH MICHEL
*La Cage*
JERRY HERMAN    HARVEY FIERSTEIN
ARTHUR LAURENTS

A CHORUS LINE

New York's
Erotic Musical Comedy!

ARTKRAFT STRAUSS

## PALACE

*La Cage aux folles*
THE BROADWAY MUSICAL

ORIGINAL BROADWAY CAST ALBUM ON **RCA** RECORDS AND TAPES

© PAN AM.

WINNER **6** 1984 TONY AWARDS
BEST MUSICAL

Oh!
Calcutta!

Edison Theatre
47th St. West of Br.
PHONCHARGE 757-

## PALACE

*La Cage aux folles*
THE BROADWAY MUSICAL

WINNER-6
1984 TONY AWARDS
INCL. BEST MUSICAL

Canon CA
PHOTOGRAPH THE UNIVERSAL LA
ROYAL ART GAL

Kodak Film    PROG

SONY
PANASONIC
AKAI
TECHNICS

AIWA
SHARP
TOSHIBA
SANYO
JVL
ER

Universal Amphitheatre gets a good notice, and a third review says that Pearl Bailey in Schenectady "is not as energetic as she used to be. But she has grown older gracefully."

There is a page on Auditoriums and Arenas (a former movie palace in Utica is being restored), one page on Clubs and Concerts (four new comedy clubs in Pittsburgh), and then come the New Act reviews. Here *Variety* notes the arrival of new talents. A New Acts review is often a young entertainer's first nod of national recognition. When reviewer Fred Kirby called Ellen and me "talented songwriters . . . whose slick performance is bright with good comedic touches" in our 1977 New Acts review, it felt like a welcome into *Variety*'s world.

The top review in this issue: David Walden and Arlene Meadows at Garbo's Bistro in Toronto. Walden and Meadows, *Variety* reports, are packing them in at the "large and friendly" club with a "tour de force" cabaret revue, a mixture of songs, comedy, and satirical sketches. Walden is a "writer/actor/composer/singer of considerable proportions," and Meadows "hilarious . . . without apparent effort." The second review is a pan. Rhythm-and-blues singer Thurston Harris's show at Los Angeles's big country-music nightclub, the Palomino, was, "to put it politely, an extremely loose affair." Harris had had several hit records in the 1950s; since one of them, "Little Bitty Pretty One," was in the soundtrack of the movie *Christine*, he was attempting a comeback. But, said *Variety*, "it was not an auspicious return."

"Legitimate"—plays, musicals, and opera—gets five pages. The box office was jumping on Broadway over Christmas: $6 million for twenty-three shows, the second highest total in history. A new musical at New York's Public Theatre, *The Human Comedy*, gets a good review for its music by Galt McDermott (composer of *Hair*), but *Variety* notes that the lyrics are weak. The Philadelphia Orchestra is scheduling two operas for its 1984–1985 season, and the Frankfurt Opera has made a success of Berlioz's opera *The Trojans*, even though it is six hours long.

The "Casting News" column lists six theatrical shows looking for actors, dancers, and singers. Two of the shows are Off-Broadway, one is for a dinner theatre in East Windsor, Connecticut, another is for a summer stock company in Millburn, New Jersey, and two are for touring companies that will present *Jerry's Girls* and *The King and I* all over the country. A seventh show, *I Love New York*, is an "industrial," one of many shows put together to entertain customers and clients at business conventions. Industrials are major employers;

some performers specialize in them, others use them for valuable experience and for making contacts.

There are "open calls"—auditions at which any performer can try out—for all seven shows, but for the six theatrical shows, the first auditions are limited to members of Actors' Equity, the actors' union. Several of the auditions will be held in the Actors' Equity Building at 165 West 46th Street, across the street from *Variety*'s building.

Then the obituaries. Drummer Wilson and actor Demarest were covered in the news pages. Here are noted the passing of British blues singer Alexis Koerner, who encouraged the young Rolling Stones; the founder of Britain's BBC-TV2, Lord Harry Bilkington; and a Yiddish-English comedy writer, Julie Berns. There are also four marriages listed, and TV's "Today Show" co-anchor Jane Pauley, married to cartoonist-playwright Garry Trudeau, has just had twins.

That's one issue of *Variety*. What tips are there for a show business newcomer? The ASCAP songwriting seminar that will be taped and the National Foundation for the Advancement of the Arts talent search in Miami are both events worth exploring. Home-video is a field to be aware of. The shake-up it is giving to movies, TV, and music continues. The movie finally being made of *Rhinestone Cowboy* is inspiring proof that dogged persistence can pay off. Above all, there is the sense that show business is a busy hive of business and artistic endeavor, with bees making honey all over the world.

What's in your *Variety*? What did you get out of it? What's the top-grossing film in your issue? Have you seen it? What's on Broadway, on the "webs," or on the boardwalk at Atlantic City? Any reports on what's happening in your hometown or the city nearest you? Can you sense the links that tie all this activity together?

The variety of *Variety* is the variety of show business itself and one of its greatest charms. That variety is based on the ultimate individuality of all show makers. No one puts on quite the same show. Some play the violin, others love the slightly different viola. There are singers who tell a few jokes, there are comedians who sing as a joke. There are camera people, makeup people, stunt people (despite the Stuntman's Association!), producers, actors, musicians, and magicians. Young, old, of any color, weight, sex, or religious belief, and from anywhere on earth—if you can make the audience clap and come back for more, there's a place for you in show business and news in you for *Variety*.

*chapter 3*

○ ○ ○ ○ ○ ○ ○ ○ ○ ○ ○ ○ ○ ○ ○ ○ ○ ○ ○ ○ ○ ○ ○ ○ ○ ○ ○ ○ ○ ○ ○ ○ ○ ○ ○ ○ ○ ○

# LEARNING TWENTY-FOUR HOURS A DAY

A N excellent show conveys truth observed from life and is itself well made. In other words, it is true to life and true to art, blending valuable content and pleasing form. It follows that an aspiring performer needs to observe life and shows with alert interest and a willingness to learn.

To learn from life is a great hope for any human being and a primary goal of religion, science, philosophy, mathematics, medicine, literature, and all the arts. One of man's deepest intuitions is that life has meaning and direction. The idea that the living can learn from life, belief in social progress and personal growth, and faith in the future are all based on this intuition. "It is good to live and learn," said Cervantes in *Don Quixote;* sayings in every language echo the thought that life is the great teacher.

Learning from life can embrace every experience. We can learn by looking within: "Know thyself," said Socrates; we can learn from our fellows: "The proper study of mankind is man," wrote Alexander Pope; and we can learn from the world around us: "Let Nature be your teacher," William Wordsworth advised. Each of us, however, learns from what we experience individually; each outlook on life is unique. Many of the experiences we learn from are ones we can't

An empty stage—where the show maker begins (Entermedia Theatre, N.Y.C.)

. . . . . . . .

31

control, the circumstances of our birth and the weather, for instance, or ones we don't wish for—illness, pain, and the death of people we love. It is impossible to tell someone what they will learn from life, and only barely possible to suggest how.

The key, I think, is *openness*, a state of relaxed receptivity to stimuli. This is at first a passive state; it is enough to be aware of what is coming in. There is no immediate need to judge anything or draw conclusions actively. Whatever is happening, notice and let happen. Ideas about what you are receiving may begin to take shape of their own accord. Let them happen too—they may be what you are learning—and let them go when new ideas take shape.

Here is an exercise to try.

1. Be by yourself in a room.
2. Sit still and be quiet.
3. Let yourself relax; breathe evenly.
4. Open your senses to all that is around you.
5. Let all you see, hear, smell, and sense on your skin soak into you.

The table, patiently continuing; the half-open scissors resting on its surface; the leaves on a tree outside the window trembling back to stillness after a breeze; your own heart beating. That is life.

Try the same exercise at the seashore, in an open field, or in the woods. After you have a quiet sense of all that is happening, let yourself follow what interests you in more detail. You may find yourself fascinated by the colors in a single stone, studying a purposeful column of ants, discovering the spirals in a pine cone. Try it again on a city street crowded with people of every shape and size walking, talking, running, reading, eating, driving, saying hello, waving goodbye. Try it again at a dinner gathering of family and friends, people you have known all your life. Mentally step back from the hubbub of cutlery and conversation for a moment and take it all in: these familiar faces and familiar voices, all rich in association and memory, each so distinct and well known to you, yet ever-changing and still mysterious. Here too the table under the tablecloth patiently continues, and the flowers on the familiar china bloom as they always have.

If you are moved to lift your glass and toast, "L'Chaim"—"To life!"—good for you. Learning from life requires more than quiet reception; it takes active appreciation. This can be studious: when what you receive strongly arouses your interest, you can seek more information by repeated observation, experiment, and research. It can be adventurous: traveling to new lands, meeting new people, trying new foods, a new haircut, bright green socks! And it can be plain enjoyment with gusto: meeting life head on, making the best of what comes, moving forward with vigor, humor, and determination.

The great pianist Arthur Rubinstein lived and worked well into his nineties. Yet as a young man in Berlin, when he had no money, his career seemed stalemated, and he was homesick for Poland, he attempted suicide by hanging himself with his belt. Fortunately the belt broke. He fell to the floor, weeping and in shock. Then he went to the piano and played until he suddenly felt hungry. He went out to buy a sausage dinner. Once on the street, as he wrote in his auto-biography, *My Young Years,*

> A sudden impulse made me stop. Something strange came over me, call it a revelation or a vision. I looked at everything around me with new eyes, as if I had never seen any of it before. The street, the trees, the houses, dogs chasing each other, and the men and women, all looked different, and the noise of the great city—I was fascinated by it all.
>
> Well, on that night, right there in the street . . . my brain was full of philosophical thoughts, and it resulted in a new conception of life and a new criterion of values, all for my private use. The eternal, unsolved question—What gave birth to the universe? What is the reason for its existence?—would involve a long dissertation.
>
> Let me say only that in this chaos of thoughts I discovered the secret of happiness and I still cherish it: Love life for better or for worse, without conditions.

What you learn from life will permeate your work, becoming in time the essence of what you communicate: your true observations. It will enrich your work and give it a center—or even change it alto-gether. In January, 1936, the country comedienne Minnie Pearl was twenty-four-year-old Ophelia Colley, a touring play director for a theatre company in Atlanta. Her next assignment was a tiny village near Sand Mountain, Alabama, where she arrived with two dollars in her pocket one snowy night. The school principal drove her down a winding road to a small log cabin. The two went around to the kitchen door, and the principal knocked.

"A tall thin lady in her seventies came to the door," Minnie wrote in her autobiography, *Minnie Pearl.* "She wore a clean, faded print dress and an apron, and you could tell she had worked hard all her life by the lines in her face." The woman was hospitable and, after a few words, invited young Ophelia to stay. She did stay for the ten days it took to mount the play; over breakfast at daybreak and dinner by lantern light she got to know the old woman.

The woman's kindness and gentle manner fascinated Ophelia. She served suppers of salt pork and cornbread as "if she'd been serving a gourmet meal in a mansion." She had had sixteen children yet had never missed helping out at harvest time. Her stories were laced with a dry country wit. Ophelia was sorry to go when the ten days were up; so was the old woman to see her go. "Lord a'mercy, child, you're just like one of us," she said.

Ophelia kept thinking about the woman, and began telling stories, imitating her down-to-earth manner. Slowly a character evolved; Ophelia named her Minnie Pearl. Audiences loved Minnie Pearl, and Ophelia had a new career. While she had been at the cabin, however, no such thought had entered her mind. She had just liked the old woman and listened to her. "I had no way of knowing she would change my life."

You will not know consciously all that you learn, either. The more you learn, the less you may feel you do know. Socrates claimed to know nothing—yet think how much the world has learned from Socrates!

Learning from shows is part of learning from life and requires the same openness and appreciation. Fortunately, shows, like the weather, are all around you. Unless you've spent your life deep in the backwoods without even a radio, you've been constantly exposed to show business since you were a baby. "Sesame Street," Mr. Rogers, cartoons on Saturday morning, even Mickey Mouse night-lights—show business grabs its customers young.

Now you need to learn from shows as a performer. That will mean preparing for and performing your own shows; we'll get to those in the next two chapters. Even before that, and certainly with it, you need to increase and sharpen your awareness of the performing arts and show business as a whole.

Reading an issue of *Variety* is one step. Calling a TV station and asking if there is any way you could observe its operation is another; being in a show's studio audience is a good chance for an inside look. If a movie is being shot on location nearby, stop and watch for as long as you can. Ask questions of any friendly member of the crew. Keep an eye on the entertainment pages of your local newspaper; know what's in town and what's coming. One by one, listen to every station

on the radio dial, AM and FM, for at least five minutes. Look in the *Yellow Pages* and see what is listed for Musicians and Music Services, Theatres and Theatrical Agents, Recording Studios, Audio and Video—any show business field that interests you.

An inside look: playing the imposter on "To Tell The Truth"

Go to the library. Plays and music, of course, live in books as literature. Excellent books have been written about every facet of show business and its arts. I list a few in this book's bibliography. Others you can find in any public library. Some you may want to buy, but library browsing and borrowing has the great advantage of being free. Even a small library is a treasure-house of ideas and inspiration and a storehouse of necessary information—reference books, for example, that list, with addresses and phone numbers, colleges, opera companies, music publishers, and movie studios.

Most libraries put books on the performing arts together, often in a special room that includes racks of current performing arts periodicals as well as poster boards with calendars of upcoming local shows. The Dewey decimal system of cataloguing, in use in most American libraries, groups books on specific arts under these numbers (allow for small local variations):

Music: 780 and up
Theatre: 792
Movies: 792.9
Dance: 793

Plays are grouped with poetry in the 800s; American plays are 812, English plays 822, for instance. Biographies and autobiographies of show business figures are grouped under *B* for Biography, and then alphabetically by the last name of the book's subject.

Go to shows, as many as you can. You'll naturally go to the shows that interest you most, but be eclectic. If you've never seen flamenco dancing, go. If you're sure you won't like chamber music, go. Every show, from a school pageant to a daytime game program, contains clues about what does and doesn't work in show business. Look, listen, and learn.

Again, there is no need to decide on what you take in; let it happen. There may come times when you will want to stop this absorption process, to shut out the work of others and concentrate only on what you generate from within. Open, active learning is vital, however. It is the only way a young performer can glimpse the world he is entering and the possibilities it holds in store.

Edward G. Robinson was seventeen years old in 1912, a freshman at the City College of New York, when he began thinking of becoming an actor. He wrote in his autobiography, *All My Yesterdays:*

> Not that I really knew what it was like to be an actor. I had to find out. So I haunted the Astor Library, reading the lives of the great actors: Edwin Booth, Robert Mansfield, David Garrick, Henry Irving, for instance, and the great plays of Aeschylus to Ibsen, and the dramatic criticism of George Bernard Shaw.
>
> And with every penny I saved, I'd get second balcony seats for any play that was running in the Bronx. In addition, I secretly traveled to Broadway and peered from the highest point of the Empire and Lyceum theatres at the great actors and great plays, and some lousy actors and lousy plays.

Shows themselves will be your primary source of information. Watching shows, you will need more than increased awareness. You will need a new perspective: the show maker's point of view.

This will take time to learn because it is nearly the opposite of the audience's point of view. Shows, remember, are illusions, meant to fool people as well as tell them the truth. The audience are the people to be fooled—"gillies" in circus slang. The show makers are the ones doing the fooling. To the show maker, the illusion is a construction of reality, one he or she worked to put together. The magician knows where the rabbit is all the time.

Think for a moment of a blank movie screen or an empty stage. That's what show makers start with. All the color and action the audience sees in a film, play, or concert, all the scenery and sets, costumes and dialogue, sound effects and music, were put there by somebody on purpose. Even accidents and ad-libs happen in a prepared context. The audience experiences something that people created, in every detail, for them to experience.

Realizing that someone made the show is the first step in acquiring the show maker's point of view. The second is imagining yourself, not quite in the show maker's shoes, but an invisible friend looking over his or her shoulder, attempting to understand all the factors and decisions involved in putting the show together. The two steps make one mental leap out of the audience: a decision to watch every show as a fellow creator, a colleague in spirit of the people who made it. You'll need to make that leap consciously at first. It will be easier the more you perform yourself. Eventually it will be instinctive, part of your mental equipment as a professional.

You can try using this perspective everytime you watch a show, even flopped on the sofa watching the Late Show. There, in an old movie, may be an actor who you know as a regular on a prime-time comedy series: Beatrice Arthur, the star of "Maude," in a small role in *Auntie Mame*; Sylvia Sydney from "WKRP in Cincinnati" as the doomed heroine in Josef von Sternberg's *An American Tragedy*. How has time changed them? How did they adapt their work to the vastly different circumstances? Notice the music. How is the composer capturing the mood—with pizzicato strings or synthesized shrieks? Who is the composer? Have you heard his work in any other movie? That odd camera angle up the stairs—why did the director choose it? Perhaps to make the stairs look ominous. If so, do you think the effect works?

Then come the ads. Their pace is different from the movies, the flow of images more rapid-fire. A film editor creates this difference by how he cuts and splices his footage. Here, too, are actors hard at work. How do the celebrities use the best-known aspects of their public images to sell the products they're endorsing? How do the actors you don't know manage to be distinctive and typical at the same time?

Here's a question to test your professional powers of observation: how can you tell a movie made for television from one made to be shown first in a movie theatre? Maybe you can tell the difference already; many viewers can. But what makes the difference? A few

LEARNING

TWENTY-FOUR

HOURS A DAY

hints: TV movies tend to have more close-ups and less cluttered sets, because their makers are thinking in terms of small screens; the pace of a theatrical movie can be faster, because with a paying audience sitting in the dark away from home, its makers have a more attentive audience. Look for further differences in lighting, camera movement, and treatment of subject matter.

It takes an effort to watch from the show maker's point of view. For one thing, you are pitted against the intelligence, experience, and showmanship of the show maker. The people who made the show don't want you to see how it's done; they want to fool you. They've spent hours and years figuring out just what your reactions will be to each unfolding element of the show so they can always be one step ahead of you.

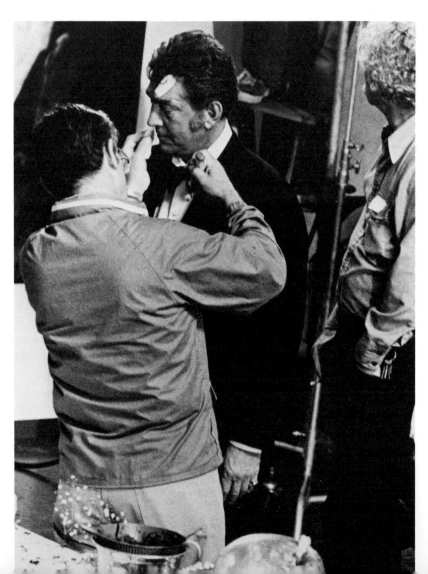

Dean Martin from the show
maker's point of view

As an instance of that: Ellen and I once plotted a comedy sequence that would land us in a realistic argument halfway through the show. "What if someone tries to intervene?" I asked in rehearsal.

"We'll drop the argument," Ellen suggested, "turn on him together, and tell him to mind his own business." Come show time, somebody did think we were fighting for real and tried to calm us down. Whammy—we gave it to him with both barrels, and the audience roared with laughter.

It is also fun to let a show entertain us unresistingly, to laugh at the Marx brothers without trying to analyze how they do it. Fortunately, watching like a pro doesn't mean being a nerveless and humorless critic. The new perspective includes enjoyment. Show makers love shows; if anything, they get more carried away than an ordinary fan. Actress Uta Hagen, in her book *Respect for Acting*, describes going to see an idol of hers, Laurette Taylor, in the play *Outward Bound*. Each time she went determined to study how Miss Taylor created her character; "each time . . . she simply caught me up in her spontaneity to the point of eliminating my own objectivity."

Experienced performers empathize with the performers and the technicians when they watch a show. They appreciate the attention to detail required to build a believable character or make a splashy effect. They know that for every part cast, perhaps twenty people auditioned, that someone sewed every last bangle on the costumes. When they applaud, they're clapping for the illusion and the work that made it real.

The best way for a beginning performer to learn this perspective— to enjoy the illusion and to see through it—is to see a show more than once.

When there's a show in town that really interests you, get tickets, the best you can afford, to two or three performances. It may be a strain on the pocketbook, but it will pay off in the long run. Most movies, of course, you can sit through until the theatre closes. TV shows can be seen on reruns, and records and tapes you can play to your heart's content. If you have a video cassette player-recorder, terrific! They are perfect for analytical watching.

Music records and tapes are a special case because we're used to listening to them over and over, but often with only half an ear. Now sit down in front of the speakers and concentrate. For a moment forget the lead melody as carried by the vocal or predominating instruments. Sense the underlying pulse. What is the meter—3/4, 4/4, 6/8? Listen for the bass line; that's the music's harmonic foundation. Pick out the different instruments one by one and follow their progress. When and how do they link up with the others? When does each speak out on its own?

Now go back to the melody. How many melodies are there? Almost all music has themes and counterthemes that occur in patterned sequences. Listen for these themes (sometimes called verse, chorus, and bridge in popular music) and how they repeat, vary, and relate to each other.

Listen to the vocal, if there is one. How many people are singing? Sometimes harmony and background voices are so skillfully blended with the lead voice that they became nearly indistinguishable. Pay attention to the lyrics. What is the story and how do they tell it? Does the melody flow with the quiet moments and climaxes of the words? How does the singer vary his or her tone and dynamics to color the song's story? If you can, find different versions of the same piece of music and compare interpretations.

Also study the record jacket, the photos, and graphic design. This is the music's sales package. What visual images did the designer use to suggest the sounds inside? Artist photos and credits show and tell you who made the record. Did you like the drumming? Who's the drummer? Are the song publishers listed? Which performance rights society do the publishers belong to, ASCAP (American Society of Composers, Authors, and Publishers) or BMI (Broadcast Music Incorporated)? If your work involves music, these details are valuable. You may work with any of these people one day. You may make a record; how do you imagine your record jacket looking? If you think this record's makers might like what you do, you could send them a well-presented sample, mentioning that you liked their work.

At the movies or a play, a music, dance, or comedy performance, sit back and enjoy the show the first time through. If it's good, it will seem fresh, lively, and surprising—done just for you at that very moment. Before you see it again, however, prepare yourself mentally.

If it's a movie, remind yourself that the whole project took perhaps two years from start to finish, and that it's been "in the can," inert reels of celluloid, for months before it gets to your neighborhood theatre. Remember that all the actors, the director, scriptwriters, producers, and assistant soundmen knew that the heroine wasn't going to die in the car crash. All the blood and bruises were makeup and she wasn't in pain—she was an actress delighted to have a job!

Between two concerts, realize that the performers are probably on tour; they might have been in Atlanta last night and will be in Pittsburgh, giving much the same show, tomorrow night. Before seeing a play the second time, recall specific bits of stage business—the slightly rattling teacup that let you know that character had a secret worry—and be on the lookout for them to happen again.

Thus armed, go back in and watch. This time you have a good idea what's going to happen; the rest of the audience doesn't. Already you are that much closer to the show maker's point of view. Now you can watch and listen to the audience too. Are they laughing, shouting, or clapping along at the same moments you and the first audience did? How did the show makers prepare those moments?

A movie, of course, is always exactly the same, but in every live show there will be variations. Look for similarities and differences. This can be particularly interesting in comedy. A stand-up comedian *must* create the illusion that his gags are spilling ad lib from his teeming brain. Now you're seeing him trot them out a second time. How does he vary his inflections, his pauses, and his double takes to suit the rapport he's creating with the new audience? Are there any true ad libs that he tosses out to meet a new situation? (If you saw him five times, you might discover that even those ad libs are really from his "ad-lib file," ready for use as needed.)

Second time through is the time to watch all the background elements of the show. Very often the show makers have worked hard to make you focus on a particular person or part of the stage or screen. Go against the focus—look at and listen to what else is going on. At a dance concert, for instance, look away from the principal dancer, pick one of the corps, and follow her wherever the choreography takes her. Watch your dancer as she stands nearly motionless, framing the central action, poised and ready to move again. She's in the background, but she's helping to create the texture on which the focal points shine like diamonds on blue velvet. You may have to push yourself to look away from the center of action; how hard you have to push is a good measure of how hard the show maker is pushing you to see the show *his* way.

Between shows, read the program; at a film, study the production credits carefully the second time through. You bought tickets to see Chuck Mangione or Linda Ronstadt or Clint Eastwood or Jessica Tandy, but check the names of everyone else who made the show possible. If any detail struck you as particularly excellent, connect it with the right name, and then look for that name in the future. Soon you'll start to see interesting examples of career progress. Here's a tip: watch for the name Westmore in the makeup credits for movies old and new. Father and son, uncle and nephew, Westmores have been a makeup clan for sixty years, as prolific and talented as the acting Barrymores. A Westmore may make you up some day.

The next step is to look beyond details to larger show elements. Show makers decide the many details of their shows by referring, consciously or semiconsciously, to overall conceptions of how they want their shows to sound and look, what they want them to say in sum. A makeup man will suggest and an actress accept or reject scarlet or coral lipstick because of a conception of character, for instance; a bandleader will call for an up-tempo number to create a mood he has in mind. Countless details of costuming, set design, acting, and musical accompaniment in plays and films are decided on the basis of historical period. If the details of a show don't advance the plot, the audience won't understand the story the show makers are trying to tell.

Every aware show maker has a conception of style, an inner sense of his or her own taste, a feeling for what is appropriate in the circumstances. Style is ultimately personal; a trumpet player decides just how much vibrato he wants to give a note as a chef adds pepper to a stew. Any more would be too much, any less not quite right. Style also has a more general meaning: what is appropriate for certain styles of show and performance. There is a style of low-key British comedy and a style of zany French farce. A string quartet and a four-piece rockabilly band: four people playing music of different styles with different styles of presentation. What are the string quartet musicians saying to you with their tuxedoes and black shoes, the calm formality of their manner? What would they be saying if they wore spangled Western shirts and cowboy boots and cracked corny jokes between every piece?

Two important show elements begin before the show and end after it: anticipation and resolution. Anticipation starts the moment an ad or publicity item stirs your curiosity, and it keeps building until the lights dim and the curtain rises. Creating, guiding, and heightening anticipation is an essential show business art. Performers often take part in it through press interviews, promotional appearances, consulting on and sometimes directing advertising campaigns. Show makers want an audience that has been teased and tantalized with just

Lobby, San Francisco
Opera House

enough tidbits about the show to have some sense of, but plenty of suspense about, what they are going to experience. Resolution begins as the show draws to a close—big finale, quiet ebbing away, or last minute twist—but also continues in the mood with which the audience leaves. A strong resolution makes people tell their friends to see the show (word of mouth), and that's what makes a hit.

Examine your own sense of anticipation and resolution about the shows you see. How do ad and publicity campaigns effect you? Some shows you dress up for, others you go to in jeans—why? Compare the lobbies of a movie theatre and an opera house. When you leave a show, are you up or down? Do you want to discuss it or forget it?

Of the many elements that do occur during any show's running time, watch for four that are crucial. They are: identification, point of view, rhythm, and structure.

Identification is the way the show maker creates the link between the audience and the show. A bald way of saying it is: the show maker must get the audience on his or her side. The audience will identify with the show maker when that link is strong, trusting his guidance even on the wildest imaginative flights. Audiences accepted a romance between a boy and a mermaid in the movie *Splash* because director Ron Howard made the two young lovers people everyone could recognize.

Director Carroll Ballard established identification with great economy in the movie *The Black Stallion*. The first shots show a small boy alone on the deck of an ocean liner. Who is he, where is he going? We don't know. Then we hear bangings and animal sounds; the boy hears them too. He and we want to know what they are. He looks up; they seem to be coming from an upper deck. He runs upstairs and along a corridor. The camera follows him. Since we see what the camera sees, we are now in effect running along behind him to find out what the sound is about. He rounds a corner, so do we, and there we discover together—ah! a beautiful black horse. In thirty seconds director Carroll Ballard has the audience *in* his movie. That is identification.

Many show makers achieve identification by beginning with something familiar. TV shows open each week with the same montage that shows the stars smiling warmly in down-to-earth locations while a catchy theme song sets a friendly mood. Classical recitalists open the evening with well-known pieces by Bach, Mozart, or Chopin; after intermission they tackle Schoenberg and Bartok. Ellen and I made it a rule long ago to begin a set with "an easy and easy-to-understand song," an icebreaker to get us and the audience past the awkward stage of introduction and on to the enjoyment of mutual recognition.

With the audience's trust, the show maker can direct how—from what vantage point—the audience sees the show. This is point of view. Skilled show makers let their show be seen from more than one angle, just as TV sportscasters let you watch a baseball game from the first base line, from inside the dugout, and even from a blimp high above the stadium. At the moment of identification in *The Black Stallion*, Carroll Ballard lets us share the boy's point of view; seeing the horse through his eyes, we feel his love and sense of adventure. Later, however, we see the boy through his mother's eyes, as she tucks a blanket around him asleep on the lawn—an adventurer, yes, we think with her, but still a wistful little boy.

Seeing from many points of view is part of show magic. We are all too used to the limits of our own individual viewpoints; we only know what *we* know. At a show, these limits are dissolved. We can glide through locked doors, hover invisibly beside people who are all alone, and, like the Shadow, "learn what secrets lurk in the hearts of men."

Point of view is, naturally, most important in dramatic shows. In Arthur Miller's play *All My Sons*, we learn what the son returning home thinks of his father, what the father thinks of the son, and how the mother sees them both. In many dramatic situations the show maker lets the audience see more than the characters see; we know the killer is behind the curtain as the heroine, happily humming a song, prepares for bed. In movies, the camera is the eye through which we see everything; the point of view (POV is the abbreviated language of screenplays) changes everytime the camera moves.

A choreographer also varies the audience's point of view. A woman dances for a man; we see her as he sees her. He dances for her; we watch him with her. The viewpoints fuse in the *pas de deux*, and when the entire company runs on to join them, it is as if the audience were dancing with them in celebration of the duo's love. A singer is sometimes telling his or her own story, sometimes telling a story about someone else. Listen to an orchestral arrangement as a series of shifting points of view, and the sequence of sounds becomes a conversation between the instruments, the flutes commenting on the trumpets, the deep voices of the bass viols agreeing with the timpani. In a multi-voiced monologue a comedian can create whole scenes in which we see a hilarious mix-up from the viewpoints of a washerwoman, a bank president, a cop, and a nosy neighbor.

Rhythm is, basically, the pace of a show. A comedy that piles split-second gag on split-second gag and ends in a wild car chase, or a rock show that races through twenty up-tempo numbers and climaxes with fireworks and smoke bombs—those are fast shows. An orchestral concert that builds the stately themes of two symphonies, or a movie drama that lingers on close-ups of thoughtful faces—those are slow shows. Most shows mix paces, alternating and contrasting quick moments and drawn-out ones.

Yet all these shows might last the same two hours on the clock.

A show maker creates a sense of time with the show and whirls the audience out of the tick-tock of daily life. This too is part of show magic. Shows can compress and expand time, take us backward and forward in time, and make us wander like dreamers in timeless zones of memory. We sense that jazzmen "come back" to the melody after extended improvisation, though the music really always moves forward. The old silent-movie title card, "Meanwhile, back at the ranch," convinced early moviegoers that two scenes they saw, one after the other, were happening at the same time. A "fast" comedy might be the adventures of one nutty night, covering in "real time" events only slightly longer than the show's length; a "slow" drama might be squeezing an epic of three generations into two hours.

Rhythm is the "timing" so essential to a comedian, the sensitivity to tempo every musician must have. How long does an actor hold a pause? How slowly does a dancer sink to the floor? Rhythm is crucial to film editing. A quick cut suggests no time has elapsed between camera shots, a dissolve suggests the passage of a few days. After a *very* slow dissolve, a young couple may reappear as grey-haired Grandma and Grandpa. If a show's rhythm is too fast and jerky, the audience can become derailed, losing the track altogether. Worst of all, if the rhythm is too slow, the audience gets ahead of the show and sits bored and squirming, waiting for the show makers to catch up.

Structure is both the most obvious and the most hidden of the four show elements. Beginning, middle, end: that's structure in a nutshell, the same "Once upon a time" to "They lived happily ever after" we first encounter in fairy tales. Structures are like the pillars and beams of a building or the skeletons of our own bodies: they vary much less than the exterior bodies hung upon them. "Boy meets girl, boy loses girl, boy gets girl" can describe the basic structure of *War and Peace*, "The Love Boat," and a hundred thousand other shows and stories.

Because we all assume the presence of structure, we don't look for it, just as car buyers, captivated by chrome, forget that Fords and Chevys are sisters under the skin. But when a show's structure is weak or awkward, the whole show is ungainly, and even the shiniest surface cannot save it. Sooner or later, it will collapse under its own badly supported weight.

Beginnings must really begin, middles must have substance, and endings must both bring the show to a summation we accept and point us toward a future we can imagine. Every line of a play, every step of a dance, every frame of a movie, each chord in a piece of music, all need to be fitted together like bricks in a wall. When the parts are carefully matched, the whole is greater than their sum because we respond to the pleasing proportions of the entire design.

Upon a stable structure, show makers can create endless variations with the confidence of children playing on a jungle gym. Today's popular musicians use and reuse the formulas of the twelve-bar blues and the thirty-two-bar song just as composers of the early nineteenth century worked within the sonata form. Playwrights write and rewrite to get the perfect "second act curtain," and comedians time and again build their gags in a series of three—opening laugh, second laugh, and punch line—with a topper added for good measure.

A good situation comedy like "The Mary Tyler Moore Show" or "Taxi" or "Cheers" is a study in the value of structure. Week after week, the show presents the same actors, sets, theme song, lighting, and camera angles, telling a story from exposition through complication to resolution in a smooth twenty-seven minutes. The premise of every episode is down-to-earth—Mary's parents are visiting when an old boyfriend shows up, for instance. Ted, Lou, and Murray react right in character. Every line, every cut from face to face advances the plot, sets up or gets a laugh, and adds to the flavor. How will Mary get out of this latest mess? Despite all the familiarity, the twist is always surprising, believable, and funny besides. The show's economy often leaves time for a quick second ending (the topper) as the credits start to roll.

Take time in the days after a show to review your reactions to it. When a show doesn't satisfy you, ask yourself why. Did you never feel a part of the show? Was it all presented from one point of view? Did it drag in the middle and thus have to rush the ending? Often questions based on identification, point of view, rhythm, and structure will give you greater insight into a show's weaknesses than a standard criticism of the acting or playing. No actor comes off well in a scene that is ten minutes too long, and even virtuoso playing or dancing is boring if we can't connect with it or if it doesn't connect to what's around it.

Be willing to be critical. Most performers and show business pros are, in their own minds, show doctors ready and able to diagnose the ills of any show. Now is the time to join their ranks. This isn't criticism from the sidelines, it is putting yourself in the thick of the fray. What would you do for the show? Fire the leading man or rewrite the script?

Put the end at the beginning and do the rest as a flashback? Would you tell the bass player to turn down his amp, the singer to hold the mike less stiffly, the dancer to watch her landings? Working out clear opinions about the shows you watch will increase your awareness of the elements in your own work and develop your sense of what's right for you—your own style.

Again, however, openness is vital. As a new student of complex crafts, you can't afford to close out information with unexamined dismissals like, "Ballet is pretentious," "Rock 'n' roll is ugly noise," or "Slapstick comedy is vulgar." Such snobberies are prejudices, in a word, when you need above all to be open-minded. If there's been a show or performing artist you've been snooty about or dismissed out of hand, look again more closely. You may enjoy yourself and learn something, even if it's only *why* that show or artist is not to your taste.

You have, of course, your own special favorites, artists who have already won you over. They seem to know what's inside you and express it better than you can. Perhaps one or two in particular have inspired you to try show business. You may already be modeling your style on theirs. Subject them to critical study too. How do they get to you, what's their identifying link? How do they pace their shows? What are the stable structural elements they use? The more clearly you see their work, the better you will understand and respect their craftsmanship. Then your work, inspired by them, won't be imitation; instead, it will be your response to excellence in a colleague.

Pay particular attention to the work of the very greatest artists, masters who have weathered the ups and downs of long careers and emerged with unshakable reputations for excellence. Luckily for us, there are many such professionals at work today and many others whose work lives on beyond them—so many that any list would be incomplete. Marlene Dietrich, Fred Astaire, Chet Atkins, and Ray Charles are four of my all-time greats. Ellen and I were lucky enough to see Jack Benny in person a few years before he died. He had refined his stingy act into an art of total economy. The smallest gesture was packed with humor. Before he played the violin, he plucked a broken hair from the bow. We assumed it just happened to be broken. In fact it was a prepared prop. Benny put the hair into his back pocket as if no one were watching. Long silence. He rolled his eyes. "I don't know why, but I *always* save them."

Johnny Carson is one contemporary master whose work is easily available for study; watch and enjoy "The Tonight Show." On it, you'll see a wide spectrum of today's stars and newcomers perform and talk about their lives and careers. The whole show is drenched in show business atmosphere. Many of the gags and anecdotes capture the absurdities of getting to and staying in the big time.

Johnny creates his link with the audience by chatting humorously about the weather and the news, letting the Nebraska farm boy that he was show through the dapper surface of the multimillionaire star he has become. He's in firm control of the show's point of view, keeping it mostly on himself. Some of the show's best moments happen, however, when a guest—a cuddly baby orangutan or an outrageous comedian like Dom DeLuise—steals the spotlight and Johnny, for a moment, lets them have it. "The Tonight Show" rhythm is a quick pace that's elastic enough to stretch out when a good moment needs more time. Structurally the show is built like the Rock of Gibraltar. "Heeeeere's Johnny," monologue, spot with Ed McMahon or Doc Severinson, and then the guests—the basic format hasn't changed in twenty years.

Learning and absorbing from life and shows is a full-time job. Everything you take in adds to the store of knowledge that will guide your actions, shape and give content to your work. This is the life of a growing artist: learning that never stops.

LEARNING

TWENTY-FOUR

HOURS A DAY

*chapter* 4

○ ○ ○ ○ ○ ○ ○ ○ ○ ○ ○ ○ ○ ○ ○ ○ ○ ○ ○ ○ ○ ○ ○ ○ ○ ○ ○ ○ ○ ○ ○ ○ ○ ○ ○ ○ ○ ○

# TECHNIQUE

EACH of the performing arts is a craft. Like other crafts, such as metal working, pottery making, and house building, the crafts of performance have a practical basis in *technique*, the specific methods by which performers create their effects. Technique is the how-to-do-it. Effective performance springs from an understanding of the principles and a careful preparation of the skills that are summed up in the one word, technique.

When Luciano Pavarotti, one of today's greatest operatic tenors, was a boy of ten in Modena, Italy, Beniamino Gigli came to the city to give a concert. Gigli was the reigning tenor of his day, and Pavarotti, already ambitious to be a singer himself, slipped into the hall the morning of the concert to hear Gigli warm up. He listened eagerly as Gigli vocalized for over an hour, and then he rushed to the stage with dozens of questions. "How long did you study?" was one. Gigli, then a man of fifty, laughed and patted young Luciano on the head. "You heard me studying now," he replied. "I am still studying."

Studying technique is a lifetime occupation for any serious performing artist, a quest pursued in long hours of highly disciplined work. For most artists, performance time is only the tip of the iceberg;

Working on technique
.  .  .  .  .  .  .  .

51

days and weeks of preparation underlie every moment on stage. Many view each performance as a test to see how far they have come in their studies. As jazz singer Joe Williams put it, "Every show is one more chance to try to do it right." Dissatisfaction with the results keeps even the most accomplished artists hard at work to perfect their skills. Other guitarists are in awe of B. B. King's mastery of his instrument, but not B. B. "I know exactly what I want to play," he told me once in an interview. "It's a goal I'm trying to reach. But I know this, I've never made it. I get close, but not there."

Continual searching for ever finer levels of craft take performers deep into the most minute knowledge of their actions. For the great violinist Yehudi Menuhin, daily practice begins with him flat on the floor. Lying on his back, he slowly raises and lowers his arms and legs, inhaling as he lifts them, exhaling as he lets them return. He notes consciously every mental impulse and bodily reaction involved in each movement. Knowledge this precise of how he works, Menuhin wrote in his autobiography, *Unfinished Journey*, is "a cardinal principle of violin playing."

> [The violinist] is part of his violin, his left hand fingering its way, without any margin for error, over the millimetric subdivisions of space that varies like a slide rule, and his bow never leaving the string but under precise, controlled conditions. To play the violin one must form a clear image of the interplay of six directions . . . . These are toward and away from oneself, horizontal push and pull, vertical carrying weight from above and vertical supporting weight from below. . . . All six must be experienced separately in the two hands and ten fingers, along the length of the fingerboard, and at each point of the bow, before they will cooperate kinetically.

We all lower our bodies by bending our knees from time to time without giving it a second thought, when we stoop to get something off a low shelf, for instance. This movement is called a *plié* in dance, and dancers give it a great deal of thought and practice. Dancer and teacher Bella Lewitsky considers the plié "one of the most taxing things the body can handle."

> To me, one of the most fragile areas of the body is that hip socket where the top of the thighbone nestles into the cup of the hip. In a plié, there is stress going from the hip down into the knee, down into the ankle. . . . I want the area around the hip socket stretched, and lengthened, so that vulnerable hip area is *very* warm. I want the thigh muscle stretched

above the kneecap so there is no shock to the knee as you go into demi-plié. I want the feet articulated so there is no stress in the ankle. In other words, I want the three major joints opened so bone is pulled slightly off bone.

The primary goal of studying technique is not to accumulate knowledge but to use it in free and satisfyingly expressive performance. In the lights and excitement of the stage, performers are like athletes with a game to win, trusting that all their analytical study has become integrated information that will guide them instinctively to the right moves. Menuhin says that when he plays he does not need to calculate but "to prepare the automatic impulse."

On the other hand, what audiences experience as unfettered emotion on stage is often superb technical control. Veteran film and stage actor Hume Cronyn, for instance, has learned how to blush at will. Many performers are reluctant to discuss the extent of their technical mastery because they don't want audiences to be conscious of it. Concealing the mechanics of a performance is a major part of the illusion. "He makes it look easy"—that's high praise. Prima ballerina Suzanne Farrell is one performer willing to be outspoken about her disbelief in "instinctive reaction" on stage. When an interviewer asked her about certain lingering falls in a slow movement of Balanchine's ballet *Symphony in C*, he suggested that her movement was a purely emotional response to the music. No, said Farrell, "I know exactly how to produce it and how to modify it."

> The music rises. I slowly take a deep breath—this raises the rib cage and the upper chest. My head is up and tilted back slightly. I turn the head slightly to make a softer line in the neck—falling with the neck and head completely straight looks corpselike to me. Then I fall, and when my partner catches me I exhale slowly. It all happens on one very, very slow breath that must be visible to the audience.
>
> Any number of people may have the same "instinctive reaction" to that moment—but it doesn't matter what you feel. You've got to produce something visually and physically to indicate what you feel.

Sometimes performers carry out a specific technical experiment on stage just to sharpen their skills. James Cagney in his autobiography, *Cagney by Cagney*, tells about the first time he saw Jack Lemmon on a television show. Cagney thought the then unknown Lemmon gave "an apple-pie performance" and also noticed that Lemmon did everything left-handed. When the two later met on the set of the movie

*Mr. Roberts*, Cagney complimented Lemmon on his work and commented on his left-handedness. "Oh," said Lemmon, "I'm not left-handed at all. I am so right-handed that I decided I was going to play everything left-handed and make it a mark of the performance. For the challenge of the thing."

Studying technique has a technique: *exercises*, to be repeated with alert attention over and over and over again. One performance, no matter how brief or apparently simple, contains dozens of separate elements and movements, just as a car motor contains many movng and nonmoving parts. Moreover, just as the motors of different cars (or trains or boats) have similar parts with similar functions, so do different performances have elements and movements in common. All ballets, for instance, are combinations of steps and movements in the vocabulary of dance, among them the plié, the *jeté*, or leap, the *pirouette*, or spin, and the *pas de chat*, the step of the cat. Musical sounds are created from tones, played one after the other in melodies or simultaneously in chords. When chord tones are played in sequence, they are called arpeggios. All words for actors and singers are made of vowels and consonants. In all plays, actors enter and exit, walk and talk, sit and stand, and try to accomplish the objectives of their characters.

Exercises isolate these common elements for study on their own. Ballet dancers may start class at the barre with slow pliés to warm up and then go on to *battements tendus* (extending the leg) and *dégagés* (extending the leg so it leaves the floor). Instrumentalists work through scales and arpeggios across the full range of their instruments; singers do the same, singing on each vowel. Before they work on scenes from written plays, actors improvise scenes in which basic objectives are in conflict: "Lend me $500." "No, I need the money for school."

Performers do exercises to develop their diaphragms for smooth, controlled breathing, exercises for dotted, syncopated, and triplet rhythms; *adagio*, or slow, exercises and quick, *allegro*, exercises. There are exercises for toes, exercises for the tongue, and exercises to learn how to fall down. Equally important are exercises for the imagination. Here are a few exercises that Esther Pease suggests in her book *Modern Dance* to let the imagination give qualities to movement: "Point your ears like a fox." "Ripple your arm like a flag." "Be a goldfish in a bowl."

Practice is repeating these exercises with alert attention so that, in fact, they are never repeated. Each time, the performer takes in information on how the exercise felt and then makes adjustments for more relaxation and greater clarity. When ready, he or she attempts to assemble the exercised elements in a practice performance of a dance, a piece of music, or a scene. Elements that are weak are re-exercised. Everything is put to the test in actual performance; the results form the directions of practice sessions to come.

Technical study is hard work. Intellectually and physically demanding, it also requires patience and confident faith in oneself and in one's long-term goals. Results of even intensive work are slow to appear and difficult to measure. Practice in the performing arts disappears into thin air, as I realize daily when I come home from a full day's workout with no more than the guitar and books I started out with. All that is left is an elusive sense of improvement, and some days do not yield even that. There is no guarantee, moreover, that technical skill will be appropriately rewarded or recognized. Experienced professonals often play supporting roles in shows starring newcomers whose youth, charm, and good looks far outweigh their know-how.

For these reasons some young performers don't see the point of subjecting themselves to the labor of acquiring technique. Self-confident beginners see uninspired performances on TV and tell themselves, "I'm better than those guys already," or point to bravura performers like rock 'n' roll singer-pianist Jerry Lee Lewis and figure, "*He* doesn't spend hours working on scales, so why should I?" Jim Payne is a drummer who has played with the orchestras of Radio City Music Hall and Broadway musicals as well as with many rock and jazz groups. A few years ago he was teaching foot-pedal technique to a teenage student. "Hey, c'mon," said the student, "I can't do *that*. I'm gonna be wearing high-heeled boots like the guys in Kiss." Jim, who at that point had been studying for twenty years, laughed an inward laugh and went on to the next student.

Self-confidence and high ambition are definite assets in show business, as are enthusiasm, sex appeal, personal magnetism, and luck. Depending on them to avoid study, however, is a dead-end street. "If you are going to succeed," says Francis Hodge, a theatre arts teacher for thirty years at Cornell University and the University of Texas, "there are no shortcuts, no halfway measures. Everything is hard, dedicated work." The more any beginner does study, the more he or she will respect the hard-won skills of others, recognizing, for intance, that Jerry Lee Lewis is a master of the techniques of up-tempo boogie-woogie piano and flamboyant showmanship.

Practicing

Technique disciplines enthusiasm and makes it more effective. It sharpens vague hopes ("I want to be an actor") into keenly specific objectives ("I want the way I drop my shoulders to show the sudden despair my character feels"). Applied technical study can extend a performer's abilities far beyond their starting point. Steve Martin became a star with his freewheeling, zany comedy, and then for the film *Pennies from Heaven* he learned to tap dance. Continually improving technical skills is the only way to stay competitive in a competitive business. "Every moment you're not rehearsing, somebody else is," warns a show business saying.

Studying technique, moreover, is an abiding source of pleasure for performers who love their craft. Chet Atkins, the great American guitarist, still practices every day until he's too sleepy to play anymore. The late John Mehegan, pianist and author of the superb four volume text on jazz technique, *Jazz Improvisation*, said in one of his last interviews, "The confrontation with the piano, those eighty-eight keys staring at me—that's enough for me forever." Looking back on a career that began in the 1930s with the Ballet Russe de Monte Carlo and included a long run dancing in the 1940s Broadway musical *On the Town*, dancer Sono Osato recalls rehearsing with choreogapher Antony Tudor as her "greatest artistic experience."

Few performers enjoy practicing more than performing, but treasures of discovery and accomplishment lurk in scales and arpeggios, warm-ups at the barre, and classroom scene studies and improvisation. The pleasure of scientific curiosity, seeing into the mechanics of movement and communication, has a fascination that is its own reward.

The unhurried pace of technical study, the slow building up of an unshakable foundation of knowledge of craft, can give a performer a stable center, secure from the ups and downs of his or her public career. Success is sometimes followed by inexplicable periods of unemployment; what one reviewer praises, another pans and a third ignores. Popularity can swell or dwindle with changes of fashion no one can predict or control. In the practice room, however, there is no critic, no producer, and no fickle public. The victories won there are private but unmistakably real; the prize is progress that no one can take away.

"People often ask me when I expect to be famous or when I plan to make my Metropolitan Opera debut," contralto Marion Dry wrote recently in an article for her college alumni magazine. "These are unsettling questions. I have no guarantee that my efforts will lead me to either of these desirable goals." Dry went on to confess that she'd love to be a superstar, but added:

> To communicate well as a singer, one needs a beautiful voice, the ability to control it throughout its pitch and dynamic ranges, awareness and control of one's entire body, knowledge of musical and vocal style, psychological insight, and a command of several languages. Coordinating all of these skills is a feat in itself. Using them all to convey a myriad of human feelings is the art of the singer. My daily work in the practice studio is to improve my ability to make everything cohere. I adore this work, and derive enormous satisfaction from the entire process of preparing for performance.

The technique of any craft is grounded on unchanging reality— the melting points of various metals, for instance, the baking temperatures of clay, the support strengths inherent in various woods. The foundations of techniques in the performing arts are human anatomy, the laws of gravity and movement, and the universal language of emotional expression. Musical instruments are scaled for human hands, dancers who leap up must come down, and, to paraphrase Tolstoy, happy smiles are all alike.

Yet no technique is static, fixed in every detail, because the how-to of a job depends on the results desired. Creative craftspeople have individual ends, and they find individual means to accomplish them. The invention of new tools, programmable synthesizers, for example, requires the development of new techniques to use them. Break dancing with its abrupt stop-go technique developed in response to the computerized music played on those synthesizers. The techniques of performing artists, like those of silversmiths, potters, and carpenters, combine traditon and innovation, ancient principles and new goals.

Studying technique has a curriculum of two primary courses: learning from teachers and learning for oneself what no one else can teach.

Of the two, learning for oneself is the more fundamental course. If there is no teacher available, a beginner must teach himself technique or not learn at all. Blues guitarist Albert King started playing the guitar by ear on his own, holding the instrument in the position most comfortable for him. Since he is left-handed, that meant he had the guitar upside down—the treble strings on the upper side of the neck. King learned to finger all the chords in reverse of standard practice, yet he became in time a brilliant and influential musician.

In her book *Where She Danced*, Elizabeth Kendall points out that Isadora Duncan developed her original approach to dance in years of work alone, when "she trusted that her body would tell her what she needed to know. . . . years when she stood quite still for hours, her two hands folded between her breasts, covering the solar plexus, that 'central spring of all movements.' "

Technique is action; its instrument is the body of each performer.

John Mehegan

All technical lessons need to be adapted to individual physical endowments. A pianist with big hands can manage to cover spreads of over an octave between thumb and little finger. A pianist with smaller hands may need to use both hands to play the same interval.

Everything we take in from outside sources needs hours and months and years of putting it into practice before we make it ours. No one else can do this for us. For instance, "sense memory" is an acting exercise: actors bring up from memory and relive the sensations of a particular experience—perhaps the juicy crunch of the first watermelon of summer with all its surprise and familiarity, the dripping chin, and the "ahhh" of a thirst perfectly quenched. The idea of sense memory can be explained, but its value is the memory each actor pulls up and how it feels to reexperience it.

Jazz musicians know the values of self-learning: their slang gets it across in colorful images: you take your "axe" out to the "woodshed" and work on your "chops." For tenor saxophonist Sonny Rollins the woodshed was the Brooklyn Bridge where he sometimes practiced alone in the early morning hours, playing for pigeons asleep in the high stone arches. The point of woodshedding is also made plain in an old jazz story. A tourist in New York stopped a hepcat with his shades, beret, and trumpet case. "Excuse me, sir, how do I get to Carnegie Hall?" asked the tourist. "Practice, man, practice," the hepcat replied.

On the other hand, all beginners need teachers. Teachers answer questions, suggest new directions, correct inefficient habits, evaluate progress, and organize coherent practice plans to lead the student from introductory basics through intermediate to advanced levels of exercises. Teachers inspire as well as guide; having overcome the first frustrations of learning themselves, they can encourage beginners daunted by the work ahead.

A natural technique, the goal for all students, is not the product of "doing what comes naturally," but of studying methods and theories developed over centuries and handed down from teachers to students who eventually become teachers. Thespis, the father of Greek theatre, "taught dancing to all who wanted instruction," according to the historian Athenaeus (quoted in A. M. Nagler's fascinating *Source Book in Theatrical History*). The playwright Euripides also taught singing and once had to remind a giggling student: "Sir, unless you were very stupid and insensible, you could not laugh while I sing in the grave Mixolydian Mode."

Shakespeare, an actor as well as playwright, put a brief but pointed acting lesson in Hamlet's speech to the actors who perform the play within *Hamlet*. An excerpt:

Suit the action to the word, the word to the action; with this special observance, that you o'erstep not the modesty of nature. For anything so overdone is from the purpose of playing, whose end, both at the first and now, was and is, to hold, as 'twere, the mirror up to nature.

Johann Sebastian Bach wrote many short pieces to teach keyboard technique to his children. Mozart's violinist father taught the young Wolfgang, and Mozart himself taught in order to support himself and his family. Beethoven taught also; his most famous pupil was Karl

Czerny, whose volumes of exercises are still basic texts for piano students.

The tradition continues. Herbert Berghof studied acting in the 1930s with Max Reinhardt, a pioneer of modern German theatre; now Berghof teaches at his own and his wife Uta Hagen's HB Studio in New York. The late George Balanchine was a student at the Maryinsky Theatre in Leningrad, then taught many decades of dancers and founded the School of American Ballet; his students now teach all over the world. Each new generation of teachers makes its own contribution to the heritage. For years Bella Lewitsky taught dance as she had learned it from choreographer Lester Horton. Then one day after watching one of her classes, Horton said, "Bella, you're not teaching my technique." Lewitsky was shocked. "Without conscious awareness, I had evidently been shifting away . . . I had begun to move in my own path."

Duke Ellington remembered all his life the "glow of enchantment" he felt studying with pianist Doc Perry in Washington, D.C. For dancer Peter Martins, it was teacher Stanley Williams who made him "feel the challenge, the potential achievement, the *importance* of being a dancer." Director Peter Palitszh, without ever telling actress Liv Ullman what to do or think, taught her "that everything we portray onstage ought to be shown from two sides, be illustrated in both black and white." For Yehudi Menuhin, Georges Enesco "wasn't just a teacher . . . he was the sustaining hand of providence, the inspiration that bore me aloft."

> What I received from him—by compelling example, not by word—was the note transformed into vital message, the phrase given shape and meaning, the structure of music made vivid.
>
> When, occasionally, he did use words to make a point, they were not cut and dried injunctions . . . but suggestions, images, which passed reasons to infuse the imagination with a completer understanding.

Performers do not need a license or to pass state examinations as do doctors, lawyers, or electrical engineers. Therefore, there is no standardized education for them. Ballet and classical music performers complete specific technical educations because their arts require mastery of definite, traditional skills. The requirements for popular music, contemporary dance, and acting are more flexible because these arts have more room for untutored spontaneity and improvisation.

Circumstances determine how many performers combine the

taught and self-taught curricula. They study with teachers and take classes when they can afford them, get books and follow the exercises in them, and get ideas from helpful colleagues. They turn pro whenever they get their first job and learn from the rough-and-ready-experience of on-the-job training.

The mixed bag of Ellen's and my learning career is not unusual. Having studied piano and clarinet at community music schools in Boston during high school, I started guitar and harmonica on my own in my late twenties, poring over Bob Dylan songbooks and seeking out other musicians. Ellen had studied piano from elementary through high school and continued after college with Goodwin Sammel in Berkeley. We started performing when we had about five songs rehearsed and sang professionally for four years before we had our first

The great jazz pianist Teddy Wilson, whose playing and teaching inspired John Mehegan

singing lesson. Now we've been studying voice for six years, making steady progress with Julia Wortman.

We've studied acting with William Hickey at HB Studios for four summers and one full year, beginning with basic improvisation and going on to scene study and building character. For one year we studied dance with Fred Timm, a former dancer with Alwin Nikolais, who gave us a grounding in dance elementals. Walter Piston's *Harmony* and John Mehegan's *Jazz Improvisation* have been our Bibles of music theory, and we go to the library constantly for books outlining different approaches to and new material for our instruments. The Third Street Music School, a community school near our apartment in New York City, is our home away from home where we spend hours in daily practice. We take classes there and also teach guitar and piano.

To someone beginning now, I would recommend a more organized approach. The first step in designing a course of study is to define one's personal goals: "What do I want to do as a performer?"

In defining goals, it is important for a beginner to find the center of his or her work. Most performers have a sense of their own specialty, what they think they are best at. That can change—Johnny Carson started out as a magician—but it often becomes the core of a varied career. Clint Eastwood sings and plays piano, writes and directs movies, but basically he is a screen actor. Woody Allen likewise does everything in film and also plays clarinet; at heart he is a comedian. By saying, "I am an actor," "I am a dancer," or more specifically, "I am a jazz trumpeter," a beginner creates a perspective on learning. The specialty becomes the area of most focused attention. Secondary interests are seen in relation to the specialty—"I am an actor learning to dance."

Here, for instance, is how one young performer defines her goals:

> I want to be a rock bassist. I want to write and sing my own songs in a group that could also get work covering Top-40 hits. I'd also like to produce records, really learn how to work in the studio. And if our records hit big, I'd like to try acting in movies.

The next step is to define the means: "What techniques must I learn in order to accomplish those goals?" The answers to that become the course of study. In school terms, this bass player's curriculum would be a popular music major with course in bass, theory, composition, and voice. Engineering and record production would be an integrated minor, and drama an extracurricular activity.

Then, "How do I learn these techniques?" The answer to this depends on where the beginner lives, on how old he or she is, how much money is available for instruction, and on the content of the proposed curriculum. For beginners with little money and no nearby teachers, the best resource is books written by good teachers. Every library has many of these, and most bookstores carry a current assortment. Instruction books can contain tremendous amounts of useful information if they are patiently mined. To get full value from a how-to book, it is necessary to do the exercises step by step as they are outlined.

Books, however, cannot "supplant the teacher," as Thalia Mara wrote in her instruction book *Third Steps in Ballet;* books "aid the teacher by making students more aware of the importance of correct understanding of the details of technique." For instance, I first tried to learn voice from Trusler and Ehret's *Functional Lessons in Singing.* It is an excellent book that I still use, but its talk of "a high degree of resonance concentrated at the hard palate and in the head and nasal cavities" baffled me until later my singing teacher led me to experience what the authors were referring to.

For a beginner with one particular goal—classical piano, for example—one teacher may be sufficient, at least at first. There are teachers for all the performing arts, music and dance particularly, in every city in the country and in every town with a liberal arts college nearby. They list themselves in the *Yellow Pages*, advertise under "Instruction" in newspaper classified ads, and post notices on bulletin boards. They are affiliated with public school systems, YMCA's and YMHA's, adult education and community learnng centers.

How to pick a teacher? The first question is, "Can he or she teach what I want to learn?" A classical guitar teacher may have little to offer someone who wants to sound like Rolling Stone Keith Richard. Check the teacher's credentials, his or her own professional experience and educational background. Interview the teacher; explain your goals, ask questions, and consider carefully the teacher's responses. It may be possible to sit in on a class or get the reactions of other students. Do not sign up for a long series of classes without a trial period first.

Is the teacher right for you? That only the student can answer. There are smiling teachers full of compliments who teach little, and there are reserved teachers full of criticisms who teach much. Learning technique has so many moments of frustration that being annoyed at a teacher is not a sure test the teacher is incompetent. Moreover, to

Rudolf Serkin leaves the theatre
after a matinee performance

learn from a teacher one needs to put aside one's own opinions and be as open as possible to the teacher's ideas. Nearly every teacher will ask the student to do things the student doesn't see the point of. The only way to learn is to try them anyway. No teacher can get through to a mind full of "yeah, buts." I advise that any student think twice before stopping work with a teacher.

Questions that are helpful in evaluating a relationship with a teacher are:

Do you trust the teacher?

Do you admire his or her own skill and knowledge?

Does the teacher understand what you want to learn?

Are you learning?

Are you satisfied with your progress?

Does the teacher recognize and enjoy your progress?

Does the teacher keep presenting new challenges?

Do you look forward to your lessons?

What is your gut reaction to the teacher as a whole person?

If the answers to these are more negative than positive, it is time to talk over the problems with the teacher. If that is not satisfactory, it may be time to look for a new teacher. A relationship with the right teacher can be a rewarding and inspiring experience. An ambitious student undercuts his or her own chances for success by continuing with an inappropriate teacher. On the other hand, teacher and student need not be close friends. Many teachers are successful with an informal style, but the relationship has a traditional formality that it is wise to respect. Master and apprentice are not equals in the workshop.

The relationship will also end; to continue growth, every student must one day leave the teacher. That ending is not always smooth. Just when Arthur Rubinstein began to feel ready for a concert career, his teacher in Berlin told him his best hope would be to become the teacher's assistant. When Rubinstein refused, the teacher screamed at him, "You will end up in the gutter, you ungrateful boy, I predict it!" Sometimes students are too dependent on the teacher and continue studying not to learn but to put off independence. Then the teacher would be right to stop the relationship, at least long enough for the student to measure his or her progress by other yardsticks.

The student with several goals will need more than one teacher. It is possible to find these one by one, but I recommend instead looking for a school with a performing arts curriculum varied enough to suit the student's interests; many teachers, in fact, teach at or through schools. There are many of these schools of every size and description all over the country. Any beginner already in school can look for whatever programs are there. Most high schools offer music, dance, and drama as electives or extracurricular club activities; New York City has a special High School of the Performing Arts, as well as one for Music and Art. Most colleges have similar programs, and many give bachelor degrees to performing arts majors. Numerous universities have postgraduate music and drama schools that give Master of Fine Arts and Ph.D. degrees.

There are also college-level schools that teach only the performing arts: New York's American Academy of the Dramatic Arts and Boston's Berklee School of Music are two. There are small professional schools grown from the vision of a single teacher like Lee Strasburg's Theatre Institute in New York; community schools like Third Street with endowed scholarships for needy students; summer schools like the Marlboro School in Vermont, directed by pianist Rudolf Serkin.

A program in the performing arts offers a student a variety of technical disciplines within a structure that relates them all. HB Studio, for instance, has seventeen different acting courses including comedy, monologues, opera. Shakespeare, improvisation, and theatre games; there are also courses in directing, makeup, fencing, ballet, play analysis, and nine voice classes—dialect study and accent correction as well as sight-singing and vocal development. Students can take one or many courses. The school suggests these courses as a full-time program:

Acting Technique
Acting Scene Study
Dance (twice a week)
Fencing or Mime
Makeup or Play Analysis
Speech (twice a week)
Theatre Games
Voice

· · · · · · ·

TECHNIQUE

An acting class with Bill Hickey at HB Studio.

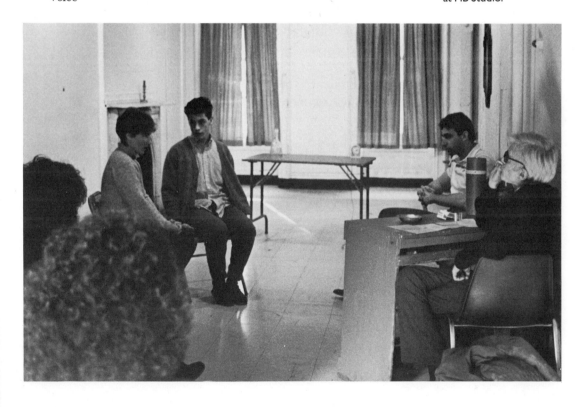

Studying the three major technical disciplines of acting, dance, and music together is a great advantage for any performer. There is a lot more work for an actress who can sing and dance as well as do a great Hedda Gabler. The poise that dance teaches is an asset for any actor, singer, or instrumentalist; dancers can use acting training to express emotion in movement and musical training to understand and memorize the rhythms and forms of the music they dance to. Whatever one's specialty is, actors, dancers, and musicians will be colleagues. Understanding their perspectives and languages will make communication with them more efficient and productive. I have seen a dance teacher waste five valuable minutes trying to explain to a rehearsal pianist the tempo he wanted for a dance exercise. Finally the pianist began to grasp the teacher's frantic sign language. "Oh, you mean 3/4 time with an even accent?" she asked, then demonstrated. "Yes, yes," said the relieved teacher, and the class could continue.

Schools can also give students hands-on learning experiences of much greater variety and responsibility than is possible in the professional performance world. In student productions young performers can take leading roles that are only given to established stars on Broadway; dancers and musicians can do solos before they could get jobs in a dance company or in a professional orchestra. Actors, dancers, and musicians all pitch in to paint sets, work lights, find props, design posters, and man the box office for school shows.

Every school, moreover, is a community, many people working together toward similar ends in one place. This is a practical help in making contacts and hearing news on the grapevine. A community is also spiritually nourishing. The countless informal interactions, chance meetings, bull sessions, and shared moments are the perfect antidote for the necessary but lonely hours of individual work. Fellow students are a great resource of any school; they challenge each other to do their best and cheer each other up when things look their worst. Shirley MacLaine caught the comradely, competitive spirit of students together at school in one pungent paragraph of her memoir, *Don't Fall Off the Mountain:*

> For the next fifteen years the long lines of girls in sweaty black leotards, straining in unison at the steel practice bar to the beat of a tinny piano, became my challenge, my competition. I needed no urging to join them. Some of the young ladies were there to lose weight, some to pass the awkward years of adolescence, others to give their mothers an extra two hours at the bridge table. But a few fragile, iron-willed youngsters truly

wanted to dance, and dedicated themselves to endless hours of toil, sweat, sore muscles, and repetition. I became one of these—not fragile, but iron-willed.

What school is right is also an individual matter. I recommend that any high school student considering a performing arts career make that career an important factor in his or her college choice. Any college student or adult graduate would be wise to consider graduate school. Degrees in the performing arts, for one thing, have tangible economic value: they open the way to college and public school teaching as a second career, and are taken in the marketplace as evidence of a basic level of expertise and experience. "We are hard pressed even to *look* at someone without an M.F.A.," a casting director for a regional theatre told acting teacher Robert Cohen for his book, *Acting Professionally, Raw Facts about Careers in Acting.*

Choosing a school, and particularly a college, is a major decision and deserves careful investigation. A guidance counselor can make suggestions and provide information. Check the "Schools" section of the Appendix in this book. Send away for brochures and visit all the schools you can. Meet students, sit in on classes, go to some productions, get the feel of the place, a sense of its morale.

The most important question to ask of any school is, "Will it challenge me?" Avoid a school that seems an easy, comfortable retreat. For an aspiring professional, the value of schoolwork is the intensity and realism of its preparation for professional work. The danger of school is its amateur spirit; as Cohen puts it, the "back-patting cosiness . . . which can lull students into a false sense of security, preventing them from developing their craft in a disciplined manner."

Other questions to ask:

*Size—big or small?* Many small schools have excellent performing arts departments—Connecticut College in dance, Oberlin in music, for instance. In general, classes may be smaller and more personal. At larger schools, however, there can be greater depth and variety of courses, more diverse viewpoints, and keener competition.

*Location—city or country?* Bennington College in Vermont is a college strong in music and dance; there are many other schools on rural and small-town campuses with good theatre arts programs. Being in or near a large city, on the other hand, is an advantage for performing arts students: there are more oppor-

A summer session workshop at
New York University

tunities to perform outside of school and to see a wide variety of professional work.

*Program—full-time performing arts or performing and liberal arts?* Conservatories like Philadelphia's Curtis Institute or Boston's Conservatory of Music provide rigorous professional preparation, while colleges provide the preparation in the context of a program of history, literature, science, and general education. Some ballet dancers and classical musicians may feel they need the total concentration of the conservatory. For most performers, a well-rounded education is a valuable addition to their art and to their knowledge and enjoyment of life beyond their career.

*Faculty—who are they?* Often one or two good teachers can make all the difference for a student's experience at a school. There are teachers of distinction at otherwise unexciting schools.

*Money—how much will it cost?* State-supported schools are often much less expensive than private schools. But nearly all schools have financial aid programs, and students at all qualified schools are eligible for a wide variety of foundation grants and student loan programs. Before giving up on any school as too expensive, it is worth investigating all financial aid possibilities.

The most important factor in learning technique is an individual's determination to do so. No obstacle will keep the truly determined beginner from learning what he or she needs to know. For many, the most important school will be the School of Hard Knocks. Singer and pianist Ray Charles got a good musical education at Florida's School for the Blind in St. Augustine, and today he is glad that many of his band members are university trained. "They play good," he wrote in his frank autobiography, *Brother Ray*, "but believe me, the real stuff ain't in the books. It's just not there. You got to go out and get your butt kicked. You got to get wiped out two or three times. And then you'll start learning what music is about."

Determination to learn will find those crucial fifteen minutes for practice in a crowded schedule, will ask those questions that may reveal embarrassing ignorance, and will take the student back over and over the same exercises. "I feel like I'm in boot camp," said acting student Sean Hagerty of his first year at New York University's Drama School. Studying technique is always being in boot camp. "The tough things on guitar seem impossible to me at first," Chet Atkins has said, "but then after enough practice, I play it like a machine." When Atkins has it that perfect, however, he starts all over. "I analyze it and ask myself, 'How did I do that?' Then I can't play it right again!"

# chapter 5

○ ○ ○ ○ ○ ○ ○ ○ ○ ○ ○ ○ ○ ○ ○ ○ ○ ○ ○ ○ ○ ○ ○ ○ ○ ○ ○ ○ ○ ○ ○ ○ ○ ○ ○ ○

# pErfOrMANCE

TODAY Laurence Olivier is Lord Olivier of Brighton, justly acclaimed one of the greatest actors of this century. Over a long career he has played an astonishing variety of roles in movies and onstage: King Lear, Hamlet, and Othello; Heathcliff in *Wuthering Heights;* music hall comedian Archie Rice in *The Entertainer;* and, in movies released back to back when he was in his early seventies, the Nazi Dr. Mengele in *Marathon Man* and Nazi-hunter Simon Wiesenthal in *The Boys from Brazil*—to name only a few.

In 1925, however, he was eighteen, fresh out of London's Central School of Speech Training and Dramatic Art, and about to make his professional debut. The play was an otherwise forgotten melodrama, *The Ghost Train;* the occasion a Sunday night charity show at an English seaside resort. Olivier's part was a walk-on. He had only to enter, sit on a sofa, say a few lines, and exit—but he had to walk on through a door in a painted canvas flat that had a very high sill. The stage manager, the other actors, and the callboy who led him from the dressing room to the side of the stage all warned him about the sill. Olivier waved their warnings impatiently away, he wrote in his autobiography, *Confessions of an Actor; he* wouldn't forget:

Ella Fitzgerald in concert

. . . . . .

My cue came and I stepped forward. I gave the canvas door a push and strode manfully through it.

Of course I did a shattering trip over the sill, sailed through the air, and before I knew what was happening to me I found my front teeth wedged firmly between a pink one and a blue one in the middle of the footlights.

In the years to come, Olivier added, he would play in many comedies and become proud of his ability to get a laugh, but "never, never in my life have I heard a sound so explosively loud as the joyous clamor made by that audience." Few performers reach the stature of Laurence Olivier; fortunately, few have so disastrous a first entrance into the life and world of performance.

*Performance* is the goal of all the performing arts and all of show business. All the crafts and commerce exist to create, prepare for, improve, sell, pay for, and make money from performance. Performance is an experience: one making a show before many.

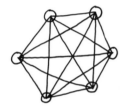

A group of people in conversation give and receive from each other relatively equal amounts of energy in talk and gesture. They are all listening and responding; each becomes in turn the momentary focus of attention. Diagrammed, the lines of energy crisscross.

When one person steps out to act and the others step together to watch, the lines of energy are very different.

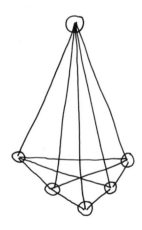

The performer and the audience are still a group, but now a group divided. The many face the one, the one faces the many. The change in the energy balance has polarized the group. In conversation, all were individuals together. Now the performer's individuality has been accentuated; the togetherness of the audience has been correspondingly tightened. Two aspects of human life that coexisted interchangeably in conversation have been sharply contrasted: the performer is man unique, the audience is mankind.

The new energy balance is dynamic and charged with currents in all directions. The performer, for instance, is constantly reaching to stay in contact with the audience—in effect trying to restore the balance disturbed by his or her stepping out. Audience members still are individuals with their own viewpoints, now with the advantage of group camouflage. Each is observed less than when in conversation. Everyone else is watching the performer, and the performer is at work, confronting many people. Even at an outdoor performance, when performer and audience are equally lit, the audience is "in the dark."

Audience membership is a cloak of anonymity that temporarily conceals the individuality of its members. Under its protection people see without being seen, enjoying a partial fulfillment of the age-old wish to be invisible.

Performance begins with "that step into the light," as actress Ruth Gordon has called it: the performer's entrance. This is an assertion of visibility, a conscious shedding of concealment. The performer steps into the open where everything can be seen. The performer's camouflage—which a high sill stripped away from Laurence Olivier—is his or her art: the costumes and makeup, stories and characters, and the technique the performer uses to create the illusion the audience does see.

Even a performer hidden in character and mask knows that he or she is there on stage, exposed like a rabbit on a mown field. Every action is visible; each new action is a decision made and effected in full view. Aware of being watched with special intensity, the performer is specially aware of what he or she is doing and what effect it has on those watching. Outnumbered and vulnerable, the performer lives moment to moment in the public eye.

This creates a sense of peril that is an essential part of the experience of performing. The step into the light is a step into the unknown. Each performance is an open situation which, however well prepared for, can never be totally predicted. All performers have to improvise, make lightning fast choices and changes of direction to adjust to tumultuous immediacy. The audience may not like the performer and what he or she does, and expess that dislike in no uncertain terms. Or, even worse, the audience may not be interested and break contact, leaving the performer truly outside the group.

On the other hand, the performer may overcome that vulnerability and turn it to advantage. With ready wit and practiced skill, the performer can shape the unknown to his or her own wish and compel the audience to fascinated and admiring attention. The triumph of that is sweet indeed; the peril undergone enhances the victorious pleasures of applause well earned.

Performers often call performing "being out there." Experience tells them that more precision could be misleading; the fullest descriptions can only approximate the whirl of emotions and actions that is performing. The description by the great American dancer and choreographer Agnes de Mille in her book, *To a Young Dancer*, is as good as any I have read:

> When you enter the stage in the presence of a live audience, everything you have ever learned is suddenly different. You lose your breath where you never did before; you have strength you never guessed; you are more aware of your body and less aware. Headaches and stomachaches disappear, but just keeping your mouth shut has become an achievement. You can see both in front of you and behind you at once. You see the whole stage and the rip under your sleeve. You hear everything—each cough, each musical instrument, the grip dropping a gelatin offstage, your partner's whispered warning, the creak of your shoes; you hear nothing—a fire engine could drive down the aisle and you would still know how many turns there were left to do; that bit of just standing around feels wonderful, but the long lifts are boring; they were fun to work out, but they are boring . . .
>
> You finish, walled safe by light. And there are the faces and the noise, and it was over so fast, this thing you prepared ten years for. It was completely changed from the way it had been that very afternoon. You are changed. You have not been yourself for some minutes. It was like a rebirth.
>
> And now you want to perform it really! Now you are ready! Now! Now! But it's done. It's over.

Singer Rod Stewart has said he lives for "those ninety minutes." B. B. King has wished for an instrument that "could measure the pressure inside a person" to capture what he feels onstage: "The pressure is like a spell, like if you've been hurt by a gal or your best friend." The late Janis Joplin said that when she was performing it was like "when you're first in love. It's that point two people can get to they call love, like when you really touch someone for the first time, but it's gigantic, multiplied by the whole audience. I feel chills, weird feelings slipping all over my body. It's a supreme emotional and physical experience.

Performing is not always a thrill. Marty Balin of the rock group Jefferson Starship (formerly the Jefferson Airplane) once estimated that the group were lucky if they got loose in one of five concerts; at the others they labored on despite bad sound, dull audiences, or lack of inspiration. Noel Coward, a polished, all-around entertainer—he sang and played the piano as well as being a songwriter, playwright, and actor—noted in his diary his reactions to six nights of solo performance at a London nightclub in the 1950s. Opening night, June

16: "I gave an assured performance, but the audience was tough; in spite of a great success I did not enjoy it much." June 17: "Better performance than last night—great fun." The next night was "successful," the fourth "the best performance I have given to date." The club was "packed and violently enthusiastic" on the fifth night but "the voice . . . certainly needs a rest." The last night was a "glamorous farewell performance that was hell for me as voice virtually non-existent."

Solo performance is performing's irreducible form, and a popular one. *Singles*—magicians, ventriloquists, hypnotists, accordionists,

PERFORMANCE

B. B. King chats between performances

**Bob Dylan**

monologists—are common in the variety arts. Classical pianists, blues and folk singers, stand-up comedians and M.C.s often perform alone. Hal Holbrook, an actor with a varied career on stage, film, and TV, has had two decades of success with his *An Evening with Mark Twain*. Its popularity inspired many similar one-man shows, including Henry Fonda's portrayal of Clarence Darrow in *Darrow*. Bob Dylan's solo performances are built on absolute individuality as a cornerstone: one man and his music.

One person is often the clear center of a performance, even when there are others onstage. Many plays, films, and operas have strong central characters: Medea, Macbeth, Willy Loman, Hedda Gabler. The actor playing those parts is the star; the other actors costar or play supporting parts. These distinctions affect technique. The star needs to work with particular energy and clarity to hold the center; the job of the supporting players is to support the star by being effective foils. When John Gielgud played Hamlet in New York in 1936, he felt some young American actors had not learned this. They worried him with questions about Rozencrantz and Guildenstern's motivation. "What is this character *about*?" they asked. He was tempted to reply, he wrote later, "It's about being a good feed for Hamlet."

Similarly, a violin soloist is the center of a violin concerto performance; so is the singer at a vocal recital. In popular music, singer-songwriters put together groups of sidemen to accompany them on stage and record. Many dance companies have rank distinctions of principal dancer, soloist, and corps de ballet.

Many performers play starring roles of one kind or another during their careers; a few become stars. What makes one performer a star is a powerful quality in the performer's work that attracts an admiring response for its unique identity. Sometimes it is clearly an inborn quality evident in early childhood; actors Gary Coleman and Mickey Rooney, musicians Jascha Heifetz and Stevie Wonder are a few of many stars widely recognized before their teens. For others it comes in the late teens and early twenties, early in the young performer's career and sometimes with overwhelming intensity. Elvis Presley, James Dean, and the Beatles all had to cope with stardom bigger and more sudden than their dreams. For others, like John Wayne and Bob Hope, stardom is a lifetime achievement built of many accumulating successes.

Agnes de Mille defines this star quality as "projection mesmerism . . . concentration combined with absolute confidence. Every faculty, every nerve is bent on communicating a definite idea." When stars enter, she wrote in *To a Young Dancer*, "a thrill goes over the nerves of all the watchers. . . . the chosen few who have the magic are freighted with power and hope . . . they join forces with the waiting audience in high anticipation."

This quality, joined with hard work, technical skill, successful business management, and luck, makes stars. The practical measure of stardom is the ability to attract audiences—name value. A performer is a star to the extent that his or her name can pull paying customers into a performance. Stars like W. C. Fields, Buster Keaton, Clark Gable, Humphrey Bogart, Maria Callas, Marilyn Monroe, and Billie Holiday are "immortals," attracting still eager audiences to their movies and records years after their deaths. Gary Cooper said he knew he was a star when he was instantly recognized and mobbed by North African villagers who loved his movies.

There are local stars and regional stars; there are national stars, like French singer Yves Montand, who become international and multilingual stars; and others, like Mexican comedian Cantinflas, who are little known outside their own country or language group. There are stars known mainly by the audiences devoted to their particular performing art, stars like jazz saxophonist-composer Benny Carter, opera singer Sherrill Milnes, or tap dancer Honi Coles. Ballet dancer Rudolf Nureyev is a star who excited audiences otherwise uninterested in dance. Country music star Dolly Parton successfully "crossed over" to become a pop music star and has become a major movie attraction as well.

Every star's power is increased by good support from his or her colleagues and other surrounding elements—good stories and well-scripted characters, great pieces of music, a fine choreography, well-designed costumes, lighting, and stage settings, plus effective publicity. The core of the appeal, however, is the interest, appreciation, and love felt by an audience for an individual performer. Louis Jordan was a singer and saxophonist whose humorous blues-jazz records (among them, "There Ain't Nobody Here But Us Chickens") sold millions of copies in the late 1940s and early 1950s. At the peak of his stardom, an agent tried to convince him to expand his quintet, the Tympany Five, into a big band for greater popularity.

Jordan said no. "My argument was, people don't go out to hear twenty-five or thirty-five or five pieces, they go to hear an individual. Of course, I admit that the music of a big band is listenable, lots of

Louis Jordan

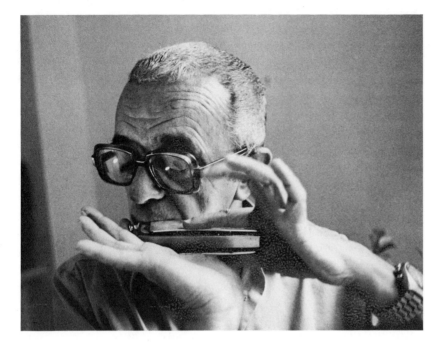

Larry Adler

pieces make nice arrangements, but if you're going to hear somebody, you say, 'I'm going out to hear Louis Jordan,' and you couldn't care how many pieces I had. You came to see me. The spotlight is on me."

Two performers together are performance's second form. Boy and girl are the heart of nearly every romantic story, Adam and Eve heading a long list that includes Solomon and Sheba, Romeo and Juliet, Rhett and Scarlet, Henry Higgins and Eliza Doolittle, even Nagg and Nell in their garbage cans in Samuel Beckett's *Endgame.* Many performances also tell the stories of two brothers or two sisters, a parent and a child, or two friends. Duos are common in the variety arts and music and dance. Harmonica player Larry Adler and dancer Paul Draper are one unusual pairing that performed successfully together in the 1940s and early 1950s. The ballet partnership of Rudolf Nureyev and Margot Fonteyn was an international attraction in the 1960s.

There have been many well-known two-person comedy teams: Laurel and Hardy, Mike Nichols and Elaine May, and the Smothers Brothers, for instance. Some comedy duos pair an active performer with a reactive performer; the comedian who delivers the jokes and the straightman who sets them up. George Burns's air of unperturbed bafflement was the perfect foil for Gracie Allen's innocent and cockeyed ramblings. A true duo is always a fifty-fifty partnership: the performance appeal of a duo is their chemistry. In a series of brilliant films (including *Pat and Mike* and *The Desk Set*), Katharine Hepburn and Spencer Tracy performed together as a strong-minded woman and a strong-minded man in love. They portrayed their alternating attraction and contention with such verve that the game between them was as entertaining as the players themselves.

Trios are common in rock and jazz music, although often, as with pianist Oscar Peterson's trio and The Jimi Hendrix Experience, one musician is the center of interest. Mozart, Beethoven, and other composers have written many chamber music trios, combining three instrumental voices in contrapuntal conversation. The Three Stooges—Larry, Curly, and Mo—are an immortal comedy trio. There are united trios in some stories, the Three Musketeers for instance. More common are triangles of three people at odds: mother, father, and son in Frank Gilroy's play *The Subject Was Roses*, or two lovers and one beloved in Francois Truffaut's film, *Jules and Jim*.

Quartets, quintets, and sextets are the beginning of larger performance ensembles. Jazz "big bands" have from ten to twenty musicians; many theatre and dance companies are equally large. Symphony orchestras can include up to eighty or ninety performers. Operas and musicals may have a hundred or more on stage and in the pit at their grand finales; circuses the same number in three rings. A "cast of thousands" has been the proud boast of many a movie epic.

For performers as well as for the audience, there is safety in numbers; more visible players mean less focus on each. "I like other people to be out there with me," singer and actor Bing Crosby said often. He was not the only star reluctant to carry a whole performance. Ensemble performance creates a unity of all the performers. For New York City Ballet corps member Toni Bentley, the big ballet *Union Jack* means "no nerves . . . the masses of people on stage are warming and close; a real feeling of 'we're in this together,' " she wrote in her book *Winter Season—A Dancer's Journal.* There are sixty-seven string players in the Philadelphia Orchestra—thirty-four violinists, twelve violists, twelve cellists, nine double bassists. "A violinist can make a mistake during a concert and never be heard except by his stand partner," notes music writer Herbert Kupferberg. "He can even stop playing for a few measures and not spoil the overall effect." As a result some string players feel a "loss of individual identity."

In most ensemble performance, however, many players have moments of individual attention. A dance may be choreographed to begin with the entire company, go on to solos and pas de deux, and then reassemble all the dancers for the conclusion; plays and films similarly constantly change the numbers and groupings of the actors in view. James Garner as private eye Jim Rockford was the star of the television series "The Rockford Files," but he often stepped back to let supporting actors Noah Beery and Stuart Margolin, playing his father and his con artist buddy, be the center of an episode. A skillful music arrangement contrasts solo voices of various instruments with ensemble passages. Duke Ellington achieved a lyrical unity in his orchestrations by writing parts perfectly suited for the many soloists in his band—alto saxophonist Johnny Hodges, trumpeter Cootie Williams, and trombonist Lawrence Brown among them.

The economics of show business and the art of performance, moreover, require that there be nothing useless in any show. No one is on the payroll or onstage whose presence is not vital for the effect desired. Every performer has a crucial job to do. A performance succeeds when every artist is working to full strength and concentration, aware of and responsive to the shape, mood, and direction of the whole show. From my own experience as a background extra in two films, *Hair* and *Willy and Phil*, I know that I did not feel "extra." When the camera began to roll, I performed with just as much intensity as when taking a guitar solo onstage with Ellen. Elsa Hilger, a cellist with the Philadelphia orchestra for thirty-three years, recalled that when she started with the last stand of the cellos, she played as if she were on the first stand. "I play every concert as if it were a solo recital, and every concert excites me, even after all these years."

Performer and audience together in the same time and place is performance's irreducible situation. Until this century it was the only one. Radio, film, television, and recorded sound have created a second situation that has achieved a stature equal in importance to its ancient predecessor. In the second situation, the performer is separated from the audience by distance and often by time; camera and microphone create images of the performer that are recorded, broadcast, and distributed to the distant audience.

The present air and light are the medium for a performer before an audience. The media that connect an audience in Maine with a performer in California are complex chains of technology based on the chemistry and physics of making images out of light and sound.

These media can be unwieldy to use—film director Josef von Sternberg said of the movie camera, "nothing has been invented that is more cumbersome." They also have enormous power; Sternberg added that the camera "is a wonderful instrument with its own formula of beauty."

The strength of these media is the extraordinarily vivid verisimilitude of their images. Despite being canned and conveyed over miles, they arrive fresh and unwilted. They can be manipulated as stage images cannot be, giving show makers vast new abilities to direct the eyes and ears of the audience. Images can be edited and selected, reversed and superimposed in time; any location can be a stage; and the audience's viewpoint can be taken zooming around the globe and to within inches of a performer's face.

Understandably, the new media have required the development of new performance techniques. "Stage actors . . . were trained to express emotion through dialogue," silent-movie star Gloria Swanson wrote in her autobiography, *Swanson on Swanson*. "Therefore, some of their best work wound up on the cutting-room floor, replaced by a printed title." Stage actors had to tone down their gestures for film. "I had to stop mugging," Edward G. Robinson wrote of his stage-to-film transition. "That expressive lift of the eyebrow on the stage turned into a caricature in a close-up."

Onstage the performer has to accept the performance as it occurs; in all the recording media, performances can be repeated in take after take and the best one used in the final product. Often the performer doesn't decide which take gets used. "A director will say 'Cut, print!' " actor Jack Lemmon told interviewer Roy Newquist, "and I know I do— all actors do—I'll say, 'My God, Billy, you're not going to print *that*! I felt horrible.' "

Singer Frank Sinatra has said he feels his performance of a song keeps improving with each new take and he often does fifteen or twenty in a recording session. Bob Dylan has recorded many songs in just one take. Record producer Phil Ramone feels that more than five takes is usually wasting time. "With repetition musicians can get too slick and intellectual, resorting to the same licks, the things they've heard and think you want."

Filmed scenes are often repeated with the camera at a new angle. Continuity of performance requires repetition of movement in as exact detail as possible. John Gielgud described the difficulties of that in his memoir, *Gielgud:*

People keep coming up, maddeningly, and saying, "You put your hand to your haversack on this line," or, "You touched your tie." You did those things not knowing you did them, so that when you are reminded of them for a week, you suddenly become frighteningly sick of the scene; it is a boring repetition of something you would rather do in a different way each time.

Continuity also requires creating a unified performance in hundreds of bits and pieces of film or tapes, often recorded over weeks or months. Some dancers like this: "I found I had more energy for each segment when I knew I didn't have to dance a piece from beginning to end," said Nancy Colahan of her experience making a public television special with the Joyce Trisler Danscompany. Many film actors attempt to stay in character off the set and even at home to keep inconsistencies of interpretation from creeping into their work. Few actors like doing scenes out of sequence, but most film budgets require shooting location exteriors at one time and then going back to the studio for interiors. "I fought it all of my time in pictures," said Edward G. Robinson. For contemporary actor Bruce Dern, it is "just something you have to put up with."

Popular musicians build up a record performance layer by layer, beginning with rhythm tracks of bass and drums, then slowly adding instruments, background and lead vocals. "Separating the sounds often means physically separating the musicians," Ramone points out. "I know how unnatural it can feel playing in a studio." Classical musicians are more likely to record together without interruption or overdubbing, although Arthur Rubinstein grew to like the freedom of recording a long piece a dozen measures at a time, stopping for a sip of coffee and a puff on his cigar between segments.

Performance on record and radio is sound performance only; the performer is invisible. Jimi Hendrix, however, said he often jumped around in the studio just as he did in his flamboyant stage act—that was how he felt the music. Radio acting is voice acting; visual gesture must be conveyed in vocal tone and timing. Comedian Milton Berle began in vaudeville and nightclubs. He worked steadily on radio in the 1930s and 1940s. "I did okay," he wrote in his autobiography, *Milton Berle*, "but I never felt I was getting across at my best. . . . Radio, being a medium for the ears, not the eyes, was not the best exposure for a visual comedian."

Berle came into his own with television. The intimate style he had developed in clubs made him TV's first big star in the early fifties.

Television performance is "theatre in close-up," write James Hindman, Larry Kirkman, and Elizabeth Monk in their book *TV Acting*. "The strong point of TV is the face," which, the authors point out, on the small screen is roughly the same size as the viewer's face. Berle came into millions of American homes as "Uncle Miltie," setting a performance style as "a comfortable old friend in the house" later used by many of the medium's biggest stars, including Walter Cronkite, Lucille Ball, Phil Donahue, and "The Fonz"—actor Henry Winkler.

The three authors add, however, "Real rapport with the TV audience is an illusion. . . . How a performer reaches the viewing audience is how he or she relates to the lens of the camera." With "and the microphone" included, that statement is true of all media performance. The audience is not there to react to the performer; the only way to the audience is through the media. "One great reward is denied the actor in film—" actress Jessica Tandy has said, "—the direct contact with the audience."

This is true even though the media performer seldom works alone. Radio and TV comedians found that they needed the live reactions of studio audiences to help them time their performances. "If the studio audience didn't laugh, chances were the home audience wouldn't either," Berle wrote. Dern reminded an interviewer that on a movie set, "You've got forty or fifty workers around you all the time. They're a different kind of audience, but they're an audience."

Working with the distant audience is the essence of media performance. That requires technical understanding of the media; performers need to know how the media will make them look and sound. Comedy actor and director Jerry Lewis advises all film actors to ride the microphone boom, to learn lenses and lighting, carpentry and costuming: "I've even licked the emulsion to see what it tasted like." Marlene Dietrich became a star on the strength of her acting, her singing, and her mastery of makeup and lighting for closeup cinematography. Today, videotape can give a performer instant feedback on what the camera sees.

Performers also need to imagine the audience that is not there. The great rock 'n' roll originator Bo Diddley spoke directly to the listener on his record "You Can't Judge a Book by Looking at the Cover": "You got your radio turned down too low, turn it up!" Disc jockeys command, "Don't touch that dial!" When dancer Colahan was dancing for videotape, she thought, "My parents will see this, and so will my grandparents, who've never seen me dance." In *Lauren Bacall by Myself*

Lauren Bacall described her first time before movie cameras on the set of *To Have or Have Not* with director Howard Hawks:

> Finally Howard thought we could try a take. Silence on the set. The bell rang. "Quiet—we're rolling," said the soundman. "Action," said Howard. This was for posterity. I thought—for real theatres, for real people to see.

Getting *through* the camera and microphone is the great skill of media performance. Early moviemakers found that if they photographed a train from the side, audiences calmly watched a picture of a train going by. If they put the camera on the track in front of the train, audiences ducked, screaming with fright and delight. Performers can come through media to the audience with similar force.

From her training as a model, Marilyn Monroe knew that to be effective on film she had to send all her energy to the camera. This could make her hard to work with. Actor Jack Lemmon, who starred with her in *Some Like It Hot*, recalls that she sometimes broke off nearly completed takes that director Billy Wilder and the other actors thought were perfect when she felt the camera had seen a flaw in her work. The printed film more often than not proved her right. With Monroe there happened "a miracle between the lens and the celluloid," as Laurence Olivier put it after directing and starring with her in *The Prince and the Showgirl*. On set she was withdrawn and often rude; she arrived hours late, apparently oblivious to the frustrations of cast and crew. She consulted her acting coach on the slightest moves. Yet on film "Marilyn! Marilyn was quite wonderful, the best of us all," Olivier wrote. "So. What do you know?"

For anyone considering a performing career, there is only one way to start: to perform. Many students continually find ways to put off gettng on their feet before the public: "I'm not ready yet." "I want to be good when I get out there." "There's no place around here where I can do *my* thing." In most cases the arguments are nonsense. They are like kids at the beach afraid to take the plunge into those inviting but chilly-looking waves, and the same rule applies—last one in's a rotten egg!

Performance is a test, the only one in the performing arts. If it works out there, it works, no matter what the level of preparation, experience, or skill. Performances that don't work can be harrowing, as performers' classic reactions indicate: "I flopped." "I bombed." "I *died* out there." On the other hand, performance is a test that can be taken over and over again. Even the most ignominious flop is not a failure if the performer learns something from the experience.

Opportunities for performance are everywhere. Country musician Barbara Mandrell says that her hand was always first in the air when high school teachers asked for oral reports—she loved talking in front of the class. Nearly all performing arts study involves classroom performance and studio recitals. Even a practice session on a new monologue, a flute sonata, or a dance combination becomes a performance if the student asks a friend or two to listen. Any street corner with a goodly flow of strolling pedestrians can be a stage. California mimes Robert Shields and Lorene Yarnell began their career outdoors in San Francisco's Union Square, and the popular chamber group Mozart on Fifth took their name from their early days playing before the show windows of New York's Fifth Avenue.

Beyond the fringe of show business is the world of amateur performance, which, in its informal way, is as widespread as its professional counterpart. Countless community centers, churches, clubs, fraternal and charitable organizations sponsor theatrical and musical events and evenings; enthusiastic volunteer performers are always welcome. Amateur performance ranges from basement get-togethers of part-time harmonica players to meticulously produced plays and musicals in well-established little theatres. Some amateur groups are actually semipro, church choirs that pay principal soloists, for instance.

There is also the unpaid borderline of the professional world. Every audition is a performance. Small nightclubs and coffeehouses in every city have talent contests, open mike, hoot, or showcase nights early in the week at which aspiring pros perform unpaid in hopes of a weekend gig. New York City's Apollo Theatre on 125th Street in Harlem recently revived its historic Wednesday Amateur Night, which was a launching pad for Ella Fitzgerald, Sammy Davis, Jr., James Brown, and many others in the forties and fifties. Simon and Garfunkle, Jose Feliciano, and Dylan all played downtown at Folk City's Tuesday-night-hoot in Greenwich Village, and David Brenner, Gabe Kaplan, and Pat Benatar stood in line to get a numbered spot Monday night at Catch A Rising Star on the Upper East Side of New York. Los Angeles has the Improv and the Palomino Club, Nashville the Exit Inn—all places where talent is regularly scouted and the beginner's pay is exposure and experience.

Similarly, Off-Off Broadway theatre, new and experimental dance

Waiting for a spot at "the Catch": performers line up at 2 p.m. to get a number at 6 p.m. so that they can perform for five minutes sometime between 10 p.m. and 2 a.m.

companies, and community-access cable TV shows seldom pay the performers. Beginners invest their time and energy in them as workshops to try out skills and ideas. The borderline, which all pros have crossed, is where beginners "have a chance to be bad," as vaudevillians say: to lay down, in places and on nights that only they remember, the foundation of their first two thousand tries.

The first lesson of unpaid and amateur performance is the fact, obvious to anyone who does it, that it is voluntary. Unpaid performers are out there solely on the strength of their desires to be onstage. They have no one else to blame for stagefright, forgotten cues, awkward pauses, the sudden sieges of anger that come when their best work to date disappears into a talkative, uncaring audience—they volunteered for it! If any decide to go home instead, most likely there will be others ready and willing to step into the vacant places.

Ellen and I volunteered first at the Seventh Seal, a Friday and Saturday-night coffeehouse in the Lutheran Campus Center just off the university campus in Berkeley, California. To get a good spot on the performer's signup list, we needed to get there an hour early and wait outside with the other hopefuls. Everybody knew just where they were in line. If we had gotten fed up and left, the people behind us would have moved up a notch; no one else would have cared. The Seventh Seal's pot of gold: occasional bookings at $7.50 an evening. We and the others scrambled for it unceasingly.

Nine months later when we played our first paid booking at the Seventh Seal, we learned that paid performance is voluntary too. Performers on every level are out there because they want to be. The performing opportunities they get they have sought out and competed for. There is something about the performing experience that keeps them working to renew it again and again. "Only do it if you couldn't be happy doing anything else," is an old show business caution to newcomers. Those who do stick to performing through thick and thin find a joy in it necessary for their full health and happiness. Pianist and composer Eubie Blake kept performing until he was nearly one hundred. When asked when he would retire, he always replied, as Duke Ellington and Pablo Casals did and George Burns still does, "Retire? Retire to what?"

What performance gives a performer that can be gotten no other way is an audience. In nearly every performer's recollection of a show, the audience is pivotal to the story. What the performer did or didn't do is important; how the audience responded is what *really* counts.

"They loved it." "They didn't get it." "I had them and then I lost them." "I worked them up to a frenzy." Audience reaction is a definition and valuation of performance. As much as technical perfection, an ever closer relationship with the audience is a performer's elusive goal; improving technique only serves that goal.

"To act without an audience is the same as singing in a room without any resonance," wrote Constantin Stanislavski in *An Actor Prepares*. "To act before a full and responsive audience is like singing in a hall with excellent acoustics . . . [the audience is] like a sounding board returing to us living, human emotions." In her autobiography *Changing*, Liv Ullman described the relationship this way:

> *We* are the theatre group. We have eaten at a strange hotel, phoned home to children and spouses, made up at temporary dressing tables.
> *They* are the public, who live their own lives down there in the darkness. Their breathing and their laughter and their stirrings are part of our experience of them. Now and then a chord is struck, we are one. The auditorium is still and the stage alive.

Actress Lynn Fontanne described her feelings about performance in Cole and Krick's *Actors on Acting*:

> When I am onstage I am the focus of a thousand eyes and it gives me strength. I feel that something, some energy is flowing from the audience into me. I actually feel stronger because of these waves. Now when the play is done, the eyes taken away, I feel just as if a circuit's been broken. The power is switched off.

"Something caught between us," Olivier wrote of the audience and himself at a successful performance, "and, like an electric wire held us together." "In a good performance there is electricity between me and the audience," ballerina Natalia Makarova has said. "I am almost like a magician. I think about what I can do to thrill them. When I feel that everyone is holding their breath waiting for me to move, I find it so inspiring."

The relationship with the audience is unpredictable: sometimes the electricity is not there. Virginia Johnson of the Dance Theatre of Harlem says she is so nearsighted that the audience is "a big black hole." But she can feel the audience as soon as the curtain goes up. "You feel either warmth or a great emptiness. You can't anticipate that feeling. You find out when you get out there."

The performer initiates the relationship and tries to take the audience in the direction he or she wants them to go. "You must control the audience," said the great actress Edith Evans. Between audience and performer there can be a contest of wills that the performer must win if he or she is to succeed. Duke Ellington called performers "gladiators" and Olivier described his feelings before one performance as, "I'll knock their bloody eyes out with it *somehow*." "Go get 'em," performers tell each other in last minute encouragement; opera singers' word of luck is *"In bucco da lupo!"*—"In the mouth of the wolf!"

"Don't let that applause fool you," says an ambitious soprano in James M. Cain's novel about the opera world, *Career in C Major:*

> They're a pack of hyenas, they're always a pack of hyenas, just waiting to tear in and pull out your vitals, and the only way you can keep them back is to lick them. It's a battle, and you've got to win.

The performer reaches out to the audience, but must also stand back and let the audience come to him or her. "The more an actor wishes to amuse his audience, the more the audience will sit back in comfort waiting to be amused," wrote Constantin Stanislavski, the great Russian director and acting teacher. "But as soon as the actor stops being concerned with his audience, the latter begins to watch the actor."

Many performers start to work on the audience by playing to them all as one person. Others identify one sympathetic face or laugh and work to it. "I always pick one person in the audience who is responding and direct my singing only to him," says rock singer Genya Ravan. "If you can maintain contact with even one person, eventually the rest of the audience will get into it."

The relationship with the audience changes with every performance; what worked one night may not work the next. With fame comes a continuing relationship that effects the interaction. A performer who has built up a well-recognized performance style over the years may be reluctant to change it, and audiences may be just as unwilling to approve any changes. Silent-film comedian Buster Keaton's trademark was his unvarying deadpan expression. He refused every request to smile, "just once," on screen. Many Beatle fans took it as a personal affront when the group disbanded, just as some thought Bob Dylan deserted folk music when he began playing with an electric band. Steve McQueen, who became a number one box office attraction as a strong silent motorcycle-riding American, could not get studio executives even to release a film he made playing Dr. Thomas Stockman in Ibsen's *Enemy of the People.*

The relationship between performer and audience can be profoundly satisfying on both sides. Audiences care deeply about performers who move them. Every experienced performer has stories of the generous help devoted fans offered them in times of need. Fan letters are not all meaningless mush. "Thank you . . . for so many beautifully artistic performances which have given me so much delight and joy," a consulting engineer wrote dancer Toni Bentley. "I'm so very beholden to you for all the long, hard, painful years of sustained effort and work in perfecting your beautiful art and talents." Bentley said that note and the little doll that came with it "have gotten me through three subsequent seasons." "My greatest debt will always be to the moviegoing public of yesterday and today," acknowledged Gloria Swanson, "without whose love and devotion I would have had no story to tell.

The performer commands the audience; he or she also serves it. "Work is life for me," Olivier wrote; the essence of his work is "service." Bandleader Sy Oliver says, "I like to play music people like. There is a great deal of satisfaction in watching people enjoy it." In his autobiography, *Country Gentleman*, Chet Atkins wrote that any performer who works his way from playing pie suppers to big auditoriums learns something on the way:

> You learn that your business is to entertain people, no matter where you are and no matter how many people are in your audience. And you do it at their level. If you go into a schoolhouse and play the greatest classical guitar in the world and put everybody to sleep, you are not an entertainer; you are merely a great classical player. But if you go in there and give those same people bluegrass because that's what they paid the admission price for, and they cheer and stomp their feet, you have performed a service. That service is called entertainment, and you can leave with a warm feeling because you have made other people happy.

There can be no hard and fast rules for performance. The experience is of essence mercurial; to preserve the elements of surprise and freedom, performers must reserve the right to do as they please. Here are some suggestions, however, culled from the experience of many performers, including my own.

*Be prepared*—Know what you are going to try to do in each performance. This may change, but have a plan when you start. "Winging it" can lead to unfocused work. "The best ad libs are the ones you make up the night before," says George Burns.

*Be on time*—Getting to the place of performance in plenty of time is a sure way to relieve yourself and your colleagues of pointless anxiety. Get there in time to unwind, say hellos, check details, and get dressed—all the while sensing the whole ambience in which your performance will take place.

*Think out your entrance*—The way a performer first appears to the audience is crucial for all that follows. Make the first impression one you can build on, not recover from. To borrow an image from tennis, the performer always has first serve. Make it an ace.

*Keep going*—All performers lose their concentration, fluff lines, skip notes, and get their feet mixed up, but experience shows that audiences seldom notice. In rehearsal, stop for mistakes until you get it right. In performance, stall, fake it, improvise—do what is necessary—but keep the show going. In the rare cases when that is impossible, stop briefly to get straight and start again. That's not fun but it can happen to the best, and audiences are usually sympathetic.

*Listen*—This was Humphrey Bogart's paramount advice to all actors; it is just as important to musicians and dancers. Listening is the key to rhythm, timing, and blended ensemble work. Listening means being open to the performance as it is actually occurring instead of mechanically going through a memorized sequence of actions. Audiences quickly spot listening performers because they seem alive and alert, engaged in what they are doing, and responsive to what's around them. In a word, they receive as well as give.

Trust your own preparation and skill enough to let go on stage. Create each moment from the vitality of the moment itself. Play!

*Be positive*—Performance is creative, an assertion of an idea, a point of view—"This is how *I* see it." Performing in terms of "I am, I want, I can, I will" is stronger than basing a performance on negatives. It takes powerful acting to create a convincingly ineffectual character, and singing softly or dancing slowly demands the controlled use of full energy.

As subheadings under this suggestion, I'll add:

*Don't apologize*—Your worries that you may not be as good as another performer who has done the same material, or that you have a cold, and that you didn't have time for full rehearsal, the audience undoubtedly doesn't share and doesn't care about. Raising them only creates doubts in their minds and can even seem like an offensive bid for sympathy. Do your best and take your lumps.

*Don't bring backstage problems onstage*—Your fights with the director or any of your colleagues over billing, dressing rooms, or pay are your business, not the audience's. Onstage complaining is by and large boring, and again, audiences often take it as a sign of weakness. Do your job, and then take care of the hassles.

*Leave 'em wanting more*—This ancient maxim is as close to a performance rule as any suggestion can be. Audiences can be amazingly tolerant of inept work, but give them a performance that wanders on and on with no end in sight and they will first get restless, then annoyed, and progress rapidly to seething dislike.

Look over your performance in advance to see where it can be tightened. If in doubt about a portion of your material, cut it. Make each action and each pause definite and to the point, and then move on.

Audiences can understand a lot from very little. Once they have gotten the point, they don't want it hammered in again and again. This does not mean rush. Give moments their full weight and keep your rhythms grounded and steady.

Often, individual performers don't control the length or shape of a whole show, but every performer makes a contribution to the forward momentum of an ensemble performance. Don't let your work bog down.

*Think out your exit*—Performance ends only when you have left the audience for the final time. Work up to the very end. Wilting in the last seconds can do much to break down everything you have built in the many minutes before. Practice your bows, plan for encores. The more spirited your exit, the more eager the audience will be for your next entrance.

Finally, as Fred Astaire said to Ginger Rogers in *The Barkleys of Broadway*—"Be cosmic!" Be bold, be big. Faint heart ne'er won fair audience. Make every performance an expansion of yourself and an expanding experience for your audience. Stretch, experiment. Reach out as far as you can imagine and then reach again. Archimedes said, "Give me a place to stand and I will move the world." Take your stand onstage and do likewise.

# *chapter 6*

○ ○ ○ ○ ○ ○ ○ ○ ○ ○ ○ ○ ○ ○ ○ ○ ○ ○ ○ ○ ○ ○ ○ ○ ○ ○ ○ ○ ○ ○ ○ ○ ○ ○ ○ ○ ○ ○ ○ ○ ○ ○

# EMOTIONS

HUMAN emotion is the lifeblood of show business. What the performing arts show the audience again and again are strong emotions, often in conflict. A show's power is its ability to stir the emotions of its audience.

Our moods, as we know, change day to day, even minute to minute. Yet their essences are constant through centuries, outlasting empires, technologies, and mighty temples of stone. Show styles change with the fashions of their civilizations, but the best shows remain timelessly vital by capturing feelings that people of all ages recognize as real.

The great stories of the Bible—Cain and Abel, the Prodigal Son, the Passion of Christ—have given their themes of hate and murder, shame and forgiveness, love and suffering to countless plays, operas, songs, and dances ever since Biblical times. A visitor from ancient Greece would feel lost in our civilization, but on the TV situation comedy "Laverne and Shirley" he'd see the same pomposities and pratfalls that made him laugh at *The Frogs* and *The Birds* by Aristophanes. The visitor would also find that Sophocles' tragedy of *Oedipus Rex*, the king who blinded himself as punishment for unknowingly marrying his own mother, still lives on our stages and in our lives as a powerful image of guilt and expiation.

*Jump 'n' Bump*, Nancy Colahan and Lonné Moretton (foreground), Ronni Favors and John MacInnis

Who would want to live in Macbeth's drafty castle, filled with bloodily uncouth Scots warriors? But who has not felt, as Macbeth did, impatience with the slow pace of time's unfolding—

Tomorrow and tomorrow and tomorrow
Creeps in this petty pace from day to day.

All of Shakespeare's plays—*Hamlet, The Merchant of Venice, Othello* among them—are vivid with passion, colored with every shade of feeling. There is something of his Romeo and Juliet in all young lovers. His immortal character Falstaff is the personification of vigorous lust for life, at its height and in its sad decline.

The show arts view the world in emotional terms, exposing wants and desires as elemental forces in human interaction. A banker studies long lists of figures, intent on grasping facts stripped of sentiment. A scientist measures truth in the pure logic of his experiments and formulae. But an actor playing the banker looks for his motivation; *why* does he study the figures? Is it ambition, greed, fear of failure? Perhaps the very neatness of the figures gives him a private and curious pleasure. To tell the scientist's story truly, a playwright would need to see much more than his test tubes and symbol-covered blackboard. Is he an only child? Does he have a cat? Does he crack his knuckles when he gets excited? Sometimes when he opens his mail box, perhaps he thinks, "Today there'll be a letter awarding me the Nobel Prize!" Or is that now one of the many disappointed dreams of his youth?

All individuals have unique, complex emotional lives. Sometimes it is hard to believe that anyone else could know what we feel or has ever felt the same way too. But when we go to a show and react to its images with an instinctive and wholehearted, "Yes, that is *just* how I feel," and we see others beside us reacting the same way, it is emotional proof that we are not alone—an enjoyable feeling.

By finding and giving form to emotions we all feel, shows turn gatherings of individuals into responsive audiences. Theatres and concert halls are forums for giving, receiving, and sharing emotions. In the one hundred and sixty years since Beethoven's *Ninth Symphony* was first performed, thousands of audiences have thrilled together as the chorus sings the glorious melody Beethoven wrote for Schiller's "Ode to Joy." When Bob Dylan, on tour in 1974 at the height of Richard Nixon's Watergate crisis, sang the biting line, "Even the President of the United States must sometimes stand naked," fans filling huge auditoriums cheered in agreement. The shock ending of the horror film *Carrie* made audiences leaving the theatres eager to talk to each other, to reassure each other that what they had seen was "only a movie."

Even households scattered across a whole country can feel united in a network of television watchers. The TV mini-series "Roots" was a national event in the winter of 1977; millions of Americans responded together to black history in America presented as the story of a proud family's struggle to survive. When a number one hit record like Barry Manilow's "I Write the Songs" is playing on radios, record players, cassette decks, and jukeboxes everywhere, it becomes, as Manilow sang, "a worldwide symphony."

Creating these emotional bonds between people is show business' service to mankind, the gold inside the glitter. In overcoming our individual isolation, entertainment refreshes our spirits. Laughter, the saying goes, is the best medicine; tears run a close second. When performers make us laugh or cry, or poise us breathlessly in between, we know we have been reached by others outside ourselves. As we understand what they feel, we experience the relaxing sensation of our own feelings being understood. Great performers like Louis Armstrong, Charlie Chaplin, Ravi Shankar, and the Beatles connect their feelings with the feelings of people of every race and from every corner of the world, reminding us all of our common humanity, our fundamental equality.

How do performers make these emotional bonds? By making art out of the content of what they perform, the technique of their craft, and the imaginative use of their own feelings.

A play, a dance, or a piece of music has emotional content, put into it by its author, choreographer, or composer. The words of Arthur Miller's *Death of a Salesman* and the notes of Beethoven's *Moonlight Sonata* are filled with feeling on the page as they were written. These are a performer's first resource. His first job is to reveal that content, to take it off the page and bring it to life. Acting teacher Bill Hickey has told his classes many times, "As actors, we serve the playwright first." This is true even when the performer writes the material. Paul McCartney wrote "Yesterday," but like any other singer, he has to put across the flavor of vain regret inherent in its melody and lyrics. Mozart never envisioned the comedy ballet that choreographer Lar Lubovitch created for his *Sonata for Glass Harmonica*, but Lubovitch's dancers, moving in mock minuet, are in full sympathy with the music's elegant good humor.

Technique communicates emotion by making the performer's gestures specific and clear enough for the audience to understand the content. Even the greatest material can fall totally flat if it is poorly performed. If a ballerina's arms flap vaguely and she falls to the floor in an ungainly heap, no one will believe she is Michel Fokine's *Dying Swan*. Ravel's *Bolero* depends for its emotional effect on the steadily increasing crescendo of its single theme, repeated over and over to a metronomic rhythm. If the players don't have the technique to keep the tempo rock steady and the volume slowly swelling, the audience will not understand Ravel's idea.

Good technique, on the other hand, gets content across *and* excites admiration for its own excellence. This admiration is aesthetic appreciation for the performance—technique is evident in a grace beautiful to behold—and respect for the performer. Even showgoers who have little inkling of how performers do what they do, know it isn't as easy as it may look. As jazz trombonist Dickie Wells once said, "You entertain them with how good you are." Audiences sense the dedication and hard work it takes to be a fine actor, dancer, or musician. When they applaud on opening night, they are applauding all the rehearsals too.

Performers learn technique because they love their work. This love is one of the strongest emotions in any performer's life. It is the foundation on which performers build their emotional relationship with their audience. They *want* to reach the audience, so they devote themselves to learning how to do so ever more effectively. Veteran singer and actress Pearl Bailey links the two goals in her autobiography, *Raw Pearl*. "Genuine performers are all in the business for the artistry of it. They are in it for the love of that public."

To win that love, performers must, like all lovers, reveal something of themselves, let down their guard, and allow themselves to be known. This is where imaginative use of their own emotions begins.

The words "imaginative use" are important because this self-revelation does *not* mean gushing every passing feeling to the public. Performance is not self-expression in that naive and egotistical sense. Letting it all hang out in front of the audience is, for one thing, seldom entertaining. A recent television documentary showed a singer-songwriter breaking the continuity of his concerts to vent his opinions on whatever came to mind. The camera eloquently caught the pained and embarrassed looks on the faces of the audience as they waited for the rambling monologue to stop.

Aretha Franklin

Emotional expression that does work is based on a performer's thoughtful understanding of his or her emotions, and then consciously putting this uniquely personal power to work in his or her art. This process is the opposite of vanity; its fundamental principle is the statement of Stanislavski: "Love the art in yourself, not yourself in the art."

Stanislavski's teachings, available in his best-known books, *An Actor Prepares* and *Building a Character*, are particularly for actors, but they can help any performer reach and use his emotions. "A person in the midst of experiencing a poignant emotional drama is incapable of speaking of it coherently," he wrote in *Building a Character*. "At such a time tears choke him, his voice breaks, the stress of his feelings confuses his thoughts." In time, however, "he can bear himself calmly in relation to past events. He can speak of them coherently." Stanislavski continues:

> Our art seeks to achieve this very result and requires that an actor experience the agony of his role, and weep his heart out at home or in rehearsals, that he may then calm himself, get rid of every sentiment alien or obstructive to his part. He then comes out on stage to convey to the audience in clear, pregnant, deeply felt, intelligible and eloquent terms what he has been through.

Stanislavski inspired many of today's techniques for controlled use of emotion on stage. One is *endowment:* the actor treating a stage-person or object, even the audience, as something or someone else you feel strongly about. Act as if a fellow actor is a slimy bug, and the audience will see one thing; act as if she is a cuddly kitten, and the audience will see something else. Another is *substitution:* the actor finds emotional equivalents from his own life for the emotion the character feels. Here's how actress Uta Hagen describes, in her book *Respect for Acting,* the opening steps of her substitution process in creating the character of Blanche DuBois, the delicate, sensual heroine of Tennessee Williams's play, *A Streetcar Named Desire:*

> I remember myself preparing for an evening at the opera (bathing and oiling and perfuming my body, soothing my skin, brushing my hair til it shines, artfully applying makeup until the little creases are hidden and my eyes look larger and I feel younger, spending hours over a silky elegant wardrobe and a day over the meal I will serve before the opera, setting out my freshest linen, my best crystal and polished silver among dainty flowers); if I recall how I weep over a lovely poem by Rilke or Donne or Browning, how my flesh tingles when I hear Schubert chamber music, how tender I feel at a soft twilight, how I respond to someone pulling out a chair for me at the table or opening a car door for me or offering me their arms for a walk in the park—*then* I am beginning to find within myself realities connected to Blanche DuBois' needs.

These techniques can be summed up in a performer's continuing need to connect himself to what he performs. Pianist-singer Bobby Short, a star attraction at New York's elegant Hotel Carlyle for years, is a fine musician. He can learn a new song technically in a few minutes. "What takes time," he has said, "is finding out how *I* am going to do it, what tempo, phrasing, and arrangement will work for me."

When a performer does connect himself strongly to his work, the audience responds strongly to the art and the performer as one. It's no accident that Luciano Pavarotti, an earthy, warmhearted Italian tenor, is best known for singing the romantic music of his countrymen, nor that flutist James Galway charms audiences with the lilting melodies of his native Ireland. Country singer Johnny Cash's signature song is "Folsom Prison Blues," the story of a hard luck Southerner; jazzman Duke Ellington's was "Take the A Train," a song bright with the gleam of Harlem high life.

Not long ago a concert of guitarist Andres Segovia was televised from the White House. A dignified man of nearly ninety, Segovia played several complex preludes by Bach. As he finished each one, the audience burst into applause at his virtuosity. Then he closed with a piece that he said was a folk song from his native Andalusia. It was a simple lullaby. His thick fingers moved slowly across the guitar strings. Suddenly the old man seemed a little boy. Segovia might have first heard the melody half-asleep in his mother's arms. As the last chord faded away, the audience sat silent for a long moment, moved to an admiration beyond applause by the depth of what Segovia had revealed.

Though it requires discipline, this artistic work with emotional power also requires an openness to emotional experience, a willingness to risk exposure of deep feeling in public. The whole language of show business is drenched in emotion. The banker may "predict" and the scientist may "mathematically prove," but show people "hope" and "yearn." They "desire" and they "want." They "rage against the fates" and they "get the blues for their babies." But, tomorrow, "everything will be coming up roses!" And, the gossip columns tell us, not always inaccurately, they have passionate romances, tempestuous divorces, seek thrills with drugs and fast cars, and get drunk and start fights in restaurants.

So do bankers and scientists! Show business, on the other hand, also has its share of unflappable sobersides. I know an operatic baritone who avoids performances on Tuesdays and Thursdays; those are his bowling nights. There is, however, truth in the cliché that lives in the performing arts are emotionally turbulent. Emotions are purposely on display in show business. Everyone has emotions; show people spend their lives and make their livings communicating them. The intensity that can get these emotions across in vivid hues to the audience doesn't turn off like a faucet the moment a performer leaves the stage. A talent for performing, in Uta Hagen's definition, requires "high sensitivity" first and "easy vulnerability" second. Show people may not be more sensitive to emotional wounds than people in any walk of life, but their work involves, even if in a closely controlled way, baring those wounds to the world.

What does this mean for you? It means, first: *admit your feelings.* That statement covers so much ground that it's worth discussing in two parts, art and career.

Your own emotions—petty and grand, fleeting and lifelong—are a basic raw material of your art. Not somebody else's emotions, not emotions you think you are supposed to have, but what you actually feel. Nobody else feels quite the same way; it's what makes you *you* that, hopefully, will make you a success.

Sometimes audiences want imitations. They go to a lounge and expect the band to play current hits note for note like the records they've already heard. Directors and producers look for "a Travolta type" or "a girl who can sing like Linda Ronstadt." If you can get work that way, fine! But imitations eventually pall. What never palls is the freshness of personal emotion delivered with conviction and insight. Think for a moment of Katharine Hepburn—her vibrant femininity strengthened by a quick intellect and New England restraint, a spirit in tune with her lithe body and flashing eyes. She is inimitable. A comedian can do an impression of her, but the only way to imitate Katharine Hepburn is to be an exciting and dedicated performer in your own way.

Your job is to discover your own feelings, know them, and use them. Discovering feelings can be painful and embarrassing. Who wants to admit all the jealousies, resentments, and annoyances that flicker through us every day? Frustrating too: feelings can be elusive imps that disappear as soon as you try to pin them down. Emotions we don't like take on clever masks that resist being stripped away. "Me nervous? Oh, no, but where are my cigarettes?"

How do you get at your feelings? You play Sherlock Holmes on yourself, taking as objective and detailed a look at yourself as possible. Anyone who can give you honest feedback can help, but only you can do the basic looking. Here are some suggestions:

1.   List, on paper preferably, as many of the facts of your life as you can think of, beginning with your age, your ethnic background, where you grew up, your family's income and social level, your height and weight, your sex.

2.   Look over these facts. How do you feel about them? Do you like your age? Do you sometimes wish you were older or younger? If so, when and why? How do you feel about your family and social background? Have you even felt ashamed of them? Do you wish you lived in another neighborhood, another town? A bigger house? How do you feel about your physical appearance?

3.   Go on to emotional events in your life—past and present romances, strong likes and dislikes, hopes and fears. Turn them over in your mind. Go beyond "I hated my second grade teacher" to why you hated her: what did she do, what was she like, did

she remind you of anyone? Think of a time you felt a specific emotion, the desire to strike and hurt someone, for instance. How did it come about? Did you act on the feelings? What happened then? Remember it in as much detail as possible. How could you tell that event as a story so that someone else could see it from your point of view?

4. Is there something you've done that you've never told the truth about, sometime you fibbed to get out of trouble? Remember that in detail. What did you do? Why were you afraid to tell the truth? Perhaps there is something you still fudge the truth of. Why?

5. Look at your habits. There are undoubtedly routines in your life that you count on to give structure to your day and week. "I always sharpen all my pencils before I begin my homework." "Every Sunday morning we have a big family breakfast and then sit around and read the paper." Then *don't* do the habitual thing and see what feelings emerge. Habits can be powerful emotion-concealers; doing things as we always do them hides the anxiety of making new decisions. Breaking habits can bring out fresh creative energy.

6. Train yourself to notice every time you say, "I have to do this," or "I should do that." "Should" and "have to" are often ways we conceal from ourselves that we are doing what we want to do. "I have to practice scales two hours every day," might really mean, "I want to practice scales because I want to be in the first violin section, and I want the conductor to like me because he's got connections in New York and a recommendation from him would really help."

Whenever you find yourself saying "have to" or "should," try to unravel the emotional knot that is creating the sense of compulsion. Is fear behind it, social or parental pressure, your own self-image? Maybe you don't really want to do what you're telling yourself you "should" do. Try substituting "I can if I want to." How does that make you feel?

7. Think of things that embarrass you or have embarrassed you in the past. Write them down. What is it that makes them so awful? How could you communicate that agony to someone else?

8. Is there any challenge you would like to take but that scares you half to death? What is it that scares you? Fear of failure or

fear of the work it would take to prepare yourself to succeed? The challenge might be trying stand-up comedy for the first time, presenting your own choreography to a dance troupe, or auditioning for a job in an orchestra. What do you need to do to be ready? Start now and see how getting to work makes you feel. When fears come up, deal with them one by one. Face each one squarely; do what is necessary to dispel it.

9.    What are your deepest goals and ambitions? Think big! Day-dream freely. How could you make those dreams real? Are there any fearful or contradictory impulses in yourself that might work to defeat those dreams? How could you strengthen your control over those impulses?

Posing and answering questions like these can become a lifelong method to find emotions you need in your work and to isolate ones that are hindering your growth. Honest answers will convince you that you're an imperfect human being. When your performance shows the results of your answers, the audience will see *you*. Fortunately, that's what they want to see. It is not easy to be open on stage, every private nerve exposed, but audiences get their fill every day of people with their defenses securely in place, smiling blandly and communicating on the "How are you? I'm fine" level. In shows, they want emotional daring just as they want life-or-death thrills from circus acrobats. Singer Bing Crosby risked his solid reputation as the cool crooner of love ballads by playing the alcoholic and suicidal Frank Dodds in the film of Clifford Odets's play *The Country Girl*. His nakedly vulnerable performance won him an Oscar nomination as Best Actor in 1954.

Audiences admire the courage of performers who are open with their emotions in their work. The outpouring of public feeling after John Lennon's death was a direct response to the deep feelings he made public in his music. When a performer expresses feelings in his or her work clearly, the audience learns something valuable about the performer and about themselves. Being open means not only revealing your weaknesses but also your pride in your work and in yourself. At one of his live comedy appearances, Woody Allen silenced a raucous group in the audience who wanted to treat Woody as if he were the absurd little man he played. "Be careful who you're talking to," he said in a quick, flat voice. "I'm a movie director."

Don't be afraid of being laughed at. A pop song a few years ago by the vocal group Tavares put it this way: "Everybody plays the fool sometime, there's no exception to the rule." Performers play the fool to reach the fool in all of us. If the audience laughs, they will really be laughing at themselves. Your work on your feelings opens them up to their own. That's why they laugh, and that's why they applaud. They love you for it.

Now your career. Dealing with your emotions as you work at your career can be as difficult as finding and using your emotions in your art.

A basic problem is that your work is everything to you but matters not at all to nearly everyone else. You're in the spotlight as you perform, but the next morning the audience has dispersed and you're on your own again. A few close friends and some members of your family may be with you all the way; other friends and relatives might be jealous or disapproving. For the rest, what you are living for, dying for, is, on a scale of interest, somewhere between "so what" and "no big deal."

Every performer feels this night-and-day contrast between fiery hope and frigid indifference. Early in our career, Ellen and I moved up from the coffeehouse circuit to a small theatre in Berkeley, California. After spending weeks on publicity, getting newspaper listings, putting up posters, and telling all our friends about the big night, there was, at showtime, a suspicious silence from the front of the house. The stage manager called us on the intercom. "There are two old people here so far," he said. "Shall I hold the curtain?" We did the show, seething inside. Where was everyone who had promised to come? The next day we got a dozen phone calls. "Sorry I couldn't make it, how did it go?"

We wanted to lash out at these fair-weather friends for their treachery. Then we realized: they don't mean it personally. They just have no idea how much we care. Anyway, they are up to their necks in their own lives. Their crises don't ruffle our pond much either. So we mustered our best smiles and said, "Oh, it was great. You missed a fantastic show."

Fame is no sure protection. "I have two Oscars on my mantelpiece," actress Bette Davis has said, "but they don't keep you warm on cold winter evenings." Noel Coward noted almost daily in his diaries that he had "to rise above" petty indignities caused by forgetful fans and colleagues. Bette Davis, of course, did have her Oscars and a mantelpiece to put them on; Noel Coward had houses in Jamaica and Switzerland to console himself in. Beginners lack even these.

You audition, all keyed up for your big break. "Thank you, next, please." You're playing a brand-new song. The people at the front table are chatting about the weather. You and your fellow actors slave over an exciting play. It closes in a week. You dance your heart out. There's a smattering of applause, and you take the bus home alone. Frustratingly, there's no one you can blame. You want this career!

The years go by. Your friends outside show business become established in their careers. You're still an unknown. They get one job and keep it. You're always looking for work. They have a house in the suburbs. You're waiting on tables to pay the rent on your tiny apart-

Waiting to audition

ment. They don't understand what you're trying to do. You wonder yourself. How can you measure your progress? Whole buildings go up while you're learning to sing *a, e, i, o,* and *u* smoothly across your range.

Other performers know what you're going through, and their support is a great help. But they're out for themselves, too. It's hard to be pals with people auditioning for the same job. If you get it, she doesn't, and vice versa. Show biz competition can be brutal. "Even if you're one in a million," a friend told us when we first got to New York, "here there are seven like you." Not everyone plays fair. Backstage psych-out battles are not for the fainthearted.

Suddenly a few things click. Your name's in the paper, agents start calling, you quit the part-time job, and you feel career momentum starting to roll. Then it stops. You break your ankle, your manager gets a new act he likes better, there's a recession. Now what?

It all adds up to artistic, social, and economic insecurity so rough on the psyche that many show business veterans discourage their kids from going through it. When an interviewer asked Walter Matthau what he'd say to young people eager to begin acting, he replied, "Don't." That won't stop a true believer, but, like a Boy Scout—Be Prepared!

Again, *admit your feelings!*

You audition for a part, get called back twice, and lose out on the third round? Of course you're disappointed. Yes, you hate the guy who got the job and the dunces who gave it to him. A bandleader drops you from the group because his old buddy came in from Chicago? That's a raw deal! A receptionist for a record company that has been sitting on your tape for six months brushes you off. Sure, you'd like to blow the place up with dynamite. So would I.

Understand, I am *not* recommending you blow anybody up or scream bloody murder at receptionists, bandleaders, or directors. Quite the opposite. Tantrums are tempting but useless. Ninety-five percent of these infuriating rejections are merely fresh instances of the world's indifference to your naked hopes. They are not personal. Actors and dancers may be rejected because they are too short or too tall to match others who have already been hired. A record company might not sign a new artist because of a temporary corporate decision to limit expansion. Next time, the match will be right or the policy changed, and you'll be working for the people who turned you down six months or a year before.

One blessing of impersonal rejections: you are barely noticed. So when you come back again, the rejection won't be held against you. No one will remember it, and you're under no obligation to bring it up. After Marlon Brando became a star in *A Streetcar Named Desire*, a casting director asked his secretary, "Why didn't I ever get to see him?" She checked the records; Brando had auditioned for him a dozen times.

But rejection, personal or not, does create emotional dynamite. Denying the pain is there doesn't make it go away. It remains inside you as a force you don't understand and can't control. In time it may begin to influence your actions, make you irritable, insecure, pessimistic, depressed, or self-pitying. Perhaps you'll begin to avoid challenges where rejection is a risk, then become angry at yourself for being afraid and angry at others who still dare to try. You may be tempted to mask this fear-anger cycle with cynicism or numb your awareness of it with alcohol or drugs.

Admitting your feelings is a crucial first step in defusing them. Saying, "Yes, I am furious," keeps the anger in view, stops it from sliding beneath the surface. It asserts your own point of view when your confidence in yourself has been shaken. At the very least, if you are furious, it's a true statement when you may be sure of little else. Saying "I'd like to strangle that guy" is a better way of making your anger harmless than saying, "Oh, I don't mind," when you do mind.

Watch out for competitors who say, "Me, I'm not ambitious." They're the ones who will launch the backstage sneak attacks. But to the fellow auditioner who says as you both wait to be called, "Man, I'm going crazy to reach the top," you can say, "Me too!" That agreement could be the start of a friendship. If that friend gets the job and you don't, you can say, "Wow, am I jealous!" With that off your chest, it will be a lot easier to be sincerely congratulatory.

So don't be a walking time-bomb. Keep a diary, write long letters home, tell a friend, go out in the woods and scream, get a punching bag, work out at a gym, play tennis and put the faces of troublesome people on the ball—do whatever is necessary to bring angry feelings to the surface and out of your system.

Ridding yourself of negative emotions is a plain necessity for your work and life. Comedienne Phyllis Diller put it bluntly: "You gotta take out your garbage every day, or you start to stink." Emotional freedom is the basis of sustained creativity; unexpressed angers and resentments can cripple it. Mulling over old grievances wastes time and mental energy, blurs concentration, and shrouds the vital present with a shadowy veil of the past. Self-pity feeds on itself and demands new failures to brood over. Creativity thrives on confident belief in possibility; negativity fosters doubt and defeatism.

Having a chip on your shoulder is also a sure way to sour your relations with other people, and getting along with people is the hidden art of all businesses, show business most definitely included. Half of being a show business success, says Sidney Kiwatt, a Warner Communications executive vice-president who works with people in every area of the industry, is being good at your job; the other half is "your ability to deal with people . . . How to present yourself, learn, grow, and not be negative or have negative things said about you." The show

EMOTIONS

After an audition

arts are collaborative arts. Performers get the spotlight, but there's a person running that spotlight. Courtesy to your colleagues is plain common sense.

As a performer, you are a salesman with a product to sell: yourself and your talent. Agents, managers, producers, directors, bandleaders, choreographers, club owners, and the secretaries who will arrange your appointments with them, are your first customers. They will expect you, as a professional, to be confident of your ability and persistent in selling it, and also pleasant, punctual, and ready to understand their point of view, their needs, and the value of their time. They still might not buy your wares, but they'll be willing to see you again. "Hard to work with"—you do not want that said about you; personal recommendations are crucial in getting show business jobs. There's no need to be obsequious, but arrogance is a luxury you can't afford. Stand up for yourself; don't push other people around.

Audiences sometimes love tough boys and mean cookies onstage. If that's your act, give it all you've got—*onstage*! When you come off, be a *mensch*, a decent human being. Your career in the performing arts is self-chosen; why choose it unless you hope to enjoy it? The best way to enjoy it is to enjoy yourself and the people you work with.

Two final points. If you find that troublesome emotions are confusing and overwhelming you, don't wait, don't be falsely proud—get help. Everywhere today there are counseling and therapy services, all of them confidential and many whose charges are adjusted to the applicant's income. Therapists are trained to be objective listeners with experience in isolating and identifying the many strands that make up emotional tangles. When the going gets rough, they can be more helpful than the best-intentioned friend.

And second: watch out for drugs and alcohol. An aura of glamour surrounds drug use in show business. Fan magazines report overindulgence by the stars with titillated awe. Gold cocaine spoons, they tell us, are a Hollywood status item; celebrities drink French champagne as if it were ginger ale. Free use of drink and drugs can seem a fitting expression of a nonconformist life-style: they will intensify the wild joys of performing, liberate your feelings, and unleash your imagination. The right mix of pills and alcohol, users say, will both calm your nerves and pep you up before a show, put you to sleep after it, and get you going again in the morning.

It is much more likely that drugs will create dependencies wasteful of time, money, and energy. Amphetamines, barbiturates, tranquilizers, hypnotics, cocaine, heroin, as well as alcohol and marijuana, are all expensive, addictive or habit-forming, and stressful to the body and the mind. They conceal more emotions than they reveal. They don't solve problems, they make problems. A performer anxious about how to get the next high isn't fully concentrating on the work at hand and is out of touch with his colleagues and his audience.

Many show business biographies have charted the self-destructive effects of chemical dependencies on the careers and lives of talented entertainers. One of the best and most recent is *Where Have I Been?* by Sid Caesar. Caesar was a sensation in the early days of television. With costar Imogene Coca and a staff of talented writers, Mel Brooks, Neil Simon, and Woody Allen among them, he blazed a trail of outrageous comedy on two top shows, "Your Show of Shows" and "Caesar's Hour," on the air from 1949 to 1958. It was live TV, broadcast with goofs and all. Caesar and his crew lived under a constant deadline, rewriting and rehearsing their skits and satires right up to showtime. The pressure of the work, the demand to stay on top, and the fear that he didn't really deserve his success haunted Caesar. To cope with his insecurities he consumed vast quantities of alcohol, stimulants, and tranquilizers. By the late sixties he was a zombie who traded on his earlier reputation for smaller and smaller bit parts in other stars' films. Life became a "Big Black Blob," he writes. He even made a whole movie in Australia that he doesn't remember at all.

Fortunately for himself, his family, and his many fans, Sid Caesar did pull out of it. A good doctor, a loyal and loving wife, and his own willpower once he decided to assert it, started him on a four-year road to recovery. Now he feels a calm and creative happiness (still with ups and downs) that he never knew in his glory days. "I like myself," he says. "I enjoy myself enjoying myself."

Others haven't gotten the chance to make the comeback: the drugs got them first. Janis Joplin, John Belushi, Jimi Hendrix, Jim Morrison—what those wonderful artists might be creating today! How can it seem anything but a stupid, needless waste?

A successful performing career will require the freest possible use of all your emotional strengths and resources. Start now to find out what they are, without props or crutches. Fly high—on your own wings.

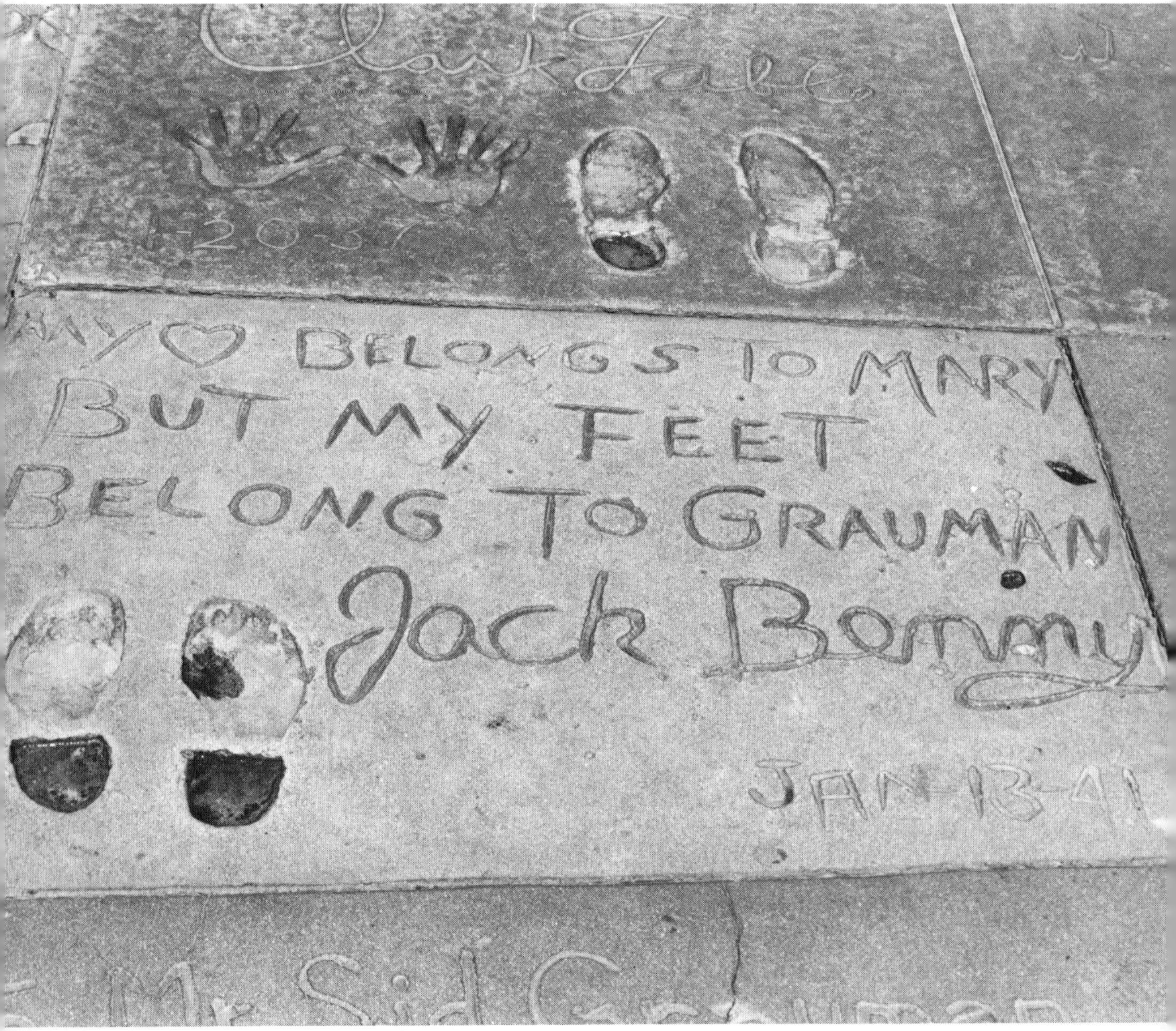

MY ♡ BELONGS TO MARY
BUT MY FEET
BELONG TO GRAUMAN
Jack Benny
JAN 13 41

# chapter 7

○ ○ ○ ○ ○ ○ ○ ○ ○ ○ ○ ○ ○ ○ ○ ○ ○ ○ ○ ○ ○ ○ ○ ○ ○ ○ ○ ○ ○ ○ ○ ○ ○ ○ ○ ○ ○ ○ ○ ○

# business—
# PART ONE

LATE in his career the great Jack Benny used to tell of a visit to his doctor. After an embarrassingly thorough examination, the doctor warned him it was time to slow down. But his work, Benny replied aghast— TV appearances, Las Vegas, playing the violin with symphony orchestras—surely the doctor didn't expect him to give it all up? The doctor did and laughed away Benny's objections. "Come on, Jack, you couldn't be doing it for the money!"

At this point in the story Benny would pause, letting his indignation swell with the laughter of the audience. They knew Benny as a man so cheap that he bought gas a dime at a time and kept his vast wealth in an underground vault guarded by a moat filled with crocodiles. When the laughter had subsided, Benny would finally speak three words, setting it off again.

"My *new* doctor . . ."

Professional performers *do* do it for the money; that is what makes them professionals. Money isn't their only motive—"Nobody's in the business just for the money," pop star Boy George said in a television interview. "There's a lot more to success than money." But receiving monetary reward for work, with a minimum goal of earning a living and the hope for even more, is a basic stimulus for every pro. When

The cement footprints at Grauman's Chinese Theatre in Hollywood—one of the great publicity gimmicks of all time

· · · · · · ·

asked what inspired him to write the jazz standard "Night in Tunisia," trumpeter Dizzy Gillespie replied, "A phone call from a publisher who wanted a song." "If we could ever glimpse the inner workings of the creative impulse, coldly and without pretense," Moss Hart wrote, "we would discover that more often the siren enticements of worldly pleasures and rewards spark it into life than the heroic and consecrated goals we are told inspire it."

Being paid to perform is a gratifying experience. The aesthetic rewards of achieving new levels of skill and the emotional rewards of heartfelt applause are important sustenance, but they do not pay the rent. Pay is tangible recognition of the worth of the performer's time and effort. It allows actors, dancers, musicians, jugglers, magicians, and acrobats to take their place among doctors and lawyers, butchers and bakers, as people supported by the community for their value to it. A performer supporting himself or herself with artistic work is in touch with one of the fundamental aspects of a happy, satisfying life: earning one's living by doing what one wants to do.

The well-publicized wealth of stars encourages many people to begin performing careers. Statistics show, however, that performance can be a risky business. Unemployment among members of Actors' Equity Association, the theatre actors' union, runs steadily at about 80 percent. Only about 4 percent of the actors make over $20,000 a year; 75 percent make less than $5000. The continuing situation for members of the Screen Actors Guild is the same: very few make middle-class incomes or better; most make only part of their income from film performance. A survey of members of New York City's local 802 of the American Federation of Musicians in 1984 showed that the average income of established pros was about $15,000 a year; beginners doing well made between $5000 and $10,000. In 1983 one principal dancer with a well-known modern dance company made $9000 for a thirty-five-week season of worldwide touring.

Low as these figures are, they are misleadingly high. For one thing, there are many nonunion actors, musicians, and dancers, most of them making less than union members. Second, these total incomes are very rarely from one job, found once and held throughout the year. They are from dozens of jobs, each one found individually through a continuous job-hunting process that is time-consuming, expensive, and unpaid. Third, as we've seen, performers prepare and maintain their technical skills on their own time and at their own expense; early in their careers they also often perform for no pay.

The reason for the low incomes of most performers is intense competition for the jobs available: there is a greater supply of performers than there is demand for their services. Twenty to sixty auditioners for a single spot in a dance company is commonplace. A & R men, the artists and repertory executives in charge of signing new artists for record companies, receive daily streams of demo tapes from groups looking for recording contracts. In the theatre and film worlds, mass auditions (popularly named "cattle calls," more politely known as "open calls") are standard practice. One story goes that a hundred actors showed up for a nine a.m. call at a casting director's office.

"Thank you all for coming," the director told the group, "but to save time for most of you I'll say now that we are only looking for Chinese women over sixty. The rest of you are free to go." Nobody moved, each one thinking, "Well, with a little makeup . . ."

Economic survival in competition this intense requires, besides excellent performing ability, intelligently accepting the competition as a fact, meeting it with organized persistence, and presenting one's abilities in an attractive way to potential employers. In short, being a realistic, businesslike, and effective salesperson.

The product? "Yourself, of course," writes actor Merrill Joels in his excellent book *How to Get into Show Business*. "There is only one you. And this is the basis on which you must build."

The first step in building on this basis is for a performer to make the mental decision, "I am a business. From now on I am one of the economic units of show business. Not as big as Warner Communications—yet!—but just as much a business." That decision sets the terms for the steps that follow and can be a steady reference point for the many difficult moments that come up in any career. What follows is an outline of those steps and business decisions.

## BUSINESS ACCOUNTS

After the initial decision, the next step is to buy a ledger, or account book, in which to record the income and expenses of the business. Keeping accurate financial accounts is essential to any business and has many benefits. It makes the initial decision real in black and white, a psychological boost in itself. It is also a basic record for all tax purposes; consistent, thorough accounts are a necessity for any taxpayer in a dispute with the Internal Revenue Service. Accounts are an invaluable source of information about the progress of a business.

Expenses that would otherwise be lost in unnoticed dribs and drabs become known and controllable quantities. Income from various sources can be compared. Expenses and income can be compared to show overall profit and loss, and the relative success, of particular projects or areas of the business.

Keeping a business ledger is not difficult. All that is necessary is a properly lined, small notebook; several styles are available at any office supply or stationery store. Label it with your name, address, and the date you are beginning it. Then, day to day, note each item of expense and income as it occurs. Here is a sample page from one musician's ledger:

Sample page from musician's ledger

| Date | Item | income | | expenses | |
|------|------|--------|--|----------|--|
| | rehearsal space rental | | | 22 | 50 |
| | guitar strings | | | 5 | 50 |
| 5-20 | payment-Port of Call gig | 75 | 00 | | |
| 5-21 | cab to/from gig | | | 7 | 75 |
| 5-22 | amp repair | | | 35 | 00 |
| 5-22 | "Guitar Player" magazine | | | 1 | 25 |
| 5-23 | teaching payment | 15 | 00 | | |
| 5-24 | copyright fee- "No Time" | | | 10 | 00 |
| 5-25 | drink with agent- Bill Moore | | | 5 | 00 |
| 5-25 | gas + tolls | | | 17 | 50 |
| 5-26 | motel | | | 33 | 00 |
| 5-27 | meals | | | 16 | 00 |
| 5-27 | payment-Mountain Inn gig | 225 | 00 | | |
| 5-27 | meals | | | 8 | 00 |
| 5-27 | gas + tolls | | | 10 | 50 |
| 5-28 | reorder photos-100 copies | | | 32 | 00 |
| 5-28 | teaching fees | 45 | 00 | | |
| 5-30 | May totals | 1025 | 50 | 512 | 44 |
| 5-31 | business rent- 1/4 total | | | 125 | 00 |
| 6-1 | rehearsal space | | | 22 | 50 |
| 6-1 | payment -Port of Call gig | 75 | 00 | | |
| 6-2 | stage clothes cleaning | | | 12 | 50 |
| 6-2 | | | | | |

Deciding what is business income is usually not difficult. Gifts or income from nonperformance, part-time jobs are not, though it is also a good idea to keep track of income from all sources. Deciding what constitutes a business expense is a bit more complicated. For a full definition with exceptions and special cases, check the books on small businesses listed in the bibliography and in the library. In brief, a business expense is any expense necessary to earn business income or to further the development of the business. For a performer, that definitely includes fees for study, instruments and instrument repair, stage clothes and stage-clothes cleaning, travel expenses for all out-of-town business trips, home office expenses (postage, stationery, business phone calls, and even the ledger itself), rental of rehearsal space, tickets to performances in the performer's field, professional periodicals, and, within reasonable limits, entertainment of business prospects.

Business expenses may also include a percentage of home rental or purchase payments, as well as utilities, if the performer uses a room in his or her house as an office or work space. Large expenses, like buying a car or van for business travel, can be spread over several years; otherwise they might create the appearance of lopsided losses in one year when in fact the expense is an investment with long-term value.

It is important to save the receipts of as many of the expenses as possible. These can be separated into relevant groups (travel, study, rental, etc.) and kept in a clearly marked envelope. Cancelled checks are excellent documentation of expenses, and it is worth paying all major business expenses by check. A special checking account for the business can be a good idea, but is not necessary at first.

The essence of keeping business accounts is clarity and continuity. Keep them detailed enough to be able to reconstruct the past realistically; keep them simple enough that you actually will keep them. A complex system filled with mysterious gaps will be baffling and of little use.

## SALES KIT—BASIC

Every salesperson needs a case full of samples to accompany his or her sales pitch. Over the years in the performing arts, a performer's sales kit has become a standardized package.

The two essential elements of a performer's sales kit are a *photograph* and a *resumé*.

JOE MULLIGAN

Actor's head shot

Pianist Richard Shirk's
standard photo

The standard photograph is a black-and-white 8″ × 10″ glossy print. For actors the best photo is a head shot, a full-face close-up that includes no more than the head and upper shoulders. There is no need for any attempt at characterization, nor for heavy makeup or special hairstyles. Stay away also from profiles and shadowy or "arty" effects that obscure the face. The photo should be a clear, lively, direct portrait that makes positive eye contact with the viewer and that looks like the actor. "Looks like the actor as he or she is now," adds casting director Gordon Hunt in his book *How to Audition;* if a new beard, a new hair color, or passing years change the actor's appearance, it is time for a new picture.

Character actors and actors looking for work in TV commercials may need a composite, a second 8″ × 10″ that combines two, three, or even four separate photos to show the actor's range—a cop and a schoolteacher, the outdoorsy cowgirl and the slinky femme fatale.

Instrumentalists, comedians, singers, and dancers may want full or half-length shots that convey the flavor of the performer's style. A pianist could be shown at the piano, for instance, a dancer or singer in concert, and a comedian taking a zany pose. Group shots similarly can create a powerful visual image of an ensemble's performance style. A drab, windswept city street can be an exciting background, suggestive of a gritty contemporary reality; a sunny, flowered field behind a performer or group might evoke an old-fashioned or folksy image.

Photos are among a performer's largest start-up costs, worth careful thought and shopping. Two points to keep in mind:

*Will it last?* Make a photo to serve your career plans for at least a year ahead. A sudden change in direction after you've made the picture may mean a wasted investment.

*Will it print?* The photo is not just for employers; it is also for newspapers, publicity posters, and flyers. Evenly lit and evenly contrasted photos, as a general rule, come out better when mass reproduced than shadowy blacks and pure white highlights.

It is definitely worth using a professional photographer. Look for one who makes a specialty of theatrical photography. They advertise in the *Yellow Pages*, show business newspapers, and on bulletin boards. Inquire about prices and services. Normally a photographer will offer one session of a full roll of film, selection from proofs or a contact sheet, and delivery of one finished print or more for an inclusive price. The success of the photo will depend a lot on rapport with the photographer; choose one you like and think it will be fun to work with.

Also in the *Yellow Pages* are companies that will duplicate the photographer's print in groups of a hundred or more. For a small extra fee they will also put the performer's name on the glossy or on a border beneath it.

Publicity photo for First Amendment—a New York City based improvisational comedy troupe

Get the best photo you can afford; money well spent here will pay off. Prices vary widely. As one standard: James J. Kriegsman, a well-established New York theatrical photographer, in mid-1984 charged $75 for one 36-shot session and one 8″ × 10″ of one selection. Kriegsman also makes glossy dupes: $33.95 for 100, $150.55 for 500.

A resumé needs to be a similarly direct verbal portrait of the performer that gets across the essence of his or her experience and qualifications in as simple and factual a way as possible—plus phone and address. Here cuteness, attempts at humor, and sales pitches are to be absolutely avoided—just the facts in outline form. And no more than the facts: resist all temptations to make up false credits. The most likely result is that they'll give the resumé a phony feeling, and whatever imagined advantage they might create is not worth the anxiety of putting yourself on shaky ground.

**DANIEL HICKS**

580-6537 HOME

HEIGHT: 6'0"
WEIGHT: 160
HAIR: BROWN
EYES: HAZEL

**OFF-OFF BROADWAY**

| | | |
| --- | --- | --- |
| CAMINO REAL | 78th ST. THEATRE | INSTRUCTOR |
| MRS. WARREN'S PROFESSION | 18th ST. PLAYHOUSE | FRANK GARDNER |
| HELLO OUT THERE | ETHICAL CULTURE SOCIETY | THE MAN |
| THE MIDNIGHT CALLER | | HARVEY WEEMS |
| 1,000,000 A.D. | DRAMATIS PERSONAE | DR. ZADA |

REP:

**COVENANT PLAYERS—LOS ANGELES, CA**
2 YEARS—4 TOURS—75 ROLES—1000 PERF.
Plays by Charles M. Tanner

| | |
| --- | --- |
| THE HIGH CALLING | ST. PAUL |
| THE PROFESSIONALS | MALKOWSKY |
| BRIDGES & CHASMS | DIAB |
| THE LEGACY | ALLEN DICKENSON |
| FACE TO FACE | JIM |

STOCK:

**SHOWBOAT THEATRE-KINGSTON N.Y.**

| | |
| --- | --- |
| THE CHERRY ORCHARD | GAYEV |
| SMILIN' THROUGH | JEREMIAH WAYNE |
| TRAIL OF THE LONESOME PINE | DAVE TOLLIVER |
| THE PATSY | TRIP BUSTY |

**ST. LAWRENCE UNIVERSITY**
CANTON, N.Y.

| | |
| --- | --- |
| A FLEA IN HER EAR | ROMAIN TOURNEL |
| SCAPIN | OCTAVIO |

COLLEGE:

**POTSDAM STATE UNIVERSITY**
POTSDAM, N.Y.

| | |
| --- | --- |
| COMEDY OF ERRORS | ANTIPHOLUS OF EPHESUS |
| THE RUNNER STUMBLES | TOBY FELKER |
| AH WILDERNESS | NAT MILLER |
| THE BACCHAE | CADMUS |
| 27 WAGON FULL OF COTTON | JAKE MEIGAN |
| ARSENIC AND OLD LACE | JOHNATHAN BREWSTER |
| THE MOUSETRAP | GILES RALSTON |

**TRAINING**

| | |
| --- | --- |
| | POTSDAM STATE UNIVERSITY |
| AMERICAN ACADEMY OF DRAMATIC ARTS | JULIE BOVASSO |
| ACTORS' PLAYHOUSE-KEN COOK | |

**SPECIALTIES**

DIALECTS: ENGLISH, SCOTTISH, IRISH, GERMAN, AMERICAN; N.Y.C., MID/FAR WEST, SOUTHERN

Actor's resumé

# CARA GARGANO

15 W. 2nd St. #8F
New York, NY 10024
(212) 787-9065

Contact: Diane Cummins
D.M.I.
(212) 446-2650

Member: AEA
          Dance Theatre Workshop
Education: BA, MA with
           distinction,
           University of
           Rochester
Ballet: Richard Thomas
        Barbara Fallis
        Sally Miller

## Currently
* Performing/choreographing for Cara Gargano Choreography:
  recent concerts in New York, New Jersey, Washington, DC,
  and Pennsylvania.
* Faculty, CW Post/Long Island University, Head of Dance Division
  Third Street Music School, Head of Dance Department

## Recent Performing Experience
* US Terpsichore Ballet Co. (Original cast in several
  Daniel Levans ballets)
* Arlington Dance Theatre
* St. Mark's Dance Co (Asst Director, Resident Choreographer)
* Empire State Ballet (guest artist, choreographer)
* Little Orchestra Society, Dino Anagost conductor (guest
  artist with Janet Soares/The Dances, Avery Fisher Hall)
* Milwaukee Repertory Theatre (Christmas Carol, Arthur Faria)
* Loving (movie for television)

## Recent Teaching Experience
* New York School of Ballet
* Usdan Camp for the Performing Arts
* Garden State Ballet, company class
* Brooklyn School of Music
* Eglevsky Ballet Summer Workshop
* Aesthetic Literacy Outreach, Long Island Public Schools

## Recent Director/Choreographer Experience
* Ballet Mistress, Garden State Ballet
* Dance Notation Bureau, staging Les Sylphides
* Director, Junior Company, Arlington Dance Theatre
* Stage Director, CW Post Opera: Dido and Aeneas, Riders to
  the Sea, Carmen
* Choreographer: Jacques Brel, Berlin to Broadway, Upstate
  Repertory Theatre

## References
* Stefan Rudnicki, CW Post/LIU, Greenvale, NY
* Richard Thomas, NY School of Ballet, 2291 Broadway, NYC

Dancer's resumé

On the other hand, present the facts in their most positive light. Put your latest and/or greatest credits on top, followed by lesser and older credits in descending order. Beginners may have only a few credits; list them proudly. There is no way to hide beginning status, and even a junior high school play or a few amateur productions show a certain degree of prior experience. List any special skills that could be useful—fluency in a foreign language, for instance. There is no need to add extraneous negative information. If an actor played Hamlet before a scattered audience for one night at a tiny neighborhood theatre

in St. Louis, he can put down "Hamlet in *Hamlet*, St. Louis Art Repertory Company" and leave it at that, an impressive credit.

The two resumés here are good models to follow. Notice how the names, addresses, and phone numbers are prominent and how the whole page is laid out for visual clarity—it is best to keep the resumé one page only. Cut less important items rather than crowd the page or go on to a second. It may well be worth having the resumé professionally typed. There can be no typographical errors or handwritten corrections, and the cleaner the original typing, the cleaner the copies.

Photo and resumé are often given out together. Many performers paste resumés to the backs of some of their photos; then the prospective employer has on one sheet everything he or she needs to know to keep the performer in mind.

The performer has no alternative but to be generous in distributing photos and resumés. They might end up in wastebaskets, but they might also end up on important desks or in files for later discovery at just the right moment. When in doubt, send the sales kit. It can do more good circulating than sitting in a box at home.

A business card is also a good idea. Cheaper than the photo and resumé, cards can be carried in a wallet at all times, ready to be given out to chance contacts. Many businesspeople keep a clip of business cards on their desks for handy reference. Business cards can be embellished with graphics or stylish lettering. The crucial items, naturally, are name, address, phone number, and indication of profession.

## SALES KIT—EXPANDED

With time, more money, more experience, and a widening of the sales market, the performer's sales kit can expand. Many performing groups create expressive insignia for themselves, like the Rolling Stones' well-known tongue in a laughing mouth. Or they use logos, their names in an evocative design, like the imitation detergent box of the rockabilly group Squeaky Clean.

Sales kits can also include *novelty items*, pens, bumper stickers, pennants, or balloons, all emblazoned with the performer's name. Ellen and I have successfully used a button as a giveaway gimmick.

A performer can write up a biography that makes a story from the facts of the resumé in two or three double-spaced pages. Readability, salesmanship, and a sense of humor are in order here. A good bio can often end up used nearly verbatim in a newspaper article announcing a performance.

Any reviews or press notices can be clipped, pasted up, xeroxed and added to the sales kit. A brochure can combine many photos, resumé and biographical facts, press quotes, and a logo in a lively foldout format. Brochures can be expensive, however; including design and printing fees, they can easily cost over a dollar each, even when ordered in lots of a thousand or more.

Many employers hiring musicians or comedians insist on hearing a sample first. For these performers a *demo tape* is as crucial as the photo and resumé. A tape is necessary when an audition is impossible because of distance or when the employer wants to listen without the performers present. With the drastically increased use of videotape and tape decks, today many actors, dancers, and musicians are using videotapes to demonstrate their talents.

The standard format for audio demo tapes today are cassettes; for video, preferably the 3/4-inch professional format, otherwise the half-inch VHS. The basic rule for demo tapes is the same as for photo and resumé: a straightforward representation of the performer that will give the employers a sense of what they will get for their money. Audio tapes can be made at home for very little money or for modest fees at studios that specialize in making demos. Many video services have low rates for short, one-camera tapes. Arranging to have a television appearance taped is an inexpensive way to get a high-quality video demo. There is no ceiling to what a performer can pay for demo tapes if he or she has the money. They can be made in $150-an-hour recording studios with three color cameras, a director, and a production coordinator.

The point to keep in mind, however, is that demo tapes, and all the items of the sales kit, are valuable only to the extent that they help the performer find work—work that creates income well in excess of the cost of the sales kit. A high-priced sales kit for low-priced work is a losing proposition. Here is one way careful accounting can be useful. A performer can set a budget for a sales kit, note the expenses of distributing it, and then measure the rate of return over six months or a year. Depending on the result, he or she can cut back to the photo, resumé, and business card basics or experiment on a brochure or a silk-screened T-shirt.

## SALES DIRECTIONS

With a sales kit, the performer is ready to present him or herself in the marketplace for work. The next questions are: where, when, and how?

The best answers to those questions are: everywhere, all the time, and with confident enthusiasm. Performing arts salesmanship, like performing arts study, is full-time work. It requires the same projective energy, the same discipline and preparation, and the same understanding of other human beings. In fact, every performance is a sales opportunity: there is no better advertisement for getting work than having work.

No performer can run in all directions at once, however, and the job avenues for a ballet dancer are very different from those for a rock 'n' roll drummer. Time spent defining and researching job possibilities, and then organizing individual approaches to each one, can save valuable days and even weeks lost in a scattered approach.

Here are suggestions for a step-by-step method that is efficient, thorough, and minimizes expenses.

1. Look up books on career possibilities for your own area of performance in the bibliography of this book and in the library. Read them carefully, taking notes on anything relevant.

2. List job possibilities in your immediate locality. Note places you are already familiar with, but don't stop there. Check the *Yellow Pages*, daily and weekly newspapers, the free advertising circulars available in many supermarkets, and bulletin boards for names and ideas. Organizations that regularly hire performers include:

> TV stations
> Radio stations
> Film production companies
> Recording studios
> Night clubs, coffeehouses, restaurants, and bars
> Theatres—neighborhood, city, regional, and summer stock
> Dance companies
> Advertising agencies
> Colleges
> College fraternities and sororities
> Private schools
> Public school systems
> Charitable and civic groups
> Fraternal groups

City and state cultural programs
Libraries
State and county fairs
Amusement parks

Individuals and families also often hire performers for private parties, as do companies of all kinds for their seasonal parties and picnics.

3.    Make up a priority list of places where you think you have the best chance of a job. Start with the most likely, and make a phone call or pay a visit. There's no need to make a sales pitch on the first contact; introduce yourself by name and profession, get the names of the people you would need to deal with, and ask any relevant questions.

On visits, meet the performers working as well as the employers. Other performers in your field, though your competition, can be valuable sources of information. Nearly all are willing to share tips and the lowdown on working conditions and pay rates.

4.    Wherever you decide to make your first sales presentations, call in advance. Most employers have definite preferences and procedures for reviewing job applicants. Find out what those are and follow them in letter and in spirit.

5.    A sales meeting is a form of performance. Be purposeful from your entrance to your exit, dress neatly, and be on time. Make no grandiose claims but, just as important, don't sell yourself short. Listen carefully to all the information you get back from the employer. You can learn a lot even if you don't get a job there and then.

No two sales presentations are exactly alike; the details of each are set by the specific situation. For the seller, however, the essence of all is to say clearly, confidently, and convincingly, "I and my work can be of value to you. I am a capable person, aware of your needs, with good ideas of my own. I will be enjoyable to work with."

6.    Keep organized notes of your efforts. An alphabetized notebook of all job contacts with the dates of every phone call, mailing, or interview is essential to make sure that your follow-ups are well timed. A sample from one actor's job contact notebook is on the following page.

Westbank Repertory Theatre
45 Radcliffe Drive
Boston, Mass. 02108
                    617-543-2189

                Artistic director-
                        Carolyn Larson
                Sec'y: Will Craig

2-5: called - spoke to W.C.; send photo/resume
     to C.L.
2-6: sent p/r
2-12 called; WC said p/r received; Country Girl
     audition 4-22 2pm; prepare Georgie/Bernie-
     Act Two, Scene One
2-22 auditioned - okay - come 4-24 2pm for call back
2-24 called back - No!! but CL encouraging - try in
     March for summer productions

7.   Keep trying! All salespeople agree: *polite persistence pays off.*
Don't expect success on the first ten tries; they lay a foundation
of familiarity that may lead to a job on the fifteenth try. Keep
widening your sales area so that you are not pinning all your
hopes on a few opportunities.

     A sales campaign like this is not easy, particularly in the early
days when the "no, thanks" far outnumber the "yes, pleases." If performers really loved selling, they'd have become salespeople full time,
not artists. So it is important to pace sales work, scheduling it into
regular mornings, afternoons, or days of the week to leave clear time
for study and rehearsal. Otherwise, selling can become dispiriting
drudgery. A tired, discouraged salesperson defeats his or her own purpose.

     Performers whose work is self-contained—soloists, duos, or music
groups, jugglers, magicians, comedians, or dancers—may find it
worthwhile to advertise in the *Yellow Pages*, newspaper classified ads,
trade papers, and professional periodicals, or to make up flyers for
posting on bulletin boards. Actors may find that ads in trade papers
announcing their parts in upcoming productions increase their name
recognition.

     Advertising is the best way to reach employers and the general
public (individual party givers, for instance) the performer has not
thought of. It can also start people calling the performer, a welcome
change. Like the items of the expanded sales kit, advertising is an
investment to be carefully weighed. It can amplify but never replace
the performer's direct sales work.

# CONTACTS

All the sales work described above has a side effect of indispensable value to every performer: *making contacts*. In fact, many sales avenues are worth pursuing even when there is little chance of immediate success because they lead to personal contacts that could be helpful later.

"Contacts are the people you know and who know you," Robert Cohen wrote in *Acting Professionally*. "Contacts are important—vital—in getting jobs." Employers tend to hire performers they have already worked with or whose work they already know. Trying an unknown is risky; feeling out a new working relationship takes time. Employers have nothing against the unknown performer; they are following a natural impulse. "If you were casting a play in a hurry and knew someone who was 'just right' for the role," as Cohen puts it, "would you really search through the drama classes at State University to find . . . somebody as good or better? No. You would call Harry. . . . you like him, you envision him doing the part, and you can settle the matter in a quick, friendly way."

This means that getting known—meeting and breaking the ice with as many people as possible in the profession—is one of a beginning performer's most important jobs. The people to get to know are not just the "big shots"—respected casting directors, influential stars, or record company vice-presidents. They are secretaries, receptionists, soundmen, stage hands, choreographers, other performers, students booking a campus coffeehouse or renting a tiny storefront for an improv comedy club. Show business is a fluid business; the unpaid apprentice going out for everybody's coffee today may be an independent producer tomorrow.

The essence of making good contacts is professional courtesy. Business relationships are seldom close friendships; they are more likely to be based on mutual usefulness—"I need you and you need me." They can be carried on, however, with a cooperative spirit, each person sympathetic to the other's point of view. That spirit can lead to friendship; it also makes business enjoyable and creates good will, an asset difficult to quantify in a ledger but as valuable as money in the bank. Be polite, be punctual, and pitch in; the people you work with will be glad to work with you again.

The new word "networking" describes how contacts grow. One meeting leads to another; an introduction to Joe means also meeting his partner Fred, whose recommendation to Louise creates a job possibility with Ted. When Ellen and I came to New York from California, we had two definite professional appointments and the names of about a half-dozen people whom friends had suggested we contact. One appointment was a washout, the other led to several good auditions. One name was that of a professional New York musician who gave us countless good tips and suggestions; another of our contacts quickly found us a place to stay and to rehearse. Most important, from the first day we knew a few people in the big, new city.

Two principles of making contacts to keep in mind:

1. *Start with the people you know:* Think of people who are contacts already. They may be able to give you suggestions and recommendations that will help you with new people you don't know.

A sales kit sent to "Columbia Records" or "The New York Shakespeare Festival" is much less effective than one sent to a specific person with a covering letter mentioning a mutual acquaintance who recommends your work.

2. *Keep up your contacts:* After a good meeting or work experience, send a thank-you note. If someone gives you a recommendation, be sure to let them know what happened. If you look through your notebook and notice a contact you haven't called in six months, call and find out what's new.

Sending out your own newsletters or postcards is an excellent and inexpensive way to stay in touch with a large circle of contacts. They may not respond right away, but they will be glad you thought of them. (See "Press and Publicity" below for details on keeping a mailing list.)

## AUDITIONS

For many performers, auditioning is the most difficult part of all their work. Auditions compress years of study, training, and hope into brief performances before a few coolly appraising auditors. Actors read their lines while the casting director slouches in his seat five rows back and whispers to the playwright, who is sipping coffee and eating a Danish pastry. Musicians audition in the morning at a nightclub while a busboy vacuums the rug and the boss talks on the phone to his liquor wholesaler. Singers and dancers are accompanied by pianists sightreading the music while two dozen auditioners wait and watch critically from the wings.

There are several different forms of auditions. There are the open calls already mentioned, and there are auditions by invitation and recommendation only. Actors have cold readings at which they are given the script moments before they have to read it aloud; prepared readings when they get the script a few days in advance; and general readings for which actors prepare pieces of their own choosing. Similarly, musicians and dancers are sometimes asked to demonstrate what they think they do best, sometimes required to perform, on the spot, music or step combinations picked by the producers. Film actors often take screen tests, not for their acting ability as such, but for producers to see how they photograph. Classical musicians auditioning for orchestral jobs, on the other hand, often play behind screens to ensure that they are judged on their sound alone.

Auditions are a fundamental part of getting work. Sales kits, interviews, and demo tapes in most cases cannot substitute for seeing a performer perform. Even when an employer knows a performer's work from a previous engagement, an audition may be necessary for producers to see whether the performer will fit into the production being planned or how he or she will match performers already hired. A bandleader, for instance, needs to know if a new bass player can work sympathetically with the group's drummer. Like it or not, auditioning comes with the territory.

A New York City audition for Nashville's Opryland

The best way for a performer to enjoy auditions, or at least to make them bearable, is first to accept their necessity and then to treat each one as a performance—which it is—deserving the best possible effort. For beginners, auditioning is a way to perform at all. The very nakedness of an audition is a special kind of performance test: an actress who can get the playwright to stop eating his Danish has won a sweet victory. Auditioning encourages boldness, quick thinking, and risk-taking. Performers audition to get jobs; they also audition for themselves and for everything they can learn.

Be prepared: even for a cold audition learn as much as possible about the style of what you are auditioning for. Be on time: promptness will be taken as a sign of professionalism. Enter and exit with a firmness that shows your respect for yourself. Keep going: auditions are not rehearsals—if you get the job, then you can work out your interpretation in detail.

Be positive: clear, strong actions are particularly important at auditions. They are, remember, *sales* performances. A timid audition will be taken as an indication of the performer's lack of confidence in his or her own ability. A bland performance will give the auditors little to react to. An audition is a showcase; show them what you've got.

Leave 'em wanting more: this too is particularly important at auditions. The auditors are not waiting to be entertained by a full-length show. They are pros making business decisions as efficiently as possible. Their time is valuable; so is the time of the other waiting auditioners. Perhaps the toughest part of any audition is being cut off in full flight with a "Thank you, next please." A performer can try to spare himself or herself that agony by being quick and to the point.

Here are several suggestions specifically for auditions:

1. *Perform for the whole room:* The few auditors—perhaps only one—are your audience, but focusing all your energy at them can be constricting for you and uncomfortable for them. Imagine the empty seats full of an audience of your own choosing, and include the auditors in it.

2. *Perform as you think is right:* Worrying whether your performance is what the auditors are looking for is just that—worry. It will show. Do it your way. You may be wrong, but you'll be yourself. Maybe the auditors don't know for certain what they are looking for, and you'll be a happy surprise.

In his excellent book *Audition*, casting director Michael Shurtleff states it categorically: "It's a total waste of time to try to find out what the auditors want."

3. *Let your dress suggest the part:* Standard audition dress is neat but comfortable street clothing; in dance, leotard and tights. Within those limits, however, accent your dress toward the work you are auditioning for. Don't audition for a Western in a business suit or in jeans for a drawing room comedy.

Suspense and the anxiety that goes with it are unavoidable in auditioning. If a performer gets the job, his or her career will take a new, perhaps exciting and lucrative direction. If not, back to the same old grind. That intense sense of possibility makes the auditioner feel that he or she is being examined under a microscope that reveals and enlarges every flaw. That can be instructive; it can also fracture one's confidence. To keep moving forward, a performer needs to learn from audition mistakes and then let them go. "Forget your bad auditions," advises Rebecca Nahas in *Your Acting Career.* "There are thousands of actors who have all given poor readings and hundreds of casting people who see bad auditions every day. Is yours really so exceptionally awful that it will make theatre history?"

Gordon Hunt makes an excellent suggestion to counteract the narcissism of auditioning anxiety: "Help someone on your way to the audition." That help can be holding open a door, writing an encouraging letter, doing a favor for a neighbor, or just a friendly smile for a tired bus driver. The idea is, forget yourself for a moment. The world will keep spinning whether you get the job or not, and you will feel more confident that you'll still be spinning with it.

## NEGOTIATION

When a performer passes an audition and gets a job offer, negotiation begins. What is the job and what is the pay? Are they acceptable? Does the performer have a counter offer? How does the employer respond to that? Can they make and shake on a deal?

Negotiation is haggling, the ancient game of trading. A subtle contest of wills, negotiation is like chess in having myriad future possibilities inherent in every move, like poker in relying both on close calculation of advantageous odds and on outrageous bluffing when the odds are a thousand to one against. For horse-traders, import-export merchants, stockbrokers, and scrap metal dealers, negotiating prices is a way of life. In negotiation, there are no set values; something is worth what you can get for it. The aim of all: "Buy low, sell high."

Few beginning performers are experienced negotiators. There is little haggling in most American consumer buying, and young performers are likely to consider employers authority figures like parents and teachers who can be opposed only with fear and trembling. Furthermore, after years of unpaid study and months of disappointed auditioning, to be offered something—anything!—to perform seems almost too good to be true.

Ignorant timidity or overeagerness are disadvantages in negotiation, and many employers, without doing anything illegal, will happily take advantage of them. That is the way the game is played. Employers have dozens of justifications for their low offers, each a potential ploy to be used as the situation requires: business is slow, the rent just went up, redecoration has left them short of cash, a new theatre across the street is taking all their customers. Attacks on the performer's confidence, either subtle or open, are also acceptable strategies: "You're green, kid. I'm crazy to be taking a chance on you. Consider yourself lucky to be working." And the crusher: "Acts like you are a dime a dozen. Take it or leave it, I can always get somebody else."

Losing the first few rounds, even the first few dozen rounds, of negotiation is part of every performer's initiation—"paying your dues," as musicians call it. Winning can begin when the performer sees that negotiation is a game, enjoyable if played coolly. Employer bluffs can be met with counter bluffs: "I'll get back to you. I'll have to check my calendar"; "At that price, I can't even pay the guys in the band." One-upmanship can work both ways: "Did you see that rave about me in the *Chronicle*?" "ABC-TV just called me." Toughness is more often than not met with a new respect rather than the dismissive contempt the timid performer fears. The legendary threat, "I'll see to it you never work in Hollywood again," is an empty one. No single employer can keep a determined performer from working.

Every negotiation is different. There are times to walk out, times to hold out, times to give a little, times to give a lot. For the best results in any negotiation:

1. *Know all you can in advance:* Find out the market rates paid to equivalent performers; make your own best estimate of the employer's economic situation.

2. *Have your own minimum price in mind:* Analyze from your financial records what you need to earn to make the job worthwhile. Don't reveal that price and do ask for more, but don't take less unless there are compensatory advantages.

3. *Hold out for your own satisfaction:* That is worth more than money; it is the feeling that you can take the job without being defeated or resentful. Compromise, yes; cave in, no.

4. *Be specific:* Be alert for employer vagueness on points important to you. Keep asking questions until you are confident that when the job begins there will be no unpleasant surprises that could have been avoided by full discussion and agreement.

5. *Stick to the point:* You are negotiating because there is a job possibility that could further your own goals. Avoid getting drawn into arguments. Don't let minor issues become major obstacles. Blow off steam outside the negotiating room, not in it.

The ideal negotiation ends in a partnership that works to the satisfaction of both performer and employer. In most cases, neither are making money from each other; they are working together to make a show that will earn both of them money from the public. Firmness and a sense of humor will go a long way to ensure that the performer gets a fair share of the loot and has a good time earning it.

## CONTRACTS

A contract is an agreement, the end result of successful negotiation. There are verbal contracts when the parties reach an agreement after discussion and seal it with no more than a handshake. Written contracts are drawn up whenever the terms of an agreement are too complex to be easily remembered; these are sealed with the signatures of both parties. *Both verbal and written contracts are legally binding.* Verbal contracts, however, are much harder to prove in case of a dispute. It is a good idea to make your own written notes of any contract you make verbally. Written contracts are often just the formal notation of a verbal agreement already reached.

There are many kinds of contracts between performers and employers. Bands get contracts for one-night gigs with nightclub owners, dancers make contracts for a season of work with a dance company, actors sign up with an advertising agency to represent one product exclusively, and singer-songwriters agree to recording contracts with special provisions for the publishing rights of their original material—these are only a few examples.

Broken, poorly made, or unfair contracts sometimes end in lawsuits that make headlines—the split-up of the Beatles, for instance, was attended by years of well-publicized legal wrangling. The mustachioed villain pressing a fountain pen into the trembling hand of a bewildered innocent and saying, "Sign here, my dear," is a common legend of contract-making, accompanied by common fears of "fine print" and legal jargon hiding exploitive clauses among the "whereases" and the "aforesaids." In fact, we all make contracts every day—a date to meet for lunch is an informal contract—and most contracts are made in good faith and fulfilled to the satisfaction of both parties.

The best way to overcome the fear of making contracts, and to make contracts that will not turn out to be frightening, is to be specific and thorough in negotiation. When two parties have fully expressed their concerns and requirements and received full acknowledgement of them in negotiation, the contract has a firm foundation. The time to discuss is *before* you sign. Be efficient in negotiation, but do not let yourself be hurried. Bring up everything you need to know. Ask every question, even if it seems to show your ignorance. Even though performers usually sign contracts presented by the employer, remember that a contract is a two-way agreement between equals and creates obligation both ways. Make sure that there are provisions clearly outlining the terms essential to you. In brief:

1. *Know what you are agreeing to:* Understand fully what the contract obliges you to do and what you will get in return.

2. *Know what you are not agreeing to:* Understand fully what the limits of the contract are, what the employer is *not* entitled to unless a new or amended contract is made.

Good advice from one experienced lawyer is, "Keep contracts simple." Unless there is evidence of or a history of bad faith, most contracts can be made without extra clauses covering every imaginable thing that could go wrong. If the theatre burns down or a blizzard closes the airport and the highways, an employer and performer who have a good working relationship are going to be able to figure out what to do next without going to court over "act of God" clauses.

On the other hand, contracts that do spell out complex business relationships that may extend over several months or years and involve large sums of money cannot be reduced to a few words. They may need several pages and legal language difficult to understand even if it is not jargon. Any time a performer feels, "This contract is over my head," there is only one remedy: *professional advice*. This can begin at the library with books on performing arts law and standard business practice, and can proceed to calls to a lawyer, agent, manager, a union or professional association. These people and how to find them are covered in the next chapter. Here I stress: *do not make any contract that could tie up your services or your work for more than a few nights or weeks without full research and advice from a competent professional in the field who is not a party to the contract.* This may not always mean being represented by a lawyer or agent; it can mean being "walked through" your first few important contracts until you feel you know the ropes.

## PUBLICITY

Publicity is the art and business of creating public awareness and excitement about performance. People can only go to shows they know about, and they will pay to go only if something in what they hear or see stimulates their curiosity. Publicity is so crucial to creating audiences that it is show business' second industry, on which the first, performance itself, depends for success. Ignoring the importance of publicity or skimping on it can be as disastrous to a show as poor preparation of the actual performance.

There is paid publicity: advertising on radio, TV, billboards, in newspapers and magazines, and even writing in the sky. Media interviews, items in entertainment columns, appearances on TV talk and game shows, and feature stories on new productions are free publicity—though often the larger advertisers get the most "free" space. There are publicity gimmicks—giveaways, contests, joke slogans, and gala premieres with stars arriving in limousines. Show business pros consider word of mouth the best publicity of all: the show itself excites audiences so much that they tell their friends to go see it. Astute show makers consider the publicity value of everything from precise wording of the title to the graphics of the ad poster, the appeal of the star, and any possible tie-in to current events. *Chariots of Fire*, for instance, capitalized on the running fad of the mid-1980s, and then was sold to be shown on TV the week before the opening of the 1984 summer

Olympics. The award shows—the Oscars, the Tonys, the Emmies, and the Grammies—are massive publicity events sponsored by the movie, theatre, TV, and record industries to shed an aura of glamour not only on the winners but on show business as a whole.

Publicity is a cooperative affair. Well-known stars can make a show a hit, and a nightclub with a reputation for presenting top talent will pull customers even on nights when the band or comedian is unknown. Shows and clubs come and go, however; a performer's primary publicity work is to become known as an individual.

A publicity campaign parallels the sales campaign. At times the two are indistinguishable; a good job is the best publicity there is. The basic tool is the *press kit*, the sales kit aimed at publicity rather than employer contacts.

Begin by identifying as many publicity avenues in your performance area as possible, starting with magazines, newspapers, and radio and television stations because they reach the most people. Call to find out to whom to submit your press kit and what the deadlines are—press material often has to be received two or three weeks in advance of publication. Keep the information you gather in an alphabetized notebook like the sales book. Ask at a copy center for a *mailing list label matrix*, a sheet of paper lined to make boxes the size of peel-off address labels. With that as a guide, type up the press contact names and addresses as a mailing list.

When there is a performance to publicize—the press nearly always covers a performer in connection with an event—make up a *press release*. The elements of a good press release are: stationery that gives the name and address of the sender; the time slug that gives the release date—"for immediate release" or "release after June 22"; the who, what, where, when, and how much set out clearly at the top; the story that gives the important facts and the background facts written as a news story; and the slant, the particular hook or angle that makes this story worthy of coverage. Be as brief and as lively as possible—press contacts get hundreds of releases a week.

Then xerox the mailing list onto labels and send the publicity kit, following up in a few days with a phone call to make sure it arrived. That is also a good time to make the contact personal and to answer any questions. One point to remember: press people take freedom of the press seriously and will resent high-pressure salesmanship. Their slant on a story or interview may not be as flattering as the one the performer had in mind, and reviewers have the unquestioned right to pan shows they don't like. Present yourself as well as possible and except in cases of flagrant misquotation or serious factual misrepresentation, don't complain about poor publicity. In most cases it is better than none.

Sometimes a show production company or club will have its own press agent or public relations office, and an individual campaign would be unnecessary duplication of effort. In that case, offer your full cooperation to them and send the show's press kit to your most important contacts with a personal note. Performers can also hire their own press agents, but it is an expensive investment of questionable worth for beginners. When breaking in, a performer's own enthusiasm is his or her best publicity asset.

Any positive story or review that the publicity campaign creates can be copied and sent out to all press contacts. A story in one publication often convinces another publication that the performer is worth writing about. As with sales contacts, keep up your press contacts even after months of few or no results. Each new release increases familiarity. Entertainment reporters sometimes forget where they get their information about a performer; a steady flow of releases persuades them, subliminally, that a performer is well known.

Performers can also have personal mailing lists of friends, relatives, and fans who can receive releases and newsletters. Ask every person you meet who expresses interest in you as a performer if they would like to be on your mailing list. Most will be delighted to get the

Press contacts typed up to serve as labels

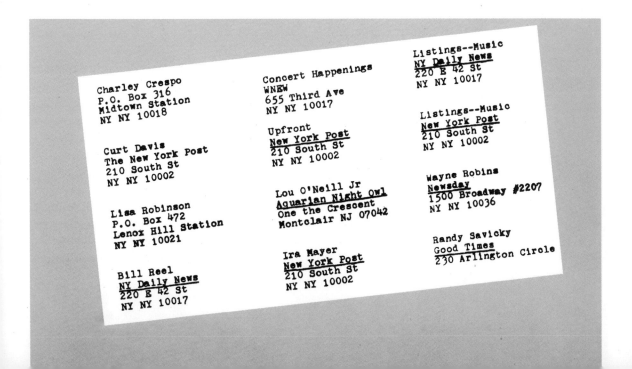

mail, and when they come to a show, they'll be there especially for you. Keep weeding out nonresponders from your list to keep down postage and printing costs.

Many performers make up posters and flyers to advertise their performances, then post them on bulletin boards, telephone poles, and bare walls, or give them to the show producers to post. A good idea here is to create a basic graphic—photo, logo, press quotes—for the top of the poster, leaving a blank space at the bottom. The design can be used for many engagements with the new "where and when" information added in the blank each time.

A goal to aim for in publicity is a *consistent image natural to the performer's personality.* An image can begin with an appropriate name— Rhythmotion for a jazz group, for instance—and be enhanced by evocative photography and press kit graphics. Consistency is not necessarily constricting; Dustin Hoffman has successfully presented himself as a versatile actor. An identifying prop can help: Willie Nelson's hairband suggests the singer's southwestern earthiness just as George Burns's cigar is inseparable from his sly and intimate comedy. A good image is never forced or artificial. Though consciously used for publicity effect, an image needs truth to be workable. The public will sense its truth, the performer will find it easy to maintain, and for both it will gain in meaning with passing time.

In sum, publicity is a form of media performance. Connect yours to the development of your performance style, and make both entertaining.

## IMAGINATION

Running a performance business requires as much imagination as performing does. It would be silly for a creative artist to be routine and uninspired in developing the commercial aspects of his or her talent.

A meat-packing company used to advertise its pork products, "We sell everything but the squeal." With imagination, performers likewise can find countless ways to market their abilities. Actors need not wait until someone else writes and produces a play or film to get a job. They can try writing one themselves or join with other actors and found their own production company. They can look for work in commercials, either acting or doing voice-overs, try stand-up comedy, or put together a one-man show. For the price of a business card and a continuing classified ad in a few newspapers, New York actress Laurette Cronin has started a business delivering "Boop-a-Grams." For $50 she'll deliver a telegram message sung in the breathless, eye-lash-fluttering style of cartoon character Betty Boop. Her best week to date: six deliveries for a total of $300. She has also been able to use her Boop character in her regular work with the First Amendment comedy troupe.

Musicians in a group are not necessarily idle when the band is between gigs. They can free-lance in other groups and in recording sessions, arrange music for others, copy lead sheets, write advertising jingles, write songs and send them to publishers. Imaginative career planning is particularly important for dancers, many of whom face retirement from performance by their late thirties. They can teach or choreograph; learn company management, lighting design, or costuming; retrain themselves in tap, folk, or ballroom dancing, where the age cutoff is older than in ballet and modern dance.

Like artistic imagination, business imagination requires flexibility, openness to possibility, and self-examination. Performers who have spent much time and effort finding and developing primary strengths and goals can work to bring out secondary interests and abilities—writing, mathematics, research, administration, or public speaking. Performance experience can be converted into a valuable asset in jobs that involve meeting and working with large numbers of people. Performing skill plus a graduate degree in business can turn a performer into a show business executive; a psychology degree added to performing skill can open up a career in speech, music, or dance therapy. It is worth any performer's time occasionally to read help wanted ads outside his or her own field for fresh ideas.

Business imagination is important at all stages of a performer's career, but it has special value in the early years when performance work doesn't pay all the bills. Part-time jobs that have nothing to do with a performer's career goals—driving a cab, working in the post office, or selling over the telephone—can be dispiriting and raise nagging doubts—"Am I a dancer or am I a magazine salesman?" With imaginative planning it may be possible to get nonperformance work that is somehow connected to show business. Running a box office, painting sets, road managing a band, or doing publicity for a dance group—these jobs create knowledge, experience, and contacts helpful to a performing career. They may not be ultimate goals, but the money they earn, and the world that comes with them, can keep a struggling performer alive, body and soul.

BUSINESS—

PART ONE

# chapter 8

○ ○ ○ ○ ○ ○ ○ ○ ○ ○ ○ ○ ○ ○ ○ ○ ○ ○ ○ ○ ○ ○ ○ ○ ○ ○ ○ ○ ○ ○ ○ ○ ○ ○ ○ ○ ○ ○ ○ ○

# busiNESS—
# PART TWO

T H E previous chapter covered the essential practical matters a performer must be aware of to run his or her own performing career as a business. The underlying assumption was that each performer is an independent businessperson capable of understanding and making dollars-and-cents decisions with the same creativity and individual freedom used in making artistic decisions.

That is also the premise of this chapter. Few performers, however, are in business solely on their own. They often work with other businesspeople who help them organize their talents into marketable form, represent them in sales and negotiation meetings with employers, read over the contracts offered them, and counsel them on career decisions. There are also guilds, unions, and professional associations that represent the interests of thousands of professional artists in acting, dance, and music as well as the variety arts.

Performing artists are also taxpayers. The ups and downs of their income, and the expenses they incur to earn it, mean they must pay careful attention to their record-keeping for tax purposes. Understanding tax law as it applies to professionals can save money and needless anxiety every April 15th.

Furthermore, many performers can find ways to earn money for

Wilson Pickett with Lee Wade,
his publicist-manager

· · · · · · ·

performance long after the performance has taken place—residuals from television shows and commercials, percentages of the profits of movies and plays, and royalties from the earnings of copyrighted songs or other composed or written works. This is a kind of magical income that can arrive as checks in the mail with little or no new expenditure of effort. "Pillow money" is an old show business term for it: money your work is earning for you even as you sleep. Not every performer will earn significant amounts of pillow money in his or her career, but the options that make it possible are definitely worth understanding and exploring.

This chapter covers these added dimensions in planning and conducting a professional performing career.

## AGENTS

An agent is a salesperson. There are agents in many businesses, men and women who earn their livings by representing, promoting, and selling to consumers the goods and services created by a company. Some agents are salaried employees of the company, but most are independent businesspeople, *middlemen*, whose income is a percentage or commission of what they sell.

Show business agents sell the work of performers to potential buyers—casting directors, advertising agencies, theatrical producers, nightclub bookers, and individuals who want entertainment for a party or a wedding. There are also agents who represent nonperforming show business artists—playwrights, screenwriters, composers and lyricists, directors, designers, and other backstage professionals. Agents help to sell everything that can be sold in show business, and the variety of their functions and specialties reflects the variety of the industry.

There are two giant agencies, the William Morris Agency and International Creative Management. Both have many agents in large offices in New York, Los Angeles, and Nashville, as well as representatives in numerous other cities and foreign entertainment capitals including London, Rome, and Munich. They represent many of the biggest stars in every area of show business—Telly Savalas, Dom DeLuise, Elvis Costello, Dolly Parton, and many, many more. Associated Booking Corporation, Regency Artists, and the Agency for the Performing Arts are three similar but lesser giants.

Columbia Artists Management, which has its headquarters across from Carnegie Hall on West 57th Street in New York City, is a leading agency for classical music performers, Mstislav Rostropovich, Marilyn Horne, and Andre Watts among others. Willard Alexander Inc. is "The Agency with the Big Bands"—Lionel Hampton, Stan Kenton, and Buddy Rich; Premier Talent is known for its rock musicians, including Bruce Springsteen, Johnny Winter, and the J. Geils Band. Fifi Oscard Associates is an important agency for New York-based actors; Agency for Artists is similarly important for actors in Hollywood.

Central Casting has offices on both coasts and is famous for representing large pools of little-known actors. Agent Irving "Swifty" Lazar, on the other hand, has become a celebrity himself by making lucrative deals for an exclusive client list currently headed by actress Lauren Bacall. Agents who work with musicians, actors, directors, and writers often package their clients' work, putting together a screenplay with a leading man and a director, for example, and presenting the whole as a single project to a production company. Lew Wasserman, the agent who founded MCA (the Music Corporation of America), became such a successful packager that his company eventually bought Universal Pictures, thereby becoming a film producer and distributor and leaving the agency business altogether.

Beyond these upper echelons there are thousands of theatrical and musical agents and agencies, most of them grouped in major cities but many scattered all over the country. Some represent a half-dozen moderately well-known actors year after year on Broadway; others handle a constantly changing stable of children for commercial work in Chicago. There are agents who supply motel cocktail lounges with bands that cover current pop radio hits, and there are agents who specialze in finding bookings for modern dance companies. Regional agents like New England's Pretty Polly Productions find jobs for performers in defined areas of the country. Many of these also act as "secondary agents" when performers represented nationally by New York, Nashville, or Los Angeles agents are looking for bookings in their areas. California's Show and Tell Productions is one of many agencies that deals exclusively with the college entertainment market. Doug Tuchman's Orange Blossom Productions earns its commissions from the gigs of several top-flight bluegrass bands.

For a beginning performer, finding and signing with a good agent can seem an indispensable key to success. In a way it is. Screen acting in Hollywood and acting in commercials in New York are two fields of performance in which representation by an agent is a virtual necessity. Competition is so stiff and time so valuable that casting directors count on agents to prescreen applicants. With rare exceptions they never see actors who submit themselves for parts. In other fields, performers can get well started without agents, but career advancement can eventually depend on professional representation. Only dancers and musicians who work for years for a single company or orchestra may find an agent unncessary. If they decide to free-lance, however, a hard-working agent will be a great help in their job hunting.

The advantages of having an agent are not hard to see. An agent works at selling full time; a performer at best can only be a part-time salesperson. A contact with one agent gives the performer the benefit of all the agent's contacts. A performer's sales pitch on his or her own behalf is always partially discounted by an employer: "Of course *you* think you're right for the job," the employer thinks and sometimes says, "but that's not exactly an unbiased opinion." The agent's opinion, colored by hopes of a commission, is not unbiased either, but it is a second opinion. An employer hears it knowing that the performer has convinced someone else in the business that he or she can do the work. In negotiation, too, an agent is not as personally involved as the the performer and can play a cooler game, less afraid that toughness could ruin the chance of a lifetime. In countless ways, an agent can be a performer's business advisor, suggesting and responding to new ideas with an eye to their commercial effectiveness.

Unfortunately, it can be hard for a new performer to find an agent. The reason is simple: most beginners make very little money from jobs that are few and far between. An agent's income is a percentage of the performer's income, usually 10 percent. Ten percent of very little is not much at all. Few agents, with rent and phone bills to pay plus themselves and their families to support, can afford the time and effort to sell a client from whom only a small return is likely. Quite naturally, they prefer established clients who earn them larger fees with less hard sell.

This means first that it is up to the performer to get started without an agent. Agents launch few careers. Even when they seem to "discover" unknowns, the chances are the unknown had discovered himself and been hard at work for years. Beginners must be their own agents; the previous chapter is aimed at just that goal. Second, it means that agents need to be a major target of the beginner's sales campaign. The phone calls, the photos and resumés, the carefully planned visits, and the follow-up postcards and thank-you notes apply to agents as much as to potential employers. Agents can have their own section of the performer's sales notebook. It is particularly important to invite them to every show: most will want to see a performer work before agreeing to represent him or her. That one employer has hired a performer is the best evidence that another might be convinced to take the same chance.

Which agent is best? The big agencies with the famous clients may seem the most attractive, but a beginner has as little chance there as an actor has of making his debut in a starring role on Broadway. Many performers who do sign with a big agency for the prestige early in their careers complain later that they got lost in the shuffle. Smaller agencies or individual agents are much more likely to invest time in a newcomer in the hope that the careers of both will grow together.

Agents are listed in the *Yellow Pages* as "Theatrical Agents" and are also under the headings "Orchestras and Bands," "Entertainment," and "Musicians." They also advertise in trade papers and periodicals or are mentioned in ads for their performers. Employers and other performers may also recommend agents they know and have worked with. All the performing arts unions franchise (in effect, approve) agents who agree to work within certain minimum standard guidelines. This is one of the most valuable services the unions render to beginners, and regularly updated lists of franchised agents are available on request even to nonmembers. A union franchise is accepted in the business as proof of an agency's legitimate status. The guidelines vary in detail among the various unions, but they agree on these basics:

1. The performer *never* pays the agent directly for services rendered. The agent only gets a percentage of the money the performer earns from work found by the agent.

This includes the provision that the agent cannot require the performer to pay for courses at a performance school or training program that is connected with the agency.

2. The agent's commission can be as low as 5 percent and for some commercial and modelling work as high as 20 and even 25 percent, but for nearly all performance work the standard commission is 10 percent.

Before agreeing to an agency fee greater than 10 percent, it is a good idea to get independent professional advice.

3. Any contract with an agent will include an agreement that the performer can be released from the contract if the agency does not find the performer a certain dollar amount of work in a certain period of time.

Performers do negotiate contracts with agents. Some are handshake understandings, others are carefully worded documents several pages long. There are two important categories of agent-performer contracts: *exclusive* and *nonexclusive*. An *exclusive contract* gives one agent the right to represent the performer. Some exclusive contracts cover every performance field. Others are exclusive only within specified areas; an actor, for instance, may be exclusively represented for films by one agent, for theatre by another. A *nonexclusive contract* is a looser relationship that a performer may have with several agents at the same time. They all can look for jobs for the performer, and he or she can choose among the offers they do turn up. Nonexclusive contracts, which have the advantages of freedom and flexibility, are common in the theatre and the lower-income levels of show business where performers need as wide a net as possible to get enough work to make a living. As success increases, performers tend to sign with one agent. Screen Actors Guild regulations require Hollywood actors to have one agent for all dramatic camera media.

Some contracts are for one year, others for two or more with options to renew if the agent has found the performer work worth a certain amount—no agent wants to lose a client who earns big commissions. Often contracts include provision for a sixty- or ninety-day trial period, after which either side can terminate the agreement. A beginning performer would be wise to ask for this trial period and to be cautious about signing a long-term agreement. Sometimes the agent's desire to go for money can conflict with a performer's desire for overall career growth. As Robert Cohen puts it in *Professional Acting*, "If you want to play classical tragedy and the agent wants to sell you for soap opera, you had better get things straight before you sign." He adds, however, that trust and patience are necessary for a good relationship with an agent: "One agent estimates that it takes about a year for an agent to establish a client . . . and another two years to get offers coming in with any regularity."

Most important, a performer-agent relationship is a partnership. As one agent told me several years ago, "If we are going to work together, you're going to need to know as much as I do." Having an agent relieves a performer of none of the necessities and responsibilities of being an effective businessperson. Agents hustle; they expect their clients to hustle. The performer who sits back and lets the agent do the work will either get no jobs at all or will have to take whatever the agent does find. Agents will be glad to use any contacts their clients come up with or to negotiate any deals for which a performer has done the groundwork. Agents are not miracle men, but teamed with alert, ambitious, and talented performers, they can work wonders economically rewarding to both.

## MANAGERS

A manager is someone who oversees and directs a business, responsible for making day-to-day decisions on details and for guiding the business toward long-term goals. A manager may not own the business—many owners hire managers to run their businesses for them—but he or she, in corporate language, is the executive director or, more simply, the boss.

In show business a manager is often called a *personal manager* because the business managed is personal: the career of a performing artist. An agent sells a performer's work and may in the course of that tell the performer what sells best and what doesn't; few agents go further than that in shaping the product they handle. A manager, on the other hand, has a much more intimate relationship with a performer. His or her job is to know everything possible about the performer as an artist and a person, to be the performer's friend and most trusted professional associate. An agent may ask the performer to supply his or her own photos; a manager may pick the photographer and the performer's wardrobe and hairstyle for the photo session. If an agent finds a performer a job, the manager will tell the performer whether or not to take it. Managers often accompany their performers on tour, booking hotel rooms, making flight reservations, and picking up stage clothes from the dry cleaners. When they don't go along, sometimes they end up walking the performer's dog and making sure the cat gets fed.

Colonel Tom Parker and Brian Epstein, who directed the careers of Elvis Presley and the Beatles respectively, are two of the best-known managers in recent show business history, and perhaps the most successful. Both found their artists when they were young and bursting with raw talent and ambition. The Beatles and Presley were far too inexperienced to know what to do with their energy except pour it out onstage. Parker and Epstein glimpsed the potential of all that energy and set about marketing it with great skill, sophistication, and business acumen. Without their performers' dazzling abilities, the managers could have done nothing, but without their managers, Elvis and the Beatles might never have achieved the focused clarity of their public images and the consistent direction of their business affairs that made them international stars.

Dick Cavett was a successful television comedy writer when he met manager Jack Rollins in the early 1960s. He was frustrated, however, writing gags and then watching Johnny Carson deliver them; he wanted to try being a comedy performer himself. Rollins, who had recently helped Woody Allen make the same transition, worked closely with Cavett to get him over the first rough spots. In *Cavett*, an interview biography with Christopher Porterfield, Cavett gives an excellent picture of what a good manager can do for a performer:

> One thing he did was sit patiently with me . . . in a back room, or a cafe, or a parked car, and talk about my act. Sometimes we'd sit up until 3:00 AM discussing that night's show and what I could learn from it. . . . I guess his main chore was to keep me from getting discouraged. Jack had a convincing way of telling you that although you had both noticed that the show was a bomb from the audience's point of view . . . it was not from his own point of view. He would say, "It was bad in a way that had value," and then point out that although it was short on laughter, I was working well, learning to survive . . .
>
> He also made decisions on where I should appear and where not, on which work would help me grow professionally and which would increase my price.
>
> To one who has worked his head off in summer stock for eighty-five dollars a week, it's a bit of a shock to hear a manager say into the phone, "My client doesn't work for a thousand a week," and then hang up. You say to yourself, "That's right, I don't work for a thousand a week. I work for eighty-five. Get them back!" When they call back saying, "You win. Twelve-fifty it is," you reach for the smelling salts.

Performers pay managers for their services, as they pay agents, with a percentage of their earnings. A manager's commission, however, is likely to be at least 15 percent and even 20 or 25 percent. Managers also often ask performers to give them power of attorney: the ability to sign contracts, receive income, open bank accounts, and invest money on their behalf. The manager's office becomes, in effect, the center of the performer's business. Because they handle the money, managers frequently make out performers' tax returns. Agents, employers, journalists, and other professionals make their proposals for the performer through the manager. If the manager for any reason decides not to pass on the proposal, the performer may never hear of it.

A manager is clearly in a position of great authority and trust. Unfortunately, show business history has countless examples of managers who have betrayed that trust. Managers have embezzled performers' money, failed to report their taxes accurately, misdirected their careers, limited one client's career growth and favored another's. At one point in her career, actress Gloria Swanson entrusted financier Joseph Kennedy with her business affairs because he promised to make her a millionaire; when she took the time to investigate them after Kennedy stopped managing her, she found a debt-ridden tangle it took her years to unravel. Doris Day initiated several lawsuits against a manager who, she claimed, made away with millions of her earnings while she had complete confidence in him. Even managers with no manipulative or criminal intent can make poor decisions and investments out of ignorance or bad judgment.

It follows that choosing a manager is one of the most crucial decisions any performer can make. Early in a performer's career, managers are unlikely to show much interest. Willy-nilly, most performers start by managing themselves. If they consider those days as time to give themselves a rigorous business education, they'll be ready to assess the value of any manager who shows interest and to be knowledgeable partners if they do sign a management contract. If, however, they treat running their own office as a burden that can be carried by the first person who says, "Be an artist, I'll take care of the paperwork," they are inviting future disasters for which they will be partially to blame.

A good question to ask is, "Do I need a manager at all?" Many performers do not. Personal managers are common in popular music; record companies are often reluctant to sign groups without the organized stability of professional management. Offbeat entertainers like Dick Cavett, whose success depends on the creation of a unique public personality, may need management to help them construct and maintain that image with prestige exposure and good publicity. With great success, particularly if it is in several media, a performer may need management simply to keep all the strands of his or her business straight. Many actors, dancers, variety artists and performers of all kinds on or below the middle income rungs, however, may well not need management.

Remember, the performer pays the manager; 20 percent of one's income is a sizable investment. Is it worth it?

If you think it is, start looking for a manager within your performance area. Managers are less likely to advertise than agents, and they are not franchised by the performance unions, but through the show business grapevine you will hear the names of many. Often a trade paper ad, a concert poster, or a record jacket will carry the line, "Personal management by . . ." Check out those who manage performers you feel an artistic connection with and then send them your sales kit. As your own reputation grows, managers may approach you.

Before signing any management agreement, analyze your own income and expenses over several years—you will need to do at least 20 percent better to continue at the same pace. Check the manager's credentials and track record with other clients. Ask the manager every question you can think of and then take the time to think up more. If the manager answers vaguely or treats your questions as a nuisance, consider how he or she will answer your questions after you sign. Check the bibliography in this book and the library for books on contracts within your own field of performance. Inquire for information at your union or the union to which you might one day belong. Consult a lawyer. Ask for a trial period.

This wariness does not imply a lack of trust in any particular manager. Most are honest and competent businesspeople. But a performer-manager relationship can work *only* if it is based on open and specific understanding of all its aspects. It is a business relationship that may involve large sums of money; it is a personal relationship that may be contracted to last for years and involve days, nights, and weeks spent together. At its best, it can be kind of a professional marriage; at its worst, it can lead to a messy, expensive, and time-consuming divorce.

Choosing and signing with a manager is one decision not to be hurried. Self-management, however slow and unglamorous, is better than risking bad management in an ill-considered rush for success.


## LAWYERS

As a businessperson negotiating and making contracts, a performer may need good legal advice many times during a career. If a performer is sued or is going to sue, he or she will need a lawyer. No sensible performer wants to end up in court over any business dispute; consultation with a lawyer before signing a contract can often forestall a dispute.

Many lawyers make entertainment law their specialty; some even use their expertise to become managers. For all show business legal matters, it is worth consulting an entertainment specialist if possible. Lawyers list themselves in the *Yellow Pages* and through state and local bar associations—seldom, however, by specialty. It may take several phone calls and references from one lawyer to another to find one knowledgeable in your area. Before visiting an attorney, ask if he or she charges for the first appointment. Some do, some do not. Also ask about the fees; they vary widely.

Many cities have legal aid offices to which lawyers donate their time to answer preliminary questions and to make referrals for little or no charge. See the Appendix for a list of special low-cost legal services for artists. Performing arts unions also have staff lawyers and legal departments that can advise members; they also have sample contracts to compare with the contracts offered by employers.

For relatively minor disputes, it may be worth investigating the small claims court in your local judicial district. Lawyers are not allowed to appear in many of these courts; plaintiff and defendant state their own cases. There is often a settlement ceiling of $1000 or $2000.

Before seeing a lawyer, and certainly before appearing in any court, be as sure as possible of your facts, have all relevant documents organized and at hand, and be ready to speak and answer questions plainly. Clarity of presentation is an asset in any legal situation; a court appearance is a form of performance.

## UNIONS

Most professional performers belong to one or more of six performing arts labor unions. These unions negotiate with employers as collective bargaining agents on behalf of all their members, setting minimum pay scales and standards for on-the-job work conditions. They also provide dozens of benefits including health insurance, pension plans, grievance procedures, credit unions, job referral, legal advice, and lobbying for legislation favorable to the arts and theatrical professions.

These unions are:

Actors' Equity Association (Equity or AEA)
American Federation of Musicians (AF of M)
American Federation of Television and Radio Artists (AFTRA)

American Guild of Musical Artists (AGMA)
American Guild of Variety Artists (AGVA)
Screen Actors Guild (SAG)

There is also the Screen Extras Guild, the Hebrew Actors Union, and the Italian Actors Union. All are affiliates of the American Federation of Labor–Congress of Industrial Organizations (AFL-CIO), and through the AFL-CIO affiliated with labor unions throughout the world. All except the American Federation of Musicians are also linked as members of an interunion association, the Associated Actors and Artistes of America, popularly known as the "Four A's." The six major unions that comprise the Four A's include stage and screen performers who are not primarily instrumental musicians. Because actors, singers, and dancers today move readily from theatre to movies to television, many of these performers belong to several of the Four A unions. The union the performer joins first becomes the performer's *parent union;* he or she is then eligible to join one of the other five, when necessary, for reduced initation fees and dues.

Today these unions are taken for granted as stable and powerful elements of show business. Representing over four hundred thousand performers on an "all for one and one for all" basis, the entertainment unions have the strength to insist that their members get a fair deal even when up against the biggest movie studios, broadcast networks, record companies, theatrical producers, and concert impresarios. This firm bargaining position is still recent history. Older members of the unions remember vividly that in the first three decades of this century there was no minimum wage, no pay for rehearsal time, no overtime pay for work at night or on holidays, and no pensions. Touring performers were often stranded on the road, actors had to buy their own costumes, and screen extras had an average yearly income of $105.63. Most important, employers could play the unorganized performers off against each other with the argument, "If you don't take what we offer, someone else will."

Today's solidarity has come only through struggle. Early organizers were often blacklisted, vilified as Communists, and sometimes tempted with special deals and under-the-table payments. All the unions have needed to call their members out on strike from time to time to enforce their demands for fair compensation. Actors' Equity's first strike in 1919 lasted thirty days, closed thirty-seven plays and stopped the opening of sixteen others. When it was over, however, union membership had risen from 2700 to 14,000, the treasury had increased to $120,000 from $13,500, and Broadway producers had agreed to accept Equity as the actors' bargaining agent. A long walkout in 1980 by SAG and AFTRA members ended in the actors winning a share of new film revenues from home video and cable television.

A fundamental rule of all the unions is that members may work as performers only for employers who have signed a contract agreeing to abide by union rules of pay and working conditions. Employers who sign are called *signatories*. Part of the contract that signatories agree to says that they can only hire union members as performers. This tight circle—union members only work for signatories and signatories only hire union members—is called the *closed shop*. The only legal limit on the closed shop is the Taft-Hartley Act, a federal law that makes it illegal to deny an individual employment solely because he or she does not belong to a union. In practice this gives a performer the right to work six weeks for a signatory without joining a union. Then the performer must join or stop work.

The term "closed shop" sounds restrictive, and to a certain extent it is. Many union members are not fully employed; while waiting for a union-authorized job to appear they are often tempted to take non-union work even if it is lower paid, some income being better than none. Nonunion moonlighting does occur—sometimes under assumed names—but the unions consider it a serious breach of discipline punishable by a fine. The unions argue that without the closed shop their solidarity and bargaining power would be fatally undercut. If union members could take nonunion work, the union would fall apart, and if employers could hire nonunion performers, they could bypass the union entirely. The "all for one, one for all principle" can mean short-term sacrifices for long-term goals.

A union card, however, "opens more doors than it closes," as Robert Cohen puts it. All over the country, and in every branch of show business, union work is not only the best paid work for performers, it is also the most prestigious. All the Broadway and Off-Broadway theatres, the major Hollywood studios and independent field producers, the national television and radio networks, and the leading advertising agencies are signatory employers. So are most city orchestras and opera companies, regional theatres, touring dance companies, local television and radio stations, circuses, large concert halls, and hotel and restaurant chains that hire musicians.

None of the unions set maximum limits for pay, and the biggest stars have personal bargaining power that lessens their reliance on union strength. Yet stars are union members too. "I've spent a lifetime on stages and sound studios with people who rode buses and subways to work instead of driving foreign automobiles," said Henry Fonda. "We all belong to the same unions." Edward Asner is the current president of the Screen Actors Guild, and Ronald Reagan was the union's president from 1947 to 1952. "I've seen what happens to working people who do not have protection," said George C. Scott. "They are almost always the first to bear the brunt of any problem encountered by their employer." Actress Beatrice Arthur, who played the outspoken Maude in a long-running television situation comedy, put it as bluntly as Maude would have: "Some people believe that stars don't need a union. I disagree. Many stars wouldn't be where they are if [the union] hadn't been behind them at crucial turning points in their careers."

How does a beginner get into a performers' union? In most cases by being offered a job by a signatory employer. Signatories can only hire union members, but they can audition anyone—union regulations, in fact, require that auditions must *not* exclude nonunion members. If the employer decides that a nonunion newcomer is right for the part, the newcomer can take the job offer to the union as proof of readiness for membership. After paying an initiation fee and dues, the union grants membership and the new member can take the job.

For instance, actor Michael David Gordon was working in a play for children at an Off-Off Broadway theatre in January, 1984. He went to an open call audition for a road company taking a play on a bus-and-truck tour and got picked for a leading role. When he came back to the theatre to give notice, he was all smiles. "The tour is only six weeks, and we're mostly playing high schools in the Deep South," he said, "but it's Equity, I get my card, and that's for keeps!"

Equity, SAG, and AGMA are unions that can only be joined by having union work. Others are "open" unions—anyone who can pay the initiation fee can join. Yet for a beginner to join a performing arts union just to belong does not make sense. Union initiation fees are not token—AFTRA's fee in mid-1984 was $500—and membership is a bar against accepting work on the nonunion fringe of show business.

This fringe is wide. The time and money available to the unions for negotiating with the thousands of entertainment employers all over the country is limited; they concentrate, therefore, on the largest and most visible employers, leaving hundreds of low-budget theatres, clubs, dance companies, film producers, ad agencies, and many other employers beyond the union-signatory pale. Beginners can work, and in many cases make satisfactory livings, on this fringe for years. The unions are well aware that the nonunion fringe exists, and that it is the current training ground for their future members.

Joining a performers' union is becoming a full professional, one fortunate result of all disciplined training and preparation outlined in the previous chapters. For any performer it is, as it was for Michael David Gordon, cause for celebration.

Here are listed the seven major performing arts unions with the addresses of their headquarters, relevant facts of their membership and scope, and, where possible, selected figures from payscales current in mid-1984 and early 1985.

*Important note:* the pay scale figures are quoted here only to give a rough sense of what union performers may earn. They are a tiny sample of many contracted figures; they are also subject to change and detailed variation. They do not include pension, health insurance, and other benefits. Remember, also, that even a successful performer works intermittently.

## ACTORS' EQUITY ASSOCIATION (Equity)

National Office:

  165 West 46th Street, New York, New York 10036
  (212) 869-8530

Los Angeles:

  6430 Sunset Boulevard, Los Angeles, California 90028
  (213) 462-2334

Regional offices also in Chicago and San Francisco.

Equity, founded in 1913, is the union of stage actors and stage managers in the legitimate theatre. According to a union handbook:

Equity administers contracts in the following areas: Broadway, touring productions, Bus and Truck tours, Resident Dramatic Stock, Indoor Musical Stock, Outdoor Musical Stock, Dinner Theatres, Resident Theatres, Industrial Shows, Theatre for Young Audiences, Off-Broadway, Hollywood Area Theatres (HAT), Bay Area Theatres (BAT), Chicago Off-Loop Theatres (COLT), University Theatres, Outdoor Drama Festivals and Cabaret Theatres.

Sample Minimum Pay Scales:

| | |
|---|---|
| Broadway and touring shows | $650 a week |
| Out of town expenses | $62 a day |
| Off-Broadway—small theatre | $202.85 a week |
| large theatre | $421.29 a week |
| League of Resident Theatres (LORT) | |
| small theatre | $306 a week |
| large theatre | $382 a week |

An alternate route to Equity membership is the union's Membership Candidate Program. Actors at many regional signatory theatres can take small roles as registered membership candidates. After fifty weeks of such work, they may join the union.

## AMERICAN FEDERATION OF RADIO AND TELEVISION ARTISTS (AFTRA)

National Office:
>1350 Avenue of the Americas, New York, New York 10019
>(212) 265-7700

Los Angeles:
>1717 North Highland Avenue, Hollywood, California 90028
>(213) 461-8111

AFTRA also has locals in twenty-seven other cities. Call the national office for further information.

AFTRA, founded in 1919, is the union of television and radio performers—according to a handbook:

>Professionals who sing, dance, act, announce, report, lecture, comment, demonstrate or moderate . . . who work as newscasters, sportscasters, weathercasters, analysts, panelists, puppeteers, specialty acts, walkons, extras . . .

AFTRA also represents color and sound effects artists, broadcast directors, producers, and writers, music librarians, and "other production or programming professionals."

Sample Minimum Pay Scales:
Network TV Daytime Serials One Hour Programs:

| | |
|---|---|
| Principal Actor Program Fee | $476 per program |
| Five lines or less | $208 " |
| Extra | $124 " |

Network Non-Dramatic One Hour Programs:
    Principal                          $490 per program
    Five lines or less             $224    "
    Extra                             $159    "
Network Prime Time Dramatic Programs:
    Principal Actor Day Rate       $361 per program
    3-Day Rate                 $915    "
    Weekly Rate               $1256    "

AFTRA is an "open" union and may be joined by paying the initation fee of $500 plus initial dues.

## AMERICAN GUILD OF MUSICAL ARTISTS (AGMA)

National Office:
    1841 Broadway, New York, New York 10023
    (212) 265-3687

Los Angeles:
    6430 Sunset Boulevard, Hollywood, California 90028
    (213) 461-3714

AGMA has regional offices in Toronto, San Francisco, Philadelphia, Chicago, Seattle, New Orleans, Washington, D.C., Boston, and Mesquite, Texas.

AGMA, founded in 1936, is the union for classical music soloists and ballet dancers. It has "sole and exclusive jurisdiction in the field of concert, recital, oratorio and grand opera, including specifically jurisdiction over all concert and solo operatic singers, instrumental soloists, dancers, and other performers in the field of concert, recital, oratorio and grand opera," according to a union brochure.

AGMA pay scales are so varied, according to a union spokesperson, that quoting a few would be misleading.

## AMERICAN GUILD OF VARIETY ARTISTS (AGVA)

National Office:
    184 Fifth Avenue, New York, New York 10010
    (212) 675-1003

Los Angeles:
    4741 Laurel Canyon Boulevard, North Hollywood, California 91607
    (213) 508-9984

AGVA has regional offices in twenty-five cities. Call the National Office for further information.

AGVA, founded in 1939, is the successor to the National Vaudeville Artists Association founded in 1916. Its membership includes acrobats, jugglers, circus performers, comedians, magicians, burlesque performers, ventriloquists, as well as singers and dancers. Its jurisdiction, according to a union official, includes "any show presentation that is minus a story or book." AGVA entertainers often work at "night clubs, cabarets, minstrel shows, dinner theatres, industrial shows, indoor and outdoor circuses, carnivals, fairs, and rodeos, ice-skating and water shows, public restaurants, music halls, resorts, private club entertainment (banquets, private stage shows, etc.), boats, barges, show boats, yacht and steamer cruises, and hotels."

Sample Minimum Pay Scales:

Variety Revues in Cabarets and Lounges:

| | |
|---|---|
| Seating Capacity 1–100 | $230 a week |
| Seating Capacity 401 and up | $475 a week |

Theatrical Shows:

| | |
|---|---|
| Artists | $650 a week |
| Out-of-town expenses | $62 a day |

Industrial Shows:

| | |
|---|---|
| First Day | $282.01 |
| Second Day | $211.77 |
| For 6-day week | $645.63 |
| For 7-day week | $806.77 |

AGVA is an "open" union and may be joined by paying the initiation fee of $300 plus initial dues.

## SCREEN ACTORS GUILD (SAG)

National Office:
    7750 Sunset Boulevard, Hollywood, California 90046
    (213) 876-3030

New York:
    1700 Broadway, New York, New York 10019
    (212) 957-5370

SAG has regional offices in nineteen cities. Call the National Office for further information.

SAG, founded in 1933, is the union of actors who work in theatrical, industrial, or educational motion pictures, filmed television programs and/or filmed television commercials. ("Filmed" means not videotaped; videotape is under AFTRA's jurisdiction. In fact, the movie and television industries are now so interdependent that many SAG members are also AFTRA members, and vice versa. Merger of these two unions is a definite possibility in the late 1980s.)

Sample Minimum Pay Scales:
Theatrical Films and Television:

| | |
|---|---|
| Day Player | $298 a day |
| Weekly Player | $1038 a week |
| 3-Day Player (TV only) | $756 for 3 days |

Educational:

| | |
|---|---|
| Day Player | $275 a day |
| Weekly Player | $962 a week |
| 3-Day Player | $688 for three days |

Commercials:
On Camera:

| | |
|---|---|
| Principal Performers | $317.40 per session |
| Group singers/dancers | $232.34 per person/per session |

Off camera (voice-over):

| | |
|---|---|
| Principal Performers | $238.68 per session |
| Group singers | $134.58 per session/per person |

## SCREEN EXTRAS GUILD (SEG)

National Office:
3629 Cahuenga Blvd., Los Angeles, CA 90068
(213) 851-4301

SEG also has branch offices in San Francisco and Hawaii. In New York and other east coast cities, SAG has jurisdiction over extra players.

SEG, founded in 1945, represents extra players who, in Merrill Joel's words, "form the human backdrop or background before which the actors play their parts." In brief, the dividing line between extra and acting work is the speaking of dialogue. Categories of extras include, beside General Extra Player, "Stand-ins, dress extras, dancers, skaters, swimmers, riders, sports participants, motorcycle drivers, and nonprofessional singers." Extras in these categories are paid separate rates.

SEG is the smallest of the major Four A unions, and many of its members are also members of SAG and AFTRA. There is a strong movement for a SEG/SAG merger that may be accomplished in 1985.

Sample Minimum Pay Scales:

| | |
|---|---|
| General Extra | $91 a day |
| Special Ability Extra | $101 a day |
| Choreographed Dancers, Swimmers, and Skaters | $244 a day |
| Silent Bit Extra | $145 a day |

## AMERICAN FEDERATION OF MUSICIANS

National Office:
   1500 Broadway, New York, New York 10036
   (212) 869-1330

New York City local #802:
   330 West 42nd Street, New York, New York 10036
   (212) 239-4802

Nashville local #257:
   11 Music Circle North, Nashville, Tennessee 37212
   (615) 244-9514

Los Angeles local #47:
   817 North Vine Street, Hollywood, California 90038
   (213) 462-2161

The AF of M has over eight hundred locals throughout the United States and Canada. Consult the phone book or call the National Office for further information.

The AF of M, founded in 1896, is the largest of all the performer unions with over 250,000 members. It represents instrumental musicians and singers in every style of music and working in every branch of show business. It is not a member of the Four A's, though some of its members are also Four A union members.

Sample Minimum Pay Scales (New York):
   Single Engagement Club Dates:

| | |
|---|---|
| Four Hours | $107 |
| Four Hours Saturday Night | $117 |
| Rehearsal (Two Hour Min.) | $ 21.25 per hour |

Ballet and Opera:
    Seven 3-hour performances        $610
    Single performance                $ 87.14
    Rehearsal ($2^{1}/_{2}$ hour min.)      $ 42.50
Theatre:
    Weekly Base Pay                  $620
    Single Performance               $ 77.50
    Rehearsal ($2^{1}/_{2}$ hour min.)      $ 32.50

## TAXES

Tax law, to say the least, is complex, and no taxpayer approaches it with spontaneous pleasure. Taxes are, in the words of Judge Learned Hand, "an exaction of the government." Two fundamentals of personal income tax law in the United States are:

1.   You are not obligated to pay a penny more than what is due the government by law.

2.   You declare to the government what tax you owe based on your knowledge of your own financial state and of the law.

Many people work year after year for one employer, nine to five, Monday through Friday. They don't take work home and have no business expenses. Their taxes are withheld—in effect, paid for them—by the company they work for. Their tax declaration is one short form.

Few performers are in that position, most having a mix of many jobs throughout the year. They need to compute and declare their own taxes on several forms. As professional people who earn their livings from the use of trained and individual skill, they can declare many of their expenses for maintaining themselves professionally as tax deductions. A performer can pay taxes as a business does, even become a corporation.

Three initial steps to understanding tax law for performers are:

1.   Get the Internal Revenue Service's booklet, *Instructions for Preparing Form 1040.* Form 1040 is the central document of self-declaration. The booklet and the form are often in post offices, public libraries, banks, accountants' offices, and are available from the IRS.

2.   Go to an accountant. Consulting an accountant long before filing time can help you prepare your record-keeping. You may

want an accountant's help in writing your return only the first year or every year. It's a worthwhile expense—and tax deductible.

3. Look in the library for a basic book on taxes. The best I know for performers is: *Fear of Filing: A Beginners Guide to Tax Preparation and Record Keeping for Artists, Performers, Writers, and Freelance Professionals.* By Volunteer Lawyers for the Arts. Edited by Theodore W. Striggles and Barbara Sieck Taylor. Dodd, Mead & Company, New York. Available in bookstores, through the publishers, or from Volunteer Lawyers for the Arts, listed in the appendix.

For tax purposes, a performer is either *self-employed, employed,* or a combination of the two.

If *self-employed,* the performer is paid in lump sums for his or her work—$300 for a weekend nightclub appearance, for instance. The employer withholds no tax because the payment is between two independent businesses. The performer adds all such income earned during the year as the business' *gross income* and enters it on *Schedule C,* the form for "Profit or Loss from Business or Profession." From this gross income the performer can subtract the business expenses noted in his or her business ledger. The result is then entered as business income on the central form, Form 1040, and added to any other taxable income to make a personal total for the year.

Because no tax is withheld, the IRS requires individual businesses to report their *estimated income* and pay any *estimated tax* each quarter: in January, April, June, and September, using Form 1040ES.

If *employed,* by a symphony orchestra, for instance, the performer is paid an hourly, daily, or weekly salary, and the employer does withhold the performer's taxes. A professional employee, however, can list many of his or her business expenses as *itemized deductions* on *Schedule A.* The allowable categories include most of those granted a business—the major exception is travel to and from the place of employment. The sum of the deductions is subtracted from the income totalled on Form 1040 before computing the tax due on the final figure, *taxable income.* If the employer has withheld more tax than is due, the performer's tax return becomes a filing for a *refund.* The sooner a refund request is filed after January 1, the faster the IRS returns the extra money withheld.

If a performer has some self-employed income and some income as an employee, he or she reports both types of income in the way appropriate to each.

The advantage of employee income is that often pension, insurance, health care, and other benefits come along with it. The advantage of self-employed income is its independence from a single employer and the broader range of allowable business expenses. Most performers, even if much of their income comes from employment, can also consider themselves self-employed. The tax advantages of self-employment are great enough to make the possibility worth careful research. The performer's own business does not need to make a profit every year; the performer only has to be able to prove a businesslike intention of making a profit.

Since performance income is subject to great variance, a windfall year sometimes following many lean years, it is also a good idea to investigate *income averaging*, the IRS's system of spreading the profits of a good year over several years.

In sum, one thing is nearly as certain as taxes themselves: ignorance of tax law will cost the taxpayer money.

## PILLOW MONEY

Many performers earn money not only for the work they do but also for work they once did and the work other people do. Sometimes they earn this extra because their recorded performance is played or broadcast over and over again, sometimes because they have created original work that other people perform, and sometimes because they are paid as performers with a percentage of the earnings of a whole production. In any of these cases, they may be earning money while they are on vacation in Europe, playing tennis, or while they are hard at work on a new show and being paid for that too.

This is *pillow money*, and a delightful form of income it is. Sometimes it comes in as a steady trickle, sometimes in nuggetlike chunks. Bob Smith, the leader of a rock band, Cat Mother, that in the early 1970s was playing only occasional gigs in Northern California, found a check for $1500 in the mail one day because an Italian songwriter had used the melody of a Cat Mother song with Italian lyrics on one of his records. The potential earnings are limitless and often dwarf what the performer earns for appearing on stage. Many middle-level actors have bought houses in the country with their take from a single commercial. Imagine all the uses of the music of John Lennon and

Paul McCartney: their own records, recordings by other artists, radio and jukebox play, sheet music, movies, television shows, Muzak, the musical *Beatlemania*, and performances by musicians in concert everywhere. Each instance of use is worth from a few cents to many thousands of dollars to the two composers.

Here are the primary ways a performer can earn pillow money, with references for further information.

COPYRIGHT

Copyright is legal recognition that an author and inventor has a right to earnings from the use of his or her creations. Article I, section 8, of the United States Constitution, grants Congress the power:

> to promote the progress of science and the useful arts by securing for limited times to authors and inventors the exclusive right to their respective writings and discoveries.

This is the basis of all copyright legislation, the most recent being the Copyright Act of 1976. The law declares that copyright comes into being with the creation of an original work: by writing a book, for instance, the author becomes the owner of the book's copyright. The "limited time" of the 1976 law is the author's lifetime plus fifty years. To secure copyright, however, an author must be sure that all copies of the work carry the c in a circle—©—that is the international copyright symbol, as well as the author's name, and the date, like so:

© John Doe 1984

He or she must also register the work with the Copyright Office at the Library of Congress. For all information regarding copyright, and the forms necessary for registration, write to:

Register of Copyrights
Library of Congress
Washington, D.C. 20559
or call (202) 287-8700

The Copyright Office has many free pamphlets on various aspects of copyright law as well as an excellent booklet, also free, *General Guide to the Copyright Act of 1976*.

Music, lyrics, musical arrangements, choreographed dances, audio and visual recordings, comedy sketches, plays, and screenplays are all eligible for copyright. Owning copyright to a work is plain ownership;

copyrights can be bought, sold, and inherited as personal property. Many creators of original works sell the copyrights to their works by being paid a salary to create it. The arrangements written by a musician employed by a record company as a house arranger, for instance, are considered "work for hire," and the copyright belongs to the employer. Sometimes creators sell their copyrights for flat fees. Screen and television writers often are paid in a lump sum for their work, and the entire film or show is copyrighted by the company that produced it. This is less common but not unknown in musical composition and writing for the stage. In all of these cases, no matter how the work sells, the creator will get nothing more; the copyright owner will get whatever pillow money the work earns.

Often, however, creators retain the copyright to their original work and sell only the *subsidiary rights*, the rights to use the work in specific ways. For example, Neil Simon owns the copyrights to his plays, and he has made millions of dollars selling the rights to have them produced on Broadway, made into movies, adapted for television, published as books, translated into foreign languages, and revived again and again in summer stock and regional theatre. Similarly, a songwriter can sell the right to make a record of one of her songs while retaining the right to use the song in a movie. Or an author can sell one publisher the right to market his work in the United States and sell the European rights to another publisher.

Subsidiary rights are most often sold on a *royalty* basis: the user of the right pays the copyright owner a royalty, or percentage, of the income the user earns from the work. A royalty deal is a gamble that pays off only if the work is a success. Yet most creators in the performing arts consider the gamble good business because of the potential pay-off and because they are, in effect, betting on themselves and their talents.

The market in subsidiary rights, however, is very complex, and a performer who is also a creator can understandably get lost (and lose money) in its intricacies. Fortunately there are guilds for musical, dramatic, and dance creators that protect and inform their members just as the performance unions do, with minimum standard contracts, legal services, and benefit plans.

For musical creators there are two major performing rights organizations: the American Society of Composers, Authors, and Publishers (ASCAP) and Broadcast Music Incorporated (BMI). Composers and lyricists can belong to ASCAP and BMI individually or through their music publishers. ASCAP and BMI are both large and powerful entities in the music business; the scope of their activities is wide. Their central function is to license users of music, concert halls, night-clubs, and radio and television stations, for instance, and then to distribute license-income to music creators and copyright owners. The money involved is millions of dollars each year. Both ASCAP and BMI maintain continuous surveys of the music used by their license holders. Every time a song shows up on the survey, the copyright owner increases his share of the year's distribution. If the film *Breakfast at Tiffany's* is shown on network television, for example, Henry Mancini, who wrote the score and the theme song "Moon River," will receive several thousand dollars. A hit record may earn the songwriter as much or more performance income as royalties from the record's sales.

The addresses of ASCAP's and BMI's major offices are:

ASCAP

    National Office:
    ASCAP Building
    1 Lincoln Plaza, New York, New York 10023
    (212) 595-3030

    2 Music Square West, Nashville, Tennessee 37203
    (615) 244-3936

    6430 Sunset Blvd., Hollywood, California 90028
    (213) 466-3936

BMI

    National Office:
    320 West 57th Street, New York, New York 10019
    (212) 586-2000

    10 Music Square East, Nashville, Tennessee 37203
    (615) 259-3625

    6255 Sunset Blvd., Hollywood, California 90028
    (213) 465-2111

Any musician who is beginning to write, perform or make demos of original compositions, needs to find out about ASCAP and BMI as soon as possible. The two are highly competitive with each other, and both are eager to have ambitious new members.

SESAC is a third performing rights organization, much smaller than ASCAP or BMI, but still large and growing. SESAC's field of concentration is gospel and church music.

SESAC

World Headquarters:
10 Columbus Circle, New York, New York 10019
(212) 586-3450

Regional Office:
11 Music Circle South, Nashville, Tennessee 37203
(615) 244-1992

Regional Office:
9000 Sunset Blvd., Los Angeles, Ca. 90069
(213) 274-6814

For songwriters there is also the Songwriters Guild, formerly known as the American Guild of Authors and Composers (AGAC). The guild has written a strong contract for songwriters to use when signing with music publishers; it also audits publishers, collects royalties, helps writers with copyrights, has an insurance plan, and conducts songwriting workshops. Its addresses:

The Songwriters Guild
276 Fifth Avenue, New York, New York 10001
(212) 686-6820

6430 Sunset Blvd., Hollywood, California 90028
(213) 462-1108

50 Music Square West, Nashville, Tennessee 37203
(615) 329-1782

For screenwriters there is the Writers Guild:

Writers Guild of America, East
555 West 57th Street, New York, New York 10019
(212) 245-6180

Writers Guild of America, West
8955 Beverly Blvd., Los Angeles, California 90048
(213) 550-1000

Similarly, for playwrights there is the Dramatists Guild, and for choreographers the Society of Stage Directors and Choreographers:

The Dramatists Guild
234 West 44th Street, New York, New York 10036
(212) 398-9366

Society of Stage Directors and Choreographers (SSDC)
1501 Broadway, New York, New York 10036
(212) 391-1070

Any performer can benefit from experimenting with creating original work. It provides fascinating new points of view on performing, and can extend and enrich one's career. If the experiments result in producible work, it can enrich the performer.

## RESIDUALS

*Residuals* is the word used to cover payment for the use and reuse of recorded performance on radio and television—the equivalent of royalty and performing rights payments. There are residuals for dramatic acting on shows that are rerun and for commercials that may get shown hundreds of times throughout an advertising campaign.

The formulas for figuring residual rates are as complex as performance pay scales in the same media. SAG and AFTRA co-negotiate commercial residual formulas, so payments to members of both unions are identical. One scale for a principal actor in a national commercial allows $300 for the first use, $116 for the second, $92 for the third through the thirteenth, and $44 thereafter.

The performance unions are the best source of information on residuals. Most nonunion performance contracts do not pay residuals. About commercials: some actors think that they are a quick way to big money. Possibly, but the field is crowded and the work required is highly professional and technically difficult. Actress Virginia Christine, known as Mrs. Olsen of the Folger's Coffee commercials, says she resents young performers who think commercials are easy:

> Acting is a craft, but doing commercials is a real discipline. They're harder to do than scenes and television shows for instance. You're dealing with a product that has to be exactly lit, you're dealing with having to repeat the same things all the time. To keep life in them, to make them real each time, you have to—forgive my expression—suck in your gut and say "Now this is real. This has got to be real."

## PERCENTAGE DEALS

There are no rules for *percentage deals*, in which a performer (or any member of a show's production team) may take a percentage of the show's earnings as partial payment or even full payment for work. It happens at the low-income end of show business when producers of an Off-Broadway show or independent film, for instance, may ask performers to take percentages because there is little money for salaries. It also happens at the top end when stars like Barbra Streisand or Marlon Brando demand a percentage of a film's gross because a share of a blockbuster's earnings is likely to be bigger than a lump sum salary any producer could pay.

Taking a percentage is always a gamble. The performer is usually dependent on the show's producers to furnish accurate information on what the show earns. Moreover, a *percentage of the gross*, or total income, is very different from a *percentage of the profits*, the gross minus production expenses. When unsure of the potential return, a performer is well advised to ask for a flat fee. On the other hand, actor Robert Shaw was offered a percentage of the film *Jaws* for his role as Quint; he turned it down, thinking the film would be a run-of-the-mill thriller, lucky to break even. Instead, it went on to be the record box-office-earning movie of all time, leaving Shaw well paid for his work, but thinking, "If only . . ." about the share he had signed away.

# *chapter 9*

○ ○ ○ ○ ○ ○ ○ ○ ○ ○ ○ ○ ○ ○ ○ ○ ○ ○ ○ ○ ○ ○ ○ ○ ○ ○ ○ ○ ○ ○ ○ ○ ○ ○ ○ ○ ○ ○ ○

# COLLEAGUES

NOT only is there no business like show business, according to Irving Berlin, there are no people like show people. Show people come in every human type and are, undoubtedly, no better or worse than people in any other occupation or social group. Yet they are a tribe, set off by their own stepping out to perform and linked by a mutual understanding, both sympathetic and jealous, of what it's like to put on shows for a living. They compete with each other for the attention of the audience; in each other they see the same hopes and bafflement of hope, the constant trying and so frequent failing, the seriousness and silliness of working so hard at play.

Show people are a performer's colleagues, and as Sheward Hagerty, my first boss after college, said, "Your colleagues are the most important part of any job." Time has proved him right. It's the people we work with, as much as the work, that makes a job enjoyable or awful. Working with show people has been one of the great pleasures of my career. Getting backstage and joking with the guys in the other band, going out with the other actors for coffee after rehearsal, chatting with nervous fellow guests in the green room before going on TV—sometimes that's been as big a kick as performing itself. It certainly was a thrill the nights bluesman Muddy Waters was in the dressing room across the hall!

Mandel & Lydon at the Cellar Door, Washington, D.C. (photo by Manuel Rocca)

·   ·   ·   ·   ·   ·   ·

My colleagues have sustained and inspired me. Their commitment to their own work has kept me practicing; their humor and helpful comments have gotten me past countless moments of bewildered discouragement. I'd like to introduce a dozen whom it has been my good fortune to know. None are typical, and they represent only themselves, but together they do suggest the spunk and sparkle of show people the world over.

Actor Richard Bright had a wide grin on his face and a piece of watermelon in his hand. It was a hot afternoon in New York. A breeze no more than a breath slipped past the potted plants on the window sill. His wife, actress Rutanya Alda, sat beside him, listening and eating a peach.

"When I was eighteen," said Richard, "I went to California from Brooklyn. Like a lot of kids I thought the only way to be an actor was to go to Hollywood. I studied for a year and then got interviewed for a part in a war movie.

"I had an 8 × 10 with a lot of lies on the back, things I had never done at theatres that never existed. When I walked into the office, I tripped and fell. I got up to the desk and gave the lady the picture and resumé. It didn't have my name on it; I didn't have a pen. She had an inkwell pen—this was 1955, remember. I reached over for the pen and knocked the whole inkwell over. I was a nervous wreck. I lit up a cigarette, shook the match out, and threw it in the wastebasket. Of course it caught fire. By that time, the door flew open and the director, Sam Harmon, asked what the hell was going on. The lady said, 'Oh, nothing. Everything's under control.' I just stood there.

"Well, he talked to me. A few days later he called me for the part, to play a dead boy. I'd just lie there and they'd pay me a hundred dollars. I turned it down, can you believe it? Yeah, and went back to New York. That's how I got started."

Back in New York, James Dean was coming up through live television drama, and Bright, a muscular man with a strong male presence, figured, "He ain't doing nothing different from what I'm doing." For a month he circled the casting offices daily, "endearing myself out of perseverance to the secretaries." No luck. "I was so depressed I stayed home. Then I got a call from Liam Dunn, a casting director at CBS. 'Where have you been? We've missed you,' he said. He had a job for me as a thug. From then on I never stopped working in TV."

In thirty years of work, Richard Bright has distinguished himself as a fine and versatile actor. When we first met in San Francisco in 1967, he was playing Billy the Kid in Michael McClure's play, *The Beard*, a role he originated and later took to New York, Los Angeles, London, and Paris. He has been on Broadway three times with Al Pacino: in *Richard III*, *First Murder*, and *The Basic Training of Pavlo Hummel*, in which he also originated the role of the crippled sergeant Brisbey. In Hollywood, Bright has played an incompetent cowboy in the comedy *Rancho Deluxe*, a con man slugged by Steve McQueen in *The Getaway*, Mafia man Al Neri in *The Godfather I* and *II*, and a sadistic thug in *Marathon Man*. Most recently he was Chicken Joe in Sergio Leone's movie *Once Upon a Time in America*.

Mysteriously, however, after his part in *The Godfather*, Bright didn't get an acting job for two years, despite the film's huge success. "That was the low point of my career. I worked in a doll factory. I still don't understand it."

Rutanya Alda took a bite of a peach. "Richard has always been one of my greatest inspirations," she said. Alda is a slender woman with wavy brown hair and lively eyes. Born in Riga, Latvia, she grew up in postwar displaced persons camps. "When I was three or four, I saw my first play, a fairy tale acted by people in the camp. As soon as I saw it, the make-believe, the costumes, the story, I thought, 'That's for me.' Ever since I've wanted to be an actress."

. . . . . .

COLLEAGUES

Rutanya Alda and Richard Bright

"Ever since" took her to Arizona, where her parents settled, to Northern Arizona State University, on to the Phoenix Little Theatre, and then to New York. Like Richard—they met and married in the early 1970s—she's worked on and Off-Broadway, in television and the movies. Her best known role may be Carol Ann, Joan Crawford's ever loyal secretary in *Mommie Dearest*, but she has also had good character roles in *The Deer Hunter*, *Racing with the Moon*, *The Fury*, and *Pat Garrett and Billy the Kid*. At the time of the interview she was rehearsing *Sacraments*, a new play soon to open on Broadway. That morning Richard had held the book for her as she memorized her lines.

For both, acting is a craft they love. "People think actors don't work on what they do," said Rutanya, "but you have to train and study. Paul Mann, in New York, is my great teacher. His method gives the actor a specific work plan to follow in creating a role."

"I've seen people who don't train," said Richard. "They get lead parts but develop bad habits. They fail upwards: they get work but get worse as actors."

Rutanya's advice to beginners is, "Pay attention to life and the people around you, look outside of yourself."

"I know a lot of people say don't try performing unless you're really sure it's for you." said Richard, "but I say, if you aren't sure, give it a shot. I meet businessmen who think that deep inside they really could be Elvis Presley, but they never dared find out by trying."

Alda and Bright live on Manhattan's Upper West Side in a small apartment comfortably crowded with books, records, a TV and video player, old scripts, and plants. The walls and shelves are covered with photos, posters, and knickknacks from their careers. Richard pointed out a play poster for *The Beard*, and Rutanya got out a photo of herself as the aged Carol Ann. "They had to do that wrinkle makeup fresh every day. It took hours." She looked around at everything in the apartment. "It's amazing how it accumulates. Of course we've been here ten years."

"Eleven," said Richard.

"I started piano lessons at five," said Richard Shirk. "My parents encouraged me, but I wasn't treated as a remarkable talent. They did buy me a Steinway when I was fifteen and took me to a lot of wonderful concerts. We sat on stage and heard Rubinstein play an all-Chopin program and Dame Myra Hess play Beethoven sonatas. She projected

Richard Shirk

an incredible aura—all in black. But it wasn't until I saw Maria Callas at the Met that I realized magic things could happen on stage. She was electrifying."

After Shirk graduated from Juilliard, however, he wasn't sure he could perform. "I was wrung out from the competition. There was so much negative feedback and intimidation from the teachers. They encouraged only a few to consider careers. Some used what they called 'the fear technique,' saying things like, 'You have the worst hands I've ever seen. Why don't you go into your father's business?' "

Meeting teacher Seymour Bernstein through a friend changed Shirk's life. Bernstein, also a composer and pianist, bases his teaching on the principle that learning music can be the disciplined center of a whole life, "harmoniz[ing] everything you think, feel, and do," as he wrote in his book, *With Your Own Two Hands.*

"Seymour showed me how to pursue music for the sake of music. That's still the most important thing for me, the internal creative process. If you're in it for fame and glory and money, for any external reason, you'll burn out. Setting my sights on a solo career as the only thing to do? It sounds horrible. I want to be as productive as possible—chamber music, accompanying, teaching, and concerts."

After a few years with Bernstein, Shirk began auditioning for concert managers ("Classical auditioning is crazy—they stop you in the middle and tell you to jump to the coda"), landing spots and getting good reviews in small concert series. In 1978, he won the Leschetizky Competition, held in a Carnegie Hall studio, which led to a New York debut at Alice Tully Hall and then a European tour. A second Alice Tully concert, however, was a near disaster. "I had the flu, the piano hadn't been tuned, and, understandably, the reviews were lukewarm." His next major concert, an all-Mozart recital at Lincoln Center library, was well received. "Getting involved with Mozart has been a big high-point in my career. It's not just the clarity of the music, its perfection, but it's also the challenge. Mozart is so difficult to interpret, and to play physically, even when the music doesn't sound difficult."

Shirk says he doesn't care how he looks on stage—"I'm thinking of the music"—but he carries himself with a low-key dignity that matches the quiet neatness of his dress. His playing has a quick sensitivity; its calm surface is a window to open emotional depths. He excels as an accompanist and has toured with soprano Susan Gregory, a former soloist with the New York City Opera. Together they have performed songs by Schubert, Schumann, Debussy, Brahms, and, naturally, Mozart. "I love accompanying because on your own you can be isolated. And there's so much wonderful repertoire. Accompanists used not to be listed on the programs, and they're still generally underpaid. But it's not really second fiddle, it's a partnership."

Shirk also teaches at Mannes School of Music, the Third Street Music School (where we met him), and has a roster of private students who come to his west side apartment. In the fall of 1984 he went back to London, Brussels, and Salzburg for recitals with Miss Gregory. "Luckily we got dates spread out over three weeks, so it was a vacation, too."

"I play piano," said André Morgan, "but I consider myself an all-around entertainer. I sing, dance, and act. Right now I'm concentrating on my songwriting, working with a lyricist on material for the pop singer Shannon. That feels like a college project. The record producer knows just what he wants: title in the hook, sixteen-bar chorus, two verses that tell a story. So many rules!"

André is a neighbor; occasionally we hear his electric piano shimmering across the air shaft. His first professional experience was playing piano in his family's gospel group, the Morgan Singers, when he was a teenager. "I was also El Gajo in a high school *Fantastiks* in Denver, but I never thought of a career in show business until I started studying voice and theatre at the University of Colorado." He came to New York with the Cleo Parker Robinson Dance Ensemble, then quit to join an Off-Broadway show, *Snowjobbers.* "It went nowhere, the worst show I've ever been in."

He made it to the fourth call back for a role in *Dreamgirls*, but then got sick with nervous tension and walked away from the final audition. "I really freaked. I was shaking all over and nearly threw up onstage. It was all I could do to grab my bag and get out of there. It taught me that I never again wanted to put all my hopes in whether one person would say 'yes' or 'no' about me." Working for the public relations office of an oil company to pay the rent, André put together a four-piece band (guitar, bass, drums, keyboards/sax), and started playing good New York clubs like J. P.'s and s.n.a.f.u., drawing the attention of a small management company, One Thousand Hats. "They're as concerned about me making it as I am. They believe in my potential—it's wonderful!"

Recently André put together a vocal tape—three minutes long with snatches of ten songs from the band's repertoire, and so far he's distributed over two hundred cassette copies looking for jingle and background singing work. "I've just joined AFTRA and the prospects look good. I'm also a featured singer with a jazz group, Rhythmotion, and today I'm tired because I got back at six a.m. from being an extra in a Richard Pryor film."

His favorite performer is Michael Jackson; he also likes Bruce Springsteen, John Cougar Mellencamp, and Tina Turner. "I like people who are *real* on stage." The only thing he doesn't like about show business is traveling. "I lived out of a suitcase for a year on the road with *Up with People.* I hated it! I like to have my own space, to be at home. Maybe it's my midwestern upbringing."

· · · · ·

COLLEAGUES

André Morgan

Nancy Colahan

180

"Movement is it!" said Nancy Colahan over a midmorning cup of coffee. She had just come from teaching an hour and three-quarters ballet class in a six-week summer session at New York University. "Boy, some of these kids don't want to *move*. There's no spirit, no concentration. I always got things quickly in class. Patience, that's what I had to learn."

Nancy Colahan is a professional dancer. Her shining blonde hair and her cheerful smile accentuate the decisive clarity of her intelligence. Growing up in San Jose, California, she studied ballet with her mother's teachers, Dimitri and Francesca Romanoff. "Mr. Romanoff is still my greatest inspiration, but I am moved by any dedicated performer in any field. I love motivated people."

After discussing it with her parents, Nancy decided to go straight to New York after high school. "For the first year I trained, then I auditioned for the Alvin Ailey Repertory—that's his second company—and made it. I'd recommend anyone with talent and drive getting to New York as soon as possible. College training is great, but it's not the real route. And for a dancer, those eighteen-to-twenty-two years are valuable."

Nancy met choreographer Joyce Trisler through working with Alvin Ailey, and Trisler asked her to join her Danscompany. "The company had a grant to revive the Denishawn technique—the early modern dancing of Ruth St. Denis and Ted Shawn. It was wonderful—we twirled loads of streamers! I was with the Danscompany for five years. Lar Lubovitch saw me there. One day he lost a dancer through an injury and called me up to replace her." She is now a principal dancer with Lubovitch's company and has traveled with it all over the world. "It hasn't all been perfect. This year I was exhausted at the end of the season; but there's one great thing about Lar, he challenges you physically—it's really dance."

Ellen played for Nancy's classes one summer and then for her husband Lonné Moretton's ballet classes for the next year at Dennis Wayne's Dancerschool in New York. Lonné is an easygoing fellow with a dark brown mustache and a quick smile. He started dance by competing in ballroom dancing exhibitions during high school in Sonoma, California. "But when I went to college, San Jose State, all I cared about was football. Then I was injured, and the coach recommended I get back in shape with dance. When I got to class, there were about thirty women and only four men. I said to myself, 'Holy Smokes, this is the place for me!' "

Lonné and Nancy met when he started studying with the Romanoffs, and in New York they've worked together with Alvin Ailey and Joyce Trisler. Lonné has also danced with the Bridgeport Ballet in Connecticut and the Long Island Ballet in New York. "I also toured for three years with Dennis Wayne's company. Dancing with them at the Spoleto Festival in 1981—that's been the high point of my career so far."

Now thirty-seven, Lonné dances only occasionally. "I'm concentrating on choreographing and teaching. This is my second year in a two-year Master of Fine Arts program at New York University. Teaching's not a second choice for me—it was a goal from the beginning. When I started, I didn't think I'd ever be good enough to dance professionally myself. I still think of my career as a lucky fluke—if it hadn't been for that football injury, it might never have happened."

Lonné's choreography is bold and action-packed; he has created dances to big band jazz, the records of Elvis Presley, and Chicago blues. "With my ballet and my modern and jazz background, I think I've got good depth. My biggest inspirations are movie musicals, Fred Astaire and Gene Kelly, and I'd love to work in TV or Broadway. Right now I'm circulating videos of my most recent work."

Lonné's students had finished their warm-ups and were waiting for him to begin rehearsal of the Elvis pieces. There was time for one more question. "Advice for beginners?" Lonné laughed. "Hard work and more hard work and then a little bit more hard work!" he said, going back to work himself.

. . . . . .

COLLEAGUES

Lonné Moretton

Jim Payne

Jim Payne is an old friend. We met in college when he used a cubbyhole under the basement stairs in our dorm to practice his drums. I'd stop by to listen and we'd get talking about music, Jim telling me all about James Brown, Jimmy Reed, Little Anthony, Jackie Wilson, and his other rhythm-and-blues heroes, and me coming back with Duke Ellington, Billie Holiday, and Lester Young.

Jim had started playing with bar and party bands in high school in Connecticut, and continued all through college. He still tried out the Navy and business school before knowing for sure he was a drummer. "I loved rock 'n' roll, something my parents didn't understand. They thought music was okay, but just as a sideline, definitely *not* for a career."

Encouraged by his teacher, Jim Strassburg, Payne moved to New York in 1970, renting a studio apartment (again in a basement) on the Lower East Side. For the next ten years, two of them in California, Jim played every kind of gig imaginable, from studio demo dates to last-minute pick-up bands for New Year's Eve to playing in the pit at Radio City Music Hall and on Broadway. "I also took extension courses at the Manhattan School of Music—sight-singing, ear training, song-writing. They were very valuable." In the process, Jim became a member of local 802 of the AF of M and a superb drummer—his time rock steady, his touch light and varied, his sound melodic.

He kept hoping to put a stable group together in which he could be a partner, not a sideman. That came in 1980 with the Slickaphonics, a funk-jazz band with the unusual lineup of sax, trombone, guitar, bass and drums, plus vocals. The Slickaphonics' sound is a rhythmic stew spiced with offbeat solos and offbeat lyrics. "Step on Your Watch!" a Payne original, is the band's humorous salute to time.

"Now we're recording our third album," Jim said recently. "The first two are doing great in Europe, but haven't caught on here. So we've been playing a lot more gigs in France and Germany than in New York. In 1983, we played the Montreux Festival in Switzerland. It was fantastic."

Jim's wife, Joanna Fitzpatrick, worked for several years setting up tours for the pop singing group Manhattan Transfer. Together Jim and Joanna are Fitzpayne Management, the Slickaphonics' central office. Jim and Joanna live in a loft in downtown Manhattan with their two kids, Amie and Sam, and their dog, Katy.

"If I had known how important music was going to be for me, I would have started studying theory in college," Jim said. "That's the key, *start studying*. And start playing with other people. Set up ten jam sessions a week, three will actually happen. Learn how to read, be able to play any kind of gig. Remember, you've got to make it happen. Don't wait around to be discovered. Be confident, look sharp, be a gentleman."

"I've wanted to be in show business ever since I saw 'I Love Lucy' in 1955," said dancer Paul Wilson. "Lucille Ball and the Ed Sullivan show were my greatest inspirations. And the Bay of Pigs."

The Bay of Pigs? We learned not to expect logic from Paul Wilson on the first day of rehearsal in the fall of 1982. Choreographer and dancer Joanne Edelmann, herself barely five feet tall, asked Paul, who is six-two, to be her partner for *Jump!*, a dance show to Mandel & Lydon music. "This is Michael Lydon," said Joanne, introducing me.

"Hi, Jim," said Paul, and that was it: I was "Jim" for a month.

Paul was born in Carbondale, Pennsylvania, and grew up in Newark, New Jersey, becoming serious about dance at Jersey City State College. His goal then was "to become an overnight sensation." That's still his goal ten years later. Besides dancing, he's been a receptionist,

Paul Wilson

typist, office manager, paralegal, teacher, bookstore cashier, and a domestic to help himself get there.

"Oh, that's the way it is," he said with a laugh, "but I'm working, I'm learning, and I'm having fun, so I call that a success, don't you?"

Paul started dancing professionally with the Charles Weidman Theatre Dance Company. "Sharing the stage with the late, great Charles Weidman has been the biggest moment in my career." He went on to work with numerous modern dance choreographers, most recently Mimi Garrard. "But I think working with modern dancers full time is always a mistake—too limiting! I've done a lot of dinner theatre musicals, *Applause* and *Hello Dolly*, for instance, all around New York. I like those because I get to sing in the chorus."

Performing, Paul moves with a muscular, rough-and-ready grace that fits his rangy build. For one piece in *Jump!*, Joanne had Paul and me both out on the floor as if we were sidewalk entertainers, me playing guitar as Paul danced. He circled me in bright flashes of energy and color, an invisible link of concentration between us. "I'm exhausted," he puffed as we came off, "but, whew, I *never* regret dancing."

Paul's inspirations include the Beatles, Phil Donahue, Barbra Streisand, the ocean, Jerome Robbins, Ernest Hemingway, and Mother Theresa. His biggest annoyance is "seeing certain people who shall remain nameless get acclaim for the absolute trash they pass off as art. There ought to be a Society for the Prevention of Phonies Getting Future Work, but I don't let it bother me. There's really only one thing to do: shut up and dance."

In 1977, Glenn Manion and Suzanne Smithline were two fresh-faced young folk musicians a year out of New York University, where they had both sung in the chorus. Suzanne strummed an autoharp, Glenn fingerpicked on guitar, and they had good, clear voices that blended sweetly in harmony. They called themselves Bes' Friends and auditioned all around the city. We met them at a huge open call for Nashville's Opryland.

But it was 1977, not 1967, the year of the Sex Pistols, the Clash, and punk rock. Fresh-faced folkies were not in demand. "We'd get really discouraged," Suzanne recalled. "We could do great playing on the sidewalk in Greenwich Village, but we couldn't get into the clubs."

One midtown manager sensed their boy-and-girl-in-love potential and made an offer: sign with him for five years and he'd get them motel lounge work—*if* they'd drop the folk image, wear snazzy outfits

Glenn Manion and Suzanne
Smithline

and makeup, and cover Top-40 hits. "It was a really hard decision,"
said Glenn, "because being a cover act with big pasted-on smiles wasn't
*us*, but we really wanted to make our living from music. We had both
been office temporaries just about full time."

They signed with the manager in 1978 and began touring motels
all over the Northeast and as far west as Iowa. "We did the best we
could," said Glenn. "We even got a rhythm machine for a bigger sound,"
said Suzy. "The trouble was," Glenn continued, "we still didn't go over.
Some places didn't let us finish out the week. They loved us at one
motel in Presque Isle, Maine, but mostly they thought we were still
too folky. The manager insisted it was because we were doing something wrong. He'd really yell at us, and we believed him. In retrospect,
the situations were wrong for us."

The five years were up in 1983, and Suzy and Glenn started to
look for new directions, without a manager. Talking over possibilities
on one long trip back from Wisconsin, they came up with rockabilly.
Suzy would switch to electric bass, Glenn to electric guitar, and they'd
get a drummer. "We loved the music—Carl Perkins and Jerry Lee
Lewis—and there was a market for it. The Stray Cats has started a
rockabilly revival," said Suzy. "We started rehearsing with a drummer
in the spring of 1983 and looking for gigs in the summer. Right away
bookers and agents were more interested. They started loving our
tapes, not losing them."

The new focus totally changed Glenn and Suzy's performance. In tight sweaters and short skirts, Suzy became a fifties bobby-soxer, Glenn a hepcat in a drape jacket, baggy pants, and shades. They danced together, bobbing the necks of their bass and guitar in unison. Suzy's playing had real rock whammy, Glenn's sparkled with Chuck Berry flash, all over the rocketing drums of Michael Columbo, a curly-haired dynamo who had previously played with another rockabilly group, Freddy Froggs and the No Frills Band.

They called the band "Squeaky Clean"—crisp *k* sounds and still the good-kids image. Fans and friends could call their phone and get the Clean Line: recorded information on upcoming gigs. And there were many of them—rock clubs on Long Island, lounges in New Jersey, and low-pay, prestige dates in Manhattan. For these they put ads in the music section of the *Village Voice* with their Tide box emblem. After a nine-month shakedown period, they decided to make a record in the spring of 1984. "This was our biggest investment ever," said Suzy. "We tried to do it cheaply, but not cut corners." That meant a professional studio and producer, six songs on an LP-size disc, and a three-color cover by a professional designer. They planned an initial pressing of one thousand copies.

In the summer, Glenn and Suzy waited impatiently for the record to be done. They could feel their momentum building with every date, and the record could be a big boost. They could get into record stores and on the radio, send it to major record companies, top-name managers, and critics at the *New York Times* and *Rolling Stone*. "I'll admit we've been getting pretty excited," said Suzy. "What if it is a hit?!"

Meanwhile, sharing a house in the suburbs with Suzy's parents helps keep their costs down. Glenn delivers newspapers one day a week. "I'm glad to be where I am now," he says. "Much of the time with the manager felt wasted going after inappropriate goals, but I learned valuable lessons making those mistakes. Everyone who has made it has been told at some point in their career they didn't stand a chance. So don't let anyone tell you there is only one path. Try anything."

"We learned that you must believe in yourself and your talents before you can expect anyone else to," said Suzy. "If it is something you really want, you can't give up. Don't ever give up."

"I have a place now," said Nancy Lombardo, "isn't it great?" She looked around the tiny livingroom with the kitchen in the corner and a hall to a bedroom beyond. "A real apartment. For five years I just had a room, cooked on a hot plate and did my dishes in the bathroom sink. And look at the shelves—my own carpentry! Carpentry's the best thing I got out of college theatre in Pensacola, Florida. I built sets in a work-study program."

Her face lit up with a smile. "I'll do anything for money!"

Nancy Lombardo is little and quick. Words spill from her in good-humored splashes; her eyes are bright with intelligence, wit, and ambition. A comic actress, her specialty is improvisation, instantly creating characters and situations based on audience suggestions. For five years Nancy has been a mainstay of *Strictly Improv* at New York's First Amendment Theatre in Greenwich Village. Sometimes she's a Valley Girl, sometimes the Spanish hostess of a cable TV talk show, and at other times Maria MacGregor, a mad Scottish poet. Her comic style is a dry irony blended with a bubbling enjoyment of her own silliness. "Sometimes on stage I break character and tell the audience, 'If you could only see what I'm imagining up here!' Improvising for me is visual. I don't think at all, there's no time."

Born in Yonkers, New York, Nancy grew up in Pensacola. "I was always leaning to theatre, but I started with TV courses at Pensacola Junior College until I was brave enough to perform. Actually, my mother had started me tap dancing when I was about two and a half. 'Me and My Teddy Bear' was my big number." At the University of West Florida she worked with teacher Shaw Robinson ("we're still in touch") and got good parts in student productions. "My first professional work was radio commercials, but I've done everything. My theory is: take any job that's offered and then learn how to do it. Once I was a wandering minstrel at Christmas in a shopping mall. Me, a wandering minstrel? But I put together something with a recorder and a puppet, and people loved it. You can't say you can't do it in this business."

Nancy also writes comedy sketches and has performed several as one-woman pieces in New York clubs. She has taken them to TV producers, but so far no sales. "A while ago Cinemax was going to shoot some two-minute comedy shorts for between movies. They liked my stuff, it was all okayed, ready to start, and then, oops, the whole project got switched to L.A. That was discouraging, but all my friends said, 'What do they know?' Now I wait for the signed contracts before I get excited."

Working as an extra in the movie *Moscow on the Hudson*, Nancy met Robin Williams and invited him to *Strictly Improv*. "He was fast, but so were we. Oh, I'm very competitive. Whoever is the best at the

COLLEAGUES

Nancy Lombardo

time, I want to work with and pass. I wouldn't say I passed Williams, but I kept up."

Nancy's new apartment is in an old building just off Times Square and across the street from the Gershwin Theatre. "I like being in the middle of it all. No matter what happens, working in the theatre is my only choice for life. I thought I'd be rich by now, but..." Nancy laughed and took a pose, transforming herself instantly into Edith Piaf. "Ah," she sang in the scratchy voice of the tragic French chanteuse, "Je ne regrette rien!"

Victor Griffin

"Oh, I learned everything the hard way—experience," said Victor Griffin, his hands tapping lightly on the tablecloth for emphasis. "In vaudeville we didn't have money to spend on classes, but it was a community. Backstage between the four shows a day, people would exchange dance steps or suggest a song. That was school for me."

Griffin, now sixty-six, started dancing when he went with his mother to pick up his big sister at dance class. "Just watching, I learned more than she did. Ballet and soft-shoe at a little school in Pittsburgh. But my father hated it, despised the idea of his son becoming a dancer." Griffin began performing at twelve, touring the RKO vaudeville circuit as a tap dancer in the Joe Laurie, Jr., troupe. Then the Garry Society, which tried to outlaw child performers, sent him back to Pittsburgh. "Two years later I was back in New York."

That was 1932, and since then Griffin has been out of work only for the two and a half years he served in the Army in Alaska during World War II. He danced with Ina Ray Hutton, later to become famous as a woman swing band leader; the Dixie Dunbar Rhythmaires; and the legendary singer Sophie Tucker. He worked with Milton Berle in the *Ziegfeld Follies of 1943* and toured as Will Parker in *Oklahoma*. In Stephen Sondheim's *Follies* he played Vincent, a retired ballroom dancer of the team Vincent and Vanessa who have bought an Arthur Murray dance school. Griffin's portrayal of Vincent's bravery touched with nostalgia for better days won him rave reviews.

"*Follies* in 1971 really started a new career for me as an actor, an acting dancer. Then in *Ballroom* I played Harry the Noodle, and one day a person in the street said to me, 'Aren't you Harry the Noodle?' That was a real victory—it meant I really *was* that guy on stage. When I played Salieri's valet in *Amadeus*, I started singing. What a discovery—I had a voice!"

We first saw Griffin in *Taking My Turn*, a musical in which eight characters reflect on how it feels to grow old. The show blended lively music, sentiment, and comedy in equal proportions. "How will I know when I'm old?" sang one character. "When your children have grey hair, then you're old," came the reply. Griffin, playing an elderly bachelor, was riveting from the moment he came onstage, the image of graceful, poised expectancy from his polished brown shoes to his gleaming bald head. Even standing still he projected cheerful energy. One character was an embittered widow. In the show's most moving moment, Grifin led her out to center stage for a dance. No, she wouldn't, she couldn't, life had hardened her heart. Griffin's every move was a caress, sympathetic and encouraging. Slowly she opened up to him and they waltzed.

"How did I do it?" Griffin laughed. "I concentrated on my partner, Sheila Smith. That's what I learned from my idol, Fred Astaire. Astaire never took his eyes off the girl, but you can't stop looking at him."

Griffin was a dancing valet in the film *Annie* and has been a butler in many TV commercials. He also teaches tap to individual students. "Lara Teeter, the lead in *On Your Toes*, is a student. He asked me to come one night. He was wonderful! I told him, 'The reviews are in, now's the time to experiment, stretch yourself.' "

"No," Griffin said, he wouldn't have lunch with us. "Go ahead, but I'm going out to dinner tonight. I try to eat only two meals a day." The dinner was for the first screening of a video version of *Taking My Turn* made for PBS. "It's at the Players Club in Gramercy Park, very fancy, and the woman in charge wrote such a sweet note with the invitation."

Beginning to sing so late is Griffin's only regret, but he seldom looks back. "Right now is the highest point in my career. I'm starting to choreograph, and I'm thinking more and more like an actor. I'm hoping to be on a television series as a continuing character. If Howard Keel can do it on "Dallas," so can I! But I'm not moving to California. My rule is: never go to LA without a job."

Griffin is a member of AFTRA, Equity, and SAG, but has no manager and only free-lance relationships with agents. He advises beginners not to come to New York without money in the bank and "to be ready when you get here." Total dedication is a must. "You have to eat, drink, and sleep your work."

Could he have done anything different? Griffin thought a moment. "Maybe," he said. "All my life I've thought I might like being a priest. I have some wonderful priest friends, and they've given me something. That's helping other people. I want to help other people with what I'm doing. I'm not off in my own little corner."

*chapter 10*

○ ○ ○ ○ ○ ○ ○ ○ ○ ○ ○ ○ ○ ○ ○ ○ ○ ○ ○ ○ ○ ○ ○ ○ ○ ○ ○ ○ ○ ○ ○ ○ ○ ○ ○ ○ ○ ○ ○ ○ ○ ○

# QUESTIONS
# AND ANSWERS

Q. I've read that you have to be "talented" to make it in show business. How will I know if I am talented, if I've got what it takes?

A. That question, and anxiety about its answer, is nearly universal in the performing arts. Even the most successful performers ask it at least once a week if not every day. They find it easy enough to answer about someone else—I *know* that Meryl Streep is a superbly talented actress—but about themselves, except at rare, happy moments, they are not sure. There is no definitive answer, and, given the constantly experimental nature of all art, there never will be.

Steady work, enthusiastic audiences, good reviews, and the respect of your peers can go a long way to still the most gnawing doubts. But then the applecart can be upset by a period of unemployment, being in a flop, or a series of inexplicable rejections. When that happens, as it most likely will from time to time, the performer is forced back on his or her own self-assessment, and that can change five times in the course of a morning.

My advice: don't let this question bug you. Don't even try very hard to answer it directly. Work hard, keep studying, keep trying. If you are really not cut out for work as a performer, the way events turn

One hour to curtain at the Booth Theatre in New York City

. . . . . . . .

191

The last run-through...

out will probably tell you that soon enough. You can then go on to a new career, undoubtedly enriched for having tried.

Stevie Wonder's definition of talent makes a lot of sense. "Your talent," he said, "is your determination." If you find that you cannot take no for an answer, if you keep banging on the door until it opens, if you feel a fierce inner drive that keeps you plugging at your craft every day, you have at least the germ kernel of talent. Nourish that with realistic self-awareness, constructive criticism from people you respect, liberal doses of humor, and you will have reason to hope that in time it will blossom and bear fruit.

Q. Every time I perform, I have awful, shaking fits of stage fright. What can I do about it? Does it ever go away?

A. Stage fright is part of performing for nearly every entertainer. A combination of fear of failure, the excitement of anticipation, and the primal awareness of being exposed and outnumbered, stage fright can have powerful physical effects including trembling, yawning, nausea and vomiting, diarrhea, and a continual urge to urinate. With these can come mental pictures of all the disasters that could possibly happen onstage—loss of concentration leading to visible confusion that strikes the audience as extremely amusing; they howl with laughter until the red-faced performer flees the stage in abject humiliation.

Sounds like fun! I know one singer who struggled with stage fright for years until she finally realized that her fear of performing was greater than her love of it. She continued as a musician but only at home. Another acquaintance only brought his fear under control after a long course of hypnosis.

For most performers, myself included, stage fright is most intense early in their careers, when the symptoms are more likely to take them by surprise. With experience, some small part of their minds can tell them, "It's just stage fright, it'll be gone as soon as I'm out there a few minutes." On the other hand, it tends to crop up again with particular force at crucial auditions or at shows that feel like breakthroughs to new career levels.

The most immediate remedy is to admit the feelings out loud— "Boy, am I nervous." That might get a laugh out of yourself or those with you, restoring a little perspective on the situation. Then try taking several long, even breaths through your nose, letting them out fully through your mouth. Exercise lightly; do a few jumping-jacks, jog in place, or let your whole upper body hang over, head to your knees, fingers touching your toes.

Some performers like to sit quietly, mentally reviewing what they will do in the whole performance. Others direct all their energy toward

and performance at last

their first moment on stage, figuring that the momentum of a strong entrance will carry them through. Harpo Marx used to tell himself, "Eleven o'clock always rolls around," promising himself a treat after the show.

*Do not take any drug or drink to make you relax.* Anything strong enough to calm your nerves will adversely affect your performance. It will only mask your feelings: they'll still be there, but you won't know what they are. There is no surer way for a performer to start a crippling drug dependence than to rely on a chemical to relieve stage fright.

But do relax. The fright is really a measure of your own hopes for success. "The best artists get the most nervous," is an old show business saying. Besides, what does it matter? As you wait to go on, think of all the other performers waiting to go on all over the world. You're not alone, you are one of thousands. Do your best and keep going. Soon enough your show will be a memory, and the worst goofs may one day provoke hearty reminiscent laughter.

Q. Should I take a stage name?

A. Only if you want to. Many performing artists change their given names for stage names, and for many reasons. Sometimes their names are too long, awkward to spell or pronounce, too obviously revealing of ethnic background, or are colorless and hard to remember. Others change their names out of a deep desire to establish their performing personalities as new identities, and they find names that better express their new selves. Some early movie stars had their names changed by studio heads when they were unknown actors, and then found themselves stuck with the new names because that's how the public knew them.

Examples of stage names are endless. Cary Grant was Archibald Leach; Bob Dylan was Robert Zimmerman. Television actor Robert Guillaume created a distinctive stage name by using the French spelling of his family name, Williams. Edward G. Robinson was born, and to himself always remained, Emmanuel Goldberg. On the other hand, actor Rip Torn's real name really is Rip Torn.

If you want to change your name, don't be dissuaded by family pressure. You have a right to call yourself what you please. But think out your decision fully. It may be difficult to change again. If in doubt, stick with what you've got: it has the advantage of being, in a fundamental way, *you*.

Q. Where I live seems so small-time, and the opportunities are really limited. When should I go to New York (or Los Angeles or Nashville)?

A. Not until you're ready! Only you can answer that, of course, but I advise thinking twice and even three times before leaving your hometown for the Big Apple, the Coast, or Music City.

The attractions of the three big entertainment centers are obvious. They are the "big time" where the big names work for the big money. They are where the possibilities are endless, where the cream of each year's crop of ambitious newcomers struggles to rise to the top, where a lucky break can lead to stardom. The special flavor of excitement in these cities is not a myth. Hundreds, even thousands of performers are competing for the attention of knowledgeable audiences with expectations of excellence. The high stakes sharpen the focus of every performer, increasing his or her sense of exposure and bringing out new levels of energy.

In show business terms, New York, L.A., and Nashville are na-

QUESTIONS

AND ANSWERS

William Basie, known to all as "Count" Basie

tional cities. Others are regional or touring cities. Boston, Massachusetts, for example, is a big city with a lively professional performing life. Being on the top there, however, will barely raise an eyebrow two hundred miles away in New York. As Merrill Joels wrote in *How to Get into Show Business,* "In most instances, your out-of-town experience may be considered amateur." Conversely, living in and working from New York confers glamour by association even on middle-rung performers. When Ellen and I have played Boston, we've asked to be announced, "Direct from Manhattan . . ."

For the beginner, the advantages of being in the national cities can seem intangible compared to the all too tangible day-to-day difficulties those cities present. New York and Los Angeles especially are very expensive places to live. I have met numerous actors, dancers, and musicians who have arrived with a small bankroll that was exhausted long before they found paying performing work. They had to take part-time or full-time work that left them no time to practice and audition. Within a year they realized they were out of touch with their hopes and had lost momentum. Some have gone home, others have stayed but quit performing.

Regional cities also have advantages often overlooked by impatient beginners. Theatre, opera, dance, and even movie production have grown tremendously in large and middle-size cities all over the country. Chicago is justly proud of its Second City comedy, Cleveland of its orchestra and Cleveland Playhouse, Minneapolis of its Guthrie Theatre. Rock bands come from every region and often are successful just because their sound expresses the flavor of their background. Competiton is still tough but not so overwhelming. Performers in their hometown are closer to family support and a lifetime network of contacts.

If you cannot be satisfied where you are, consider trying a city bigger than your own but still smaller than the big three. Louis Jordan did just that when he came East from the Midwest. "I was headed to New York but stopped in Philadelphia for a few years—I was scared!"

If the big-city itch still won't let go, visit the city of your choice for a week or two first. See everything you can; meet performers, agents, secretaries, stage hands; read newspapers and trade papers, and collect them to take home with you; find out what food costs and what apartments rent for. Ask yourself realistically, "Could I get by here, am I ready?"

If the answer is yes, go! Nothing ventured, nothing gained. Have as much money as you can in advance, have a secondary skill for part-time work, and know how to cook so you can eat at home. Be mentally prepared for a long haul.

Q. Should I set myself a time limit to "make it"?

A. This question was the basis for a funny episode of the television situation comedy "Taxi." A young actor had set himself a three-year time limit to get an acting job in New York, driving a cab meanwhile. Came the last day, no job. At just past midnight, with all his friends gathered around wondering what he'd do next, the fellow faced a future with no acting, no auditioning, no trying in it. He made his decision in seconds. "Hey, I'm gonna give myself three more years!"

The idea of an arbitrary time limit doesn't suit the continuing urge to perform that motivates show artists. Moreover, what do you mean by "making it"?

Setting goals is a good idea, and so is periodic review of those goals. I also suggest continual financial analysis to measure the return from investment. If any career avenue you attempt turns out to be a dead end, try new avenues.

Setting limits for yourself is self-limiting. Instead, be flexible, experimental, expansive. That way you'll continue to be creative no matter where your career takes you, and being creative is making it in the arts.

Q. I only got serious about my career when I was thirty. There are so many younger people who are ahead of me. Do I have a chance?

A. Yes! There is a premium on youth in show business and there are advantages to starting young, but on the other hand there are no set age limits. Even some dancers continue into their sixties and seventies, musicians can play until health and strength fail them, and actors are needed to play all the ages of man.

Comedian Rodney Dangerfield's current career began with a second try at performing when he was in his fifties. His first try as a young man had failed. Danny Aiello decided to be an actor in his forties. Singer-pianist Dardanelle came back to performing after raising a family.

Take your age into account realistically when setting your goals, but don't use it as an excuse for not doing your best. "If you can hold the fort long enough, they're going to need you," said veteran trouper Sophie Tucker. "It ain't how good you are, it's how long you can last."

* * * * * *

Q. What do I do if someone is harsh in criticizing my work? It really hurts!

A. Nobody relishes criticism, and the openness required for performing makes performers particularly vulnerable targets. Criticism is tough to take before a performance, when you need all your confidence and concentration; it is tough afterward, when you feel drained and are well aware of all the flubs and weak points without anyone else bringing them up. In between times, classroom and rehearsal critiques can set off agonizing chain reactions of self-doubt—"What did she mean my energy was down? Was it the way I held my head? Maybe my breath was wrong . . ." Marvin Gaye said it in song: "We're all sensitive people."

Criticism, however, comes with performing. By stepping out to be noticed, performers invite comment. Given human nature, that is not all going to be positive. You may never grow to like it, but it is important to learn to live with it.

First, always try to make the old distinction between constructive and destructive criticism. Constructive criticism can be stated in the most blundering and tactless words—many people don't know how to express themselves well or without exaggeration—but with practice it is possible to sense underlying honest and helpful intent. True reactions, even when clumsily worded, can be helpful to any performer. As you listen, and afterward, compare your own feelings about your work with these outside comments. Accept what you can use, file or reject the rest. Other people have their own points of view, but if you are honest with yourself, you are as likely to be right as they are.

You have a perfect right to avoid listening to criticism at moments when you are not ready to take it in—just before or after a show, when you are working out a problem on your own, or when you are tired or hurried. It is possible to say politely, "Excuse me, but I can't listen right now, catch me at rehearsal tomorrow." If the person criticizing is the boss, you may have no choice, but a constructive boss will want to work with you when you are best able to respond.

Destructive criticism is another story. Many people respond to performers out of their own jealousies, hates, pomposities, and frustrations. They can be fellow performers, supposed friends or fans, and even family members. The most determined are devilishly adept at finding ways to a performer's own deepest doubts while maintaining a front of innocent and thoughtful concern.

This criticism, however mixed with syrupy sweetness, is a poison that can sap a performer's strength with manufactured anxieties. It needs to be rejected absolutely. Train yourself to recognize its hypocritical and bullying flavors and the telltale buildup of tension after its injection. Watch out for people who load their advice with "You should" or "You have to," or who present themselves with superior airs. Be as firm as necessary with whoever is using it, letting them know that you are on your guard. If they persist, limit your relationship with them as much as possible.

There will be no need for suspicion of all comers, but be aware of the dangers of naive trust. If your talent is of value, there will be times that you'll need to fight for it. A confident, street-smart realism is your best defense. Most psych-out bullies are cowards who avoid people clearly unwilling to play the victim.

Q. It embarrasses me when people praise my work lavishly. What do I say to them?

A. Say "Thank you, thank you very much" and keep saying it. The words may come out of you mechanically. You may really be thinking that the fan must be deaf as well as blind to have missed that incredible mix-up in Act II. Apology and explanation, however, are out of place when compliments are being handed out. They sound like false modesty or lack of confidence, and they also diminish the pleasure of the appreciative fan. If she did miss that goof, it didn't exist for her, so why bring it up?

Don't shortchange yourself of the pleasure of admiration. You worked for it, enjoy it! You can take it in without letting it go to your head. Soon enough you'll be back at work—gather the rosebuds while you may.

Q. I get annoyed sometimes at the stage crew and other performers when they mess up details of a show I've worked so hard on. Don't I have the right to throw a temperamental fit to make sure things are done right?

A. If it will help, and as a last resource, yes. One person's laziness or carelessness can make your work difficult or even impossible. For your own professional self-defense, and for the good of the whole show, it may be worth speaking up loudly about a production problem and then holding your ground until it is corrected.

But—and that is a big but—make sure you have earned the right to be temperamental. This means first being sure of your ground; having to crawl back with an "Oops, excuse me" will create bad feeling and weaken you in any future encounter. Second, be sure you are fighting for the show and for the respect due you as one of its working parts. Your colleagues will see through a fuss created to shore up your own vanity. Third, be sure your own work is fully professional. Jumping on the person running the lights and then forgetting your own cues will make you no friends.

Opera singer Beverly Sills once needed to lay down the law when she was singing at La Scala in Milan. She had asked for a costume embroidered with silver. The designer said yes but delivered one done in gold. Miss Sills asked again; again yes, but again gold. This went on until the fifth time, when she decided it was time to play prima donna. "I took the gold costume," she wrote in her autobiography, *Bubbles, A Self-Portrait*, "folded it carefully into a square, lifted a pair of scissors the costume lady had dangling around her neck, and slowly and deliberately I cut the costume in half. Then, with a smile, I said, 'Now you go back upstairs and make the costume in silver.' " The next time it came back right.

Remember, however, that Miss Sills was already an international star. Beginners in the chorus would have been wise to accept the gold costume with a smile.


Q. I'm a dancer, and my company tours six months a year. Being away so much creates a lot of problems between me and my girl friend. Besides, my future is so uncertain, I don't know how we can get married. How can I resolve the tension between my love life and my career?

A. Even Dear Abby would have a tough time with that question! It's no secret that show business is rough on romantic relationships. Performers involved with people outside of the profession sometimes find that their lovers never quite understand what drives them on year after year. Wives want musician husbands to leave the road and take them out on New Year's Eve instead of playing for other couples. Husbands ask their actress wives to quit so together they can raise a family. Performers who fall in love with each other don't find it all a bed of roses either. All may be well while they are both struggling beginners; let one become a star while the other is lucky to get bit parts—that's when the heartaches begin.

Show business, of course, can't take all the blame. "The course of true love never did run smooth," said Shakespeare. If it did, most performers, without the tales of star-crossed lovers to tell, would be out of work!

At this distance, romantic advice means little. I will say, however, be as honest as possible with yourself and the one you love about your own needs for a career. In many films and plays, the performer who sacrifices love and family for success has been portrayed as an egocentric doomed by ambition to a glittering but hollow life. Don't let this exaggeration make you feel guilty about your own urges to work, travel, and to pour heart and soul into performing. Denying or minimizing those urges if they are truly important to you will not make you or the one you love content.

The more realistic you are about your need to perform, the more likely you will be to find someone similarly realistic about his or her needs. Then perhaps love and career will not be an anxious question of either/or but a fulfilling answer of both/and.

Q. I feel my art is above business. Many of the performers I see on television and in movies seem to have cheapened their art to make it commercially acceptable. How can an artist work in show business without selling out?

A. This is a perennial question, debated endlessly by performers faced with the difficulties of making a living and following the challenges of their work. It rests on two assumptions: first, that art, being a search for the ideal, is superior to business, which deals plainly with "reality"; and second, that the two are in conflict, business always trying to debase art by insisting that it sell.

Like "Am I talented?" this is a bugaboo question, scarier sounding that the facts behind it warrant. Show people and journalists are in part to blame for its existence. Art and Business are hero and villain in many shows: the Starving Artist in his garret scorns Fame and Fortune to Follow his Vision while the Sell-Out dines on pheasant under glass and snickers, "I'm only in it for the money." A recent *New York Times* piece profiled a classical pianist who regularly records and tours Europe and America, earning enough to live in quiet luxury in

Ray Charles

London. But when he plays, said the *Times* writer, his artistic dedication is such that "show business is far away indeed."

There *can* be conflict between business and art. Art is experiment, business puts a premium on results—now! What sells best is not necessarily the best, and work of high artistic value can be judged as having no business value. Warner Bros., for instance, had filed away its 1930s series of Humphrey Bogart gangster films as forgotten quickies until Harvard students in the late 1950s discovered them as classics.

Looking for conflict, however, is much less helpful than looking for possibilities. Art and business can and do work together. Being businesslike is a commonsense necessity for artistic survival.

A telling sequence in Pier Paolo Pasolini's film *The Decameron* showed a Renaissance artist waking in ecstasy from a dream in which he had conceived in one complete vision an enormous wall painting for a church. To paint it, however, he not only had to convince the church fathers to pay for it, but also to erect a six-story-high scaffolding, hire dozens of assistants, and then labor months to complete it. Because Pasolini played the artist himself, the story of the painting became a metaphor for Pasolini's own commercial enterprise in creating his film.

On the other hand, being able to enjoy living inexpensively grants any artist precious independence from the unending pressure to "make a buck." The potluck camaraderie of struggling troupers is a proud tradition. The old saying is true: "The best things in life are free."

My advice: try to get work that satisfies as many of your artistic, personal, and economic values as possible, and then do your best with the work you get.

Rich or poor, we are all linked in a worldwide commercial network. Humans live by trading what they have for what they need. Commerce is fundamental to the ecology of the human community. No artist stands outside this network; its links are among his or her strongest connections with the people in the audience.

Q. Show people are always talking about dreaming and following your dream. I read Ruth Gordon's advice to a young performer, "Whatever you do, never stop dreaming." It sounds vague to me. Why is dreaming so important?

A. Show people do talk about dreams a lot. "You can be in my dream if I can be in yours," sings Bob Dylan. Ray Charles ended his auto-biography:

> Sometimes my dreams are so deep that I dream I'm dreaming. I wake up inside myself. I watch myself sleeping and I look like a baby or a boy, tired from playing all the day long, a small soul hungry for peace and rest.

Sometimes performers mean by *dream* the quest for great achievement, the artist striving ever upward like the bold knight of Longfellow's poem, *Excelsior*. Sometimes they mean the sleeping dreams that tell us stories in shifting images. It can sound like hooey: the blaring optimism of a Broadway musical finale or the corniness of a Hollywood tearjerker trying to convince us that Wishing on a Star Will Make Tomorrow Bright!

There is a practical aspect to dreaming, however. Creating in the arts is following and developing a personal point of view, expressing an interior vision. Much of that vision appears in the dreams of waking and sleeping. Who do you daydream of being? What are your most fulfilled fantasies of a happy life for yourself? How can you make them come true? Can you find ideas and moods in your night dreams to put into your work?

Dreams are hopes and memories. Let yourself feel them. Don't be afraid to be corny; show business is for hams. The twinkle in the eye that could be a smile or a tear—an old pro can put it on at the drop of a hat. Yet it works again and again because it tells the truth: life is but a dream, bittersweet and beautiful.

○ ○ ○ ○ ○ ○ ○ ○ ○ ○ ○ ○ ○ ○ ○ ○ ○ ○ ○ ○ ○ ○ ○ ○ ○ ○ ○ ○ ○ ○ ○ ○ ○ ○ ○ ○ ○ ○ ○ ○ ○ ○ ○

# appendix

*Asking is the key to everything. If you learn to live with rejection, you can ask for anything.*

This, says Bob Moss, a former actor and now producer with Playwright's Horizons, is the greatest single lesson he's learned in show business.

It is also the motto of this appendix. All performers are in constant need of information: news of job and career possibilities, developments in their field, ideas on staging and costuming, scores, scripts, historical facts, legal advice, phone numbers and addresses, and that is only the beginning. Ask, ask again, and keep on asking until you find out what you need to know.

A public library is any performer's single greatest source of information. Each one is a treasure house, its riches offered free to all comers. Become familiar with the performing arts shelves. Also ask the librarians for relevant reference books and directories.

Here are a few guides to valuable information in the performing arts, many of which I drew on for this book, and most of which I found through public libraries.

## BIBLIOGRAPHY AND FURTHER READING

### BIOGRAPHIES

Show business biographies are an entire literary genre. While some are sensationalized puff jobs patched together from newspaper clippings, many are detailed, thoughtful books that inspire as they entertain. In general, autobiographies, even when "as told to," are the most valuable. Distinguished performers tend to be generous in telling their own stories, open about their mistakes and frustrations, and objective about the reasons for their successes. For the beginning performer, all show business biographies contain the truth that cannot be repeated too often: everyone was a beginner once.

Astaire, Fred. *Steps in Time*. New York: Da Capo Press, 1981.

Atkins, Chet. *Country Gentleman*. New York: Ballantine Books, 1974.

Bacall, Lauren. *Lauren Bacall by Myself*. New York: Alfred A. Knopf, 1979.

Bailey, Pearl. *The Raw Pearl*. New York: Harcourt, Brace and World, 1968.

Berle, Milton, with Frankel, Haskel. *Milton Berle, An Autobiography*. New York: Delacorte Press, 1974.

Burns, George. *Living it Up, or They Still Love Me in Altoona*. New York: G. P. Putnam's Sons, 1976.

Caesar, Sid, with Davidson, Bill. *Where Have I Been?* New York: Crown Publishers, 1982.

Cagney, James. *Cagney by Cagney*. New York: Doubleday, 1976.

Cavett, Dick, and Porterfield, Christopher. *Cavett*. New York: Bantam Books, 1975.

Charles, Ray, and Ritz, David. *Brother Ray*. New York: Warner Books, 1979.

Coward, Noel. *The Noel Coward Diaries*. Edited by Graham Payn and Sheridan Morley. Boston: Little, Brown and Co., 1982.

Ellington, Duke. *Music Is My Mistress*. New York: Da Capo Press, 1981.

Fein, Irving A. *Jack Benny: An Intimate Biography*. New York: G. P. Putnam's Sons, 1976.

Fonda, Henry, with Teichman, Howard. *Fonda—My Life*. New York: New American Library, 1982.

Gielgud, John, with Miller, John and Powell, John. *Gielgud—An Actor and His Times*. New York: Clarkson N. Potter, 1979.

Hart, Moss. *Act One—An Autobiography*. New York: Random House, 1959.

Horne, Marilyn. *My Life*. New York: Atheneum Publishers, 1983.

Huston, John. *An Open Book*. New York: Alfred A. Knopf, 1980.

Lynn, Loretta. *Coal Miner's Daughter*. New York: Warner Books, 1977.

MacLaine, Shirley. *Don't Fall Off the Mountain*. New York: W. W. Norton, 1970.

Martins, Peter, with Cornfield, Robert. *Far From Denmark*. Boston: Little, Brown and Co., 1982.

Menuhin, Yehudi. *Unfinished Journey*. New York: Alfred A. Knopf, 1977.

Olivier, Laurence. *Confessions of an Actor*. London and New York: Penguin Books, 1982.

Pavarotti, Luciano. *Pavarotti—My Own Story*. New York: Warner Books, 1982.

Robinson, Edward G., with Spigelglass, Leonard. *All My Yesterdays*. New York: New American Library, 1975.

Rubinstein, Arthur. *My Young Years*. New York: Alfred A. Knopf, 1973.

Sills, Beverly. *Bubbles, A Self-Portrait*. Indianapolis and New York: Bobbs-Merrill, 1976.

Stassinopoulos, Arianna. *Maria Callas: The Woman behind the Legend*. New York: Simon and Schuster, 1981.

Swanson, Gloria. *Swanson on Swanson*. New York: Random House, 1980.

Ullman, Liv. *Changing*. New York: Alfred A. Knopf, 1976.

## CAREER AND TECHNICAL GUIDANCE

Bernstein, Seymour. *With Your Own Two Hands—Self Discovery through Music*. New York: Schirmer Books, 1981.

Busnar, Gene. *Careers in Music*. New York: Julian Messner, 1982.

Cohen, Robert. *Acting Professionally: Raw Facts about Careers in Acting*. New York: Barnes and Noble Books, 1981.

Dearing, James W. *Making Money Making Music (No Matter Where You Live)*. Cincinnati: Writer's Digest Books, 1982.

de Mille, Agnes. *To A Young Dancer*. Boston: Little, Brown and Company, 1962.

Engle, Lehman. *Getting Started in the Theatre*. New York: Collier Books, 1973.

Hagen, Uta, with Frankel, Haskell. *Respect for Acting*. New York: Macmillan Publishing Company, 1973.

Harmon, Renee. *The Actor's Survival Guide for Today's Film Industry*. Englewood Cliffs, N.J.: Prentice-Hall, 1984.

Hayden, Melissa. *Dancer to Dancer—Advice for Today's Dancer*. Garden City, N.Y.: Anchor Press, 1981.

Hunt, Cecily. *How to Get Work and Make Money Making Commercials*. New York: Van Nostrand Reinhold, 1982.

Hunt, Gordon. *How to Audition*. New York: Harper & Row, 1977.

Joels, Merrill E. *How to Get into Show Business*. New York: Hastings House Publishers, 1969.

Katz, Judith A. *The Business of Show Business*. New York: Barnes and Noble Books, 1981.

Kirkman, Larry, and Monk, Elizabeth. *TV Acting: A Manual for Camera Performance*. New York: Hastings House Publishers, 1979.

Loren, Teri. *The Dancer's Companion—The Indispensable Guide to Getting the Most out of Dance Class*. New York: The Dial Press, 1978.

Mara, Thalia. *Third Steps in Ballet*. New York: A Dance Horizons Republication, 1957.

Martin, George, ed. *Making Music—The Guide to Writing, Performing, and Recording*. New York: Quill, 1983.

Mehegan, John. *Jazz Improvisation*. 4 vols. New York: Watson-Guptil, 1964.

Nahas, Rebecca. *Your Acting Career—How to Break into and Survive in the Theatre*. New York: Crown Publishers, Inc., 1976.

Piston, Walter. *Harmony*. New York: W. W. Norton, 1969.

Shemel, Sidney, and Krasilovsky, William M. *This Business of Music: A Practical Guide to the Music Industry for Publishers, Writers, Record Companies, Producers, Artists, Agents*. New York: Billboard Books, 1979.

Shilling, Dana. *Be Your Own Boss—A Step-by-Step Guide to Financial Independence with Your Own Small Business*. New York: William Morrow, 1983.

Shurtleff, Michael. *Audition*. New York: Walker & Company, 1978.

Stanislavski, Constantin. *An Actor's Handbook*. New York: Theatre Arts Books, 1963.

Weist, Dwight, and Barron, Robert. *On Camera: How to Earn Money in TV Commercials and Other Media*. New York: Walker & Company, 1983.

DIRECTORIES

Here are three excellent performing arts directories with nearly complete listings of every type of show business organization and company. The first is particularly strong in theatre and dance, the second in film, the third in music.

Handel, Beatrice, ed. *National Directory for the Performing Arts and Civic Centers*. New York: John Wiley and Sons, 1978.

*International Motion Picture Almanac,* published yearly by Quigley Publishing Company, 159 West 53rd Street, New York, N.Y. 10019.

*Talent and Booking Directory,* published yearly by the Talent and Booking Publishing Company, 7033 Sunset Boulevard, Los Angeles, California 90028.

## HISTORY

Freedly, George, and Reeves, John A. *A History of the Theatre*. New York: Crown Publishers, Inc., 1958.

Kendall, Elizabeth. *Where She Danced*. New York: Alfred A. Knopf, 1979.

Nagler, A. M. *A Source Book in Theatrical History*. New York: Dover, 1959.

Southern, Richard. *The Seven Ages of the Theatre*. New York: Hill and Wang, 1961.

## INTERVIEWS

Cole, Toby, and Krick, Helen. *Actors on Acting*. New York: Crown Publishers, Inc., 1970.

Gruen, John. *The Private World of Ballet*. London and New York: Penguin Books, 1975.

Kalter, Joanmarie. *Actors on Acting—Performing in Theatre and Film Today*. New York: Sterling Publishing Company, 1979.

Newquist, Roy. *Showcase*. Introduction by Brooks Atkinson. New York: William Morrow, 1966.

## PERIODICALS

There are countless magazines and newspapers covering every aspect of show business and the performing arts. Their interviews, articles, reviews, and advertisements contain a wealth of information. Many have sections listing the names and addresses of schools, agents, casting directors, producers, theatres, dance companies, concert halls, and clubs.

Here are a few of the best known and most valuable.

*American Theatre*     (monthly magazine)
355 Lexington Avenue
New York, New York 10017

*Backstage*    (weekly trade paper)
330 W. 42nd Street
New York, New York 10036

*Ballet Review*    (quarterly magazine)
46 Morton Street
New York, New York 10014

*Billboard*    (weekly music trade magazine)
1515 Broadway
New York, New York 10036

*Country Music*    (monthly magazine)
450 Park Avenue South
New York, New York 10016

*Dancemagazine*    (monthly magazine)
33 West 60th Street
New York, New York 10023

*Downbeat*    (monthly jazz and pop music magazine)
222 West Adams Street
Chicago, Illinois 60606

*Film Comment*    (bi-monthly magazine)
140 West 65th Street
New York, New York 10023

*Guitar Player*    (monthly magazine)
20085 Stevens Creek
Cupertino, California 95015

*Hollywood Reporter*    (daily trade paper)
6715 Sunset Boulevard
Hollywood, California 90028

*Keyboard*    (monthly magazine)
20085 Stevens Creek
Cupertino, California 95015

*Musician*    (monthly magazine)
1515 Broadway
New York, New York 10036

*Opera News*    (monthly magazine; twice monthly in the winter)
1865 Broadway
New York, New York 10023

*Ovation*    (monthly classical music magazine)
320 West 57th Street
New York, New York 10019

*Rolling Stone*     (bi-weekly pop music news magazine)
745 Fifth Avenue
New York, New York 10022

*Show Business*     (weekly trade paper)
1501 Broadway
New York, New York 10036

*Songwriter Connection*     (monthly magazine)
6640 Sunset Boulevard
Hollywood, California 90028

*Daily Variety*     (daily trade paper)
1400 North Cahuenga Boulevard
Hollywood, California 90028

*Variety*     (weekly trade paper)
154 West 46th Street
New York, New York 10036

## BOOKSTORES

Nearly every bookstore carries at least a few books on the performing arts. For the best selection, try bookstores near college campuses and stores that carry quality paperback books. Two of the best in the country are:

The Drama Book Shop
150 West 52nd Street
New York, New York 10019
(212) 582-1037

Larry Edmunds Book Store
6658 Hollywood Boulevard
Hollywood, California 90028
(213) 463-3273

## UNIONS — See pages 153-163

## SCHOOLS

As outlined in Chapter Four, *Technique*, there are schools and teachers everywhere in the country offering classes in every aspect of the performing arts.

Here are national organizations that include and list many of the best educational opportunities for aspiring performers.

Acting Coach and Teachers Association
P.O. Box 1482
Hollywood, California 90028

The association includes many teachers who work independently as well as many who teach through schools.

American Theatre Association
1010 Wisconsin Avenue NW Suite 630
Washington, D.C. 20007

ATA is a large and vigorous organization "promoting the growth and the interests of non-commercial theatre in the United States." It includes divisions in theatre for the armed forces, community theatre, children's theatre, secondary school, and university theatre.

Its Annual Directory is a good guide to many theatre arts educational possibilities. The Directory costs $7.00. ATA also publishes many other books and periodicals of interest to performing arts students. For their titles and prices, write the ATA.

Central Opera Service
c/o The Metropolitan Opera
Lincoln Center
New York, New York 10023

The Central Opera Service is a national center for information on opera. It publishes the *Career Guide for the Young American Singer,* with listings of domestic and foreign opera companies and colleges with opera and musical theatre programs ($7.50, available on request).

League of Professional Training Programs
1860 Broadway Suite 1515
New York, New York 10023

The League is an alliance of thirteen of the country's best theatre arts schools: The American Conservatory Theatre, Boston University, Brandeis University, Carnegie-Mellon University, the Juilliard School, New York University, North Carolina School of the Arts, Southern Methodist University, SUNY at Purchase, Temple University, University of California, San Diego, University of Washington, and Yale School of Drama.

The League's free information bulletin gives the addresses of these schools as well as brief outlines of their programs and requirements.

National Association of Schools of Music
11250 Roger Bacon Drive Suite 5
Reston, Virginia 22090

The NASM represents 525 colleges, universities, and independent conservatories with degree programs in music. Its membership directory costs $7.00, available on request.

National Guild of Community Schools of the Arts
P.O. Box 583
Teaneck, New Jersey 07666

The Guild has over 120 member schools, most in New York, New England, and the mid-Atlantic states. Its membership directory costs $7.00, available on request.

For dancers, an excellent source of information about dance schools and colleges with strong dance programs are the listings published at the back of each issue of *Dancemagazine* (see Periodicals). *Dancemagazine* also publishes a yearly college guide, available from the magazine for $20.00.

For musicians there is the *Musical America International Directory of the Performing Arts*. Published yearly, the Directory includes comprehensive listings of music schools with details of their programs and faculty. The 1985 edition costs $50 and is available from ABC Leisure Magazines, 825 Seventh Avenue, New York, New York 10019.

REGIONAL AND SMALL THEATRES

Regional and small theatres have been a professional starting place for countless performers and a continuous source of employment for many. Remember: these theatres hire musicians and dancers as well as actors. They are also interested in variety artists, new playwrights and composers, and eager beginners willing to trade time and work for experience and contacts.

Here are two groups that coordinate auditions, job-hunting information, and many other services for hundreds of regional, Off Broadway, and Off-Off Broadway theatres.

Alliance of Resident Theatres/New York
325 Spring Street
New York, New York 10012

The Alliance is a central information clearinghouse for nearly all non-Broadway theatre in New York City.

Theatre Communications Group
355 Lexington Avenue
New York, New York 10017

TCG represents over 200 regional theatres all over the country, publishes a monthly magazine, *American Theatre,* arranges audition time and space for out-of-town casting directors in New York, and "fosters the cross-fertilization of ideas" between the individuals and institutions involved in nonprofit professional theatre. TCG also publishes a yearly *Theatre Directory,* an invaluable guide to regional theatre, available for $3.95 from TCG's New York headquarters.

## LOW-COST LEGAL AID
(alphabetical by state)

| | |
|---|---|
| California: | Bay Area Lawyers for the Arts<br>Fort Mason Center, Building C<br>San Francisco, California 94123<br>(415) 775-7200 |
| Colorado: | Colorado Lawyers for the Arts<br>770 Pennsylvania Street<br>Denver, Colorado 80203<br>(303) 866-2617 |
| Connecticut: | Connecticut Commission on the Arts<br>340 Capitol Avenue<br>Hartford, Connecticut 06106<br>(203) 566-4770 |
| Florida: | Volunteer Lawyers for the Arts<br>Metro-Dade Council of Arts and Sciences<br>200 S. Miami Avenue #281<br>Miami, Florida 33130<br>(305) 579-4634 |
| Georgia: | Georgia Volunteer Lawyers for the Arts<br>32 Peach Tree Street NW #521<br>Atlanta, Georgia 30303<br>(404) 577-7378 |
| Illinois: | Lawyers for the Creative Arts<br>220 S. State Street<br>Chicago, Illinois 60604<br>(312) 987-0198 |
| Massachusetts: | Artists Foundation/Lawyers for the Arts<br>110 Broad Street<br>Boston, Massachusetts 02110<br>(617) 482-8100 |
| New York: | Volunteer Lawyers for the Arts<br>1560 Broadway #711<br>New York, New York 10036<br>(212) 575-1150 |

| | |
|---|---|
| Pennsylvania: | Philadelphia Volunteer Lawyers for the Arts<br>260 South Broad Street<br>Philadelphia, Pennsylvania 19102<br>(215) 545-3385 |
| Rhode Island: | Lawyers Referral Service<br>1804 Fleet National Bank Building<br>Providence, Rhode Island 02903<br>(401) 421-7799 |
| Tennessee: | Tennessee Volunteer Lawyers for the Arts<br>c/o Waddey and Newport<br>500 Church Street<br>Nashville, Tennessee 37219<br>(615) 244-7545 |
| Texas: | Volunteer Lawyers and Accountants for the Arts<br>1540 Sul Ross<br>Houston, Texas 77006<br>(713) 526-4876 |
| Washington, D.C.: | Washington Area Lawyers for the Arts<br>c/o DC Commission on Arts and Humanities<br>420 7th Street NW<br>Washington, District of Columbia 20004<br>(202) 724-5613 |
| Washington: | Washington Volunteer Lawyers for the Arts<br>66 Bell Street<br>Seattle, Washington 98121<br>(206) 223-0502 |

APPENDIX

# index

INDEX

INDEX

222

INDEX